The Complete Films of
Frank Capra

The Complete Films of
FRANK CAPRA

by Victor Scherle and William Turner Levy

A CITADEL PRESS BOOK
PUBLISHED BY CAROL PUBLISHING GROUP

First Carol Publishing Group Edition 1992

A Citadel Press Book
Published by Carol Publishing Group
Citadel Press is a registered trademark
of Carol Communications, Inc.

Editorial Offices   Sales & Distribution Offices
600 Madison Avenue   120 Enterprise Avenue
New York, NY 10022   Secaucus, NJ 07094

In Canada: Canadian Manda Group
P.O. Box 920, Station U
Toronto, Ontario M8Z 5P9

Manufactured in the United States of America
ISBN 0-8065-1296-2

10 9 8 7 6 5 4 3 2 1

Carol Publishing Group books are available at special discounts
for bulk purchases, for sales promotions, fund raising, or
educational purposes. Special editions can also be created to
specifications. For details contact: Special Sales Department,
Carol Publishing Group, 120 Enterprise Ave., Secaucus, NJ 07094

*This book is lovingly dedicated
to the most important person in Frank Capra's life,
his charming and delightful wife, Lu!*

FRANK AND LU CAPRA with their Yorkshire terrier, Joko, at
their summer home in the High Sierras, 1973.

To Bill and Victor —
Affectionately,
Frank Capra

Acknowledgments

The authors are indebted and warmly thankful to:

Frank Capra, who answered endless questions with both authority and humor, screened films for us at his home, and lent generously from his collection of photographs and stills.

Lu Capra, who with patience and kindness pursued each request for help to a successful conclusion.

All the wonderfully cooperative and generous persons whose original contributions constitute an integral part of this book.

The following persons and organizations from whose expertise this book has profited:

Jack and Paula Kramer, proprietors of Movie Star News, New York, New York. Jack's death, which occurred while this book was being written, is a loss that all his many friends feel deeply.

Cinephiles Peter Hanson and Richard Sisson, who were never stumped, no matter how esoteric the query.

Mark Ricci, proprietor of Memory Shop, Inc., New York, New York.

Hyman Goor, proprietor of Metropolitan Book Store, New York, New York.

Gerald Raftery, librarian, Martha Canfield Memorial Free Library, Arlington, Vermont.

Rosalyn Mass, who teaches film at Baruch College of the City University of New York.

L. Arnold Weissberger, author of *Famous Faces*.

Leonard Maltin, author, editor of *Film Fan Monthly*.

Richard Lamparski, author of the "Whatever Became Of . . ." series.

Lee Graham, contributing editor of *Hollywood Studio Magazine*.

John Springer, author of *They Had Faces Then*, etc.

Donald Deschner, author of *The Films of Cary Grant*, etc.

James Robert Parish, author of *Hollywood's Great Love Teams*, etc.

Screen Actors Guild

Chester Sticht, secretary to Frank Capra.

The following institutions for opening their research facilities and screening their films:

The Library of Congress, Washington, D.C., and reference librarian of the Motion Picture Section, Patrick J. Sheehan.

The National Archives of the United States, Washington, D.C., and film archivist William Thomas Murphy; and Paul Lannon.

American Film Institute, John F. Kennedy Center for the Performing Arts, and Charles Gregg, director, Theatre Arts.

The Museum of Modern Art, New York, and the head of its Department of Film, Charles Silver.

Library and Museum of the Performing Arts of the New York Public Library at Lincoln Center.

And our friends:

John and Wini Hawkes, of Dorset, Vermont, who acquired films for us and put their private screening room at our disposal.

The following persons, institutions, and organizations for providing photographs and stills:

ACTORS

Lina Basquette, Ellen Corby, Ruth Donnelly, Jack Elam, Tom Fadden, Fritz Feld, James Flavin, Connie Gilchrist, Coleen Gray, Ish Kabibble, Charles Lane, Margaret Livingston, Mike Mazurki, Arthur O'Connell, Tom Pedi, Alan Reed, Benny Rubin, Hayden Rorke, Barbara Stanwyck, Dub Taylor, Mary Treen, Ian Wolfe, Fay Wray.

AUTHORS

Homer Dickens, *The Films of Katharine Hepburn*, etc; Ken D. Jones, *The Films of James Stewart*, etc; Lawrence J. Quirk, *The Great Romantic Films*, etc; Jeffrey Richards, *Visions of Yesterday*; Ted Sennett, *Lunatics and Lovers*, etc; Ella Smith, *Starring Miss Barbara Stanwyck*; Bob Thomas, *King Cohn*, etc.

PRIVATE COLLECTORS

Edward L. Bernds, sound engineer; Peter Hanson; Frank P. Keller, film editor; Larry Kleno; Walter Lantz, artist; Richard Sisson; Joseph Walker, cameraman.

INSTITUTIONS

Academy of Motion Picture Arts and Sciences.

Directors Guild of America and Joseph C. Youngerman.

George C. Marshall Research Foundation, Lexington, Virginia, and Assistant Archivist Anthony R. Crawford.

The Library of Congress, Washington, D.C.

Loyola Marymount University, Los Angeles, California, and Professor Bernard Abbene, chairman, Communication Arts.

The Museum of Modern Art, New York, and Mary Corliss.

The National Archives of the United States, Washington, D.C.

University of Southern California Library and James C. Wagner, Department of Special Collections.

University of Wyoming, Laramie, Wyoming, Director of Rare Books and Special Collections Gene M. Gressley, and research historian David Crosson.

U.S. Army Audio-Visual Agency, the Pentagon, Washington, D.C.

ORGANIZATIONS

Bell Telephone Company, New York, N.Y., and Robert Galvin.

Collectors Book Store, 6763 Hollywood Boulevard, Hollywood, California 90028, and Malcolm Willits.

Eddie Brandt's Saturday Matinee, P.O. Box 3232, North Hollywood, California 91609.

Film Favorites, P.O. Box 517, Canton, Oklahoma 73724.

Diane Goodrich, 17071 Escalon Drive, Encino, California 91436.

The Larry Edmunds Bookshop, Inc., 6658 Hollywood Boulevard, Hollywood, California 90028.

Memory Shop, Inc., 109 East 12th Street, New York, N.Y. 10003.

Merv Griffin Productions and David S. Williger.

The Mike Douglas Show and Wendy J. Mayer.

Movie Star News, 212 East 14th Street, New York, N.Y. 10003.

Newsweek Magazine.

Theatre Poster Exchange, Inc., P.O. Box 845, Memphis, Tennessee 38101.

Contents

Introductions 1
Articles 5
Comments on Frank Capra 13
Frank Capra's Wonderful Life 23

Fultah Fisher's Boarding House 35
The Strong Man 39
Long Pants 43
For the Love of Mike 47
That Certain Thing 51
So This Is Love 55
The Matinee Idol 57
The Way of the Strong 61
Say It With Sables 63
The Power of the Press 65
Submarine 69
The Younger Generation 73
The Donovan Affair 77
Flight 79
Ladies of Leisure 83
Rain or Shine 87
Dirigible 91
The Miracle Woman 95
Platinum Blonde 99

Forbidden 103
American Madness 107
The Bitter Tea of General Yen 111
Lady for a Day 117
It Happened One Night 123
Broadway Bill 131
Mr. Deeds Goes to Town 135
Lost Horizon 143
You Can't Take It With You 157
Mr. Smith Goes to Washington 165
Meet John Doe 175
Arsenic and Old Lace 187
Why We Fight series and
    Other World War II Films 195
It's a Wonderful Life 223
State of the Union 233
Riding High 239
Here Comes the Groom 245
The Television Science Films 251
A Hole in the Head 257
Pocketful of Miracles 263
Rendezvous in Space 271

Epilogue 273
Index 275

BARBARA STANWYCK, with her favorite director, Frank Capra.

ON THE LINCOLN MEMORIAL SET for *Mr. Smith Goes to Washington*: James Stewart, left, and Frank Capra.

FRANK CAPRA: THE CARL SANDBURG OF HOLLYWOOD

by The Honorable William O. Douglas
Associate Justice, United States Supreme Court

Frank Capra, who worked at all levels of the movie industry from script writer on up, is remembered as a director of genius, character and deep insight into people and events.

I remember his first film, *Fultah Fisher's Boarding House* built around Kipling's poem of the same name. That was a silent film; but it ran the entire gamut of human emotions. Frank Capra had a great capacity for growth. He exploited camerawise the advancing technology, best illustrated by the *Why We Fight* series, for which he received the Distinguished Service Medal in World War II. But his real contribution to the screen was revealed in his search for the heart and mind of mid-America and in the manner in which he related them to the ideals represented by our institutions and men from Washington and Jefferson down to Lincoln and modern times.

Frank Capra was the Carl Sandburg of Hollywood who reminded all America of the faces of Americana we love and cherish. In a sense his productions portrayed Good *v.* Evil. Yet more accurately he set the homely virtues of small-town America against the greed of the marketplace, the corruption of politicians, and the dangers of fascism. He made a hero out of the most obscure person. Frank Capra entertained us; but he also brought tears to our eyes when we revisited with him the shrines of Jefferson and Lincoln and when he made us realize that in spite of all the overreaching and crime and immorality the heart of America was warm and her conscience bright.

—*Washington, D.C.*, March 18, 1974.

THE MASTER'S HAND WAS SO GENTLE

by Barbara Stanwyck

Mr. Capra discussed the character and its relation to the story and other characters with the performer. He recognized and respected what you (as an actor or actress) were trying to do—your interpretation. And he let you have your head—so to speak. But he was always there to guide you. He would not tell you

Introductions

DIRECTOR OF SILENT FILMS, Frank Capra, studies shot before ordering cameraman to begin rolling film in early motion picture camera.

1

how to do a scene *per se,* and he would never tell you how to read a line, as some directors do. The direction was always there, but the master's hand was so gentle that you were not aware you were being directed. Yet of course, you were.

You see, Mr. Capra understands people. I believe he has a great affection for actors, and that is terribly important. Strange as it may seem, some directors do not like actors.

Mr. Capra is a giant in his profession. His mark will always be there for all to see.

I am grateful for the privilege of working for Mr. Capra. His teachings have stayed with me in moments of trial and confusion. My respect and gratitude to Frank Capra are boundless; my love, eternal.

An old Gaelic blessing for Mr. Capra: "May the roads rise with you and the wind be always at your back; And may the Lord hold you in the hollow of His hand."

—Beverly Hills, California, January 31, 1974.

FRANCOIS TRUFFAUT, at work on his 1973 film *Day for Night.*

A RESTORER OF MEN'S SPIRITS
by François Truffaut

Frank Capra, who had directed some wonderful Harry Langdon silent films, was to achieve fame with *It Happened One Night,* a film whose style has been copied a hundred times. Unfortunately, because of poor distribution, Capra's complete work is little known in France; nevertheless, I retain a sufficiently strong memory of *Mr. Deeds Goes to Town, You Can't Take It with You, Mr. Smith Goes to Washington* (before Watergate—thirty-five years before!), *Meet John Doe,* and *It's a Wonderful Life* to know that this great filmmaker exerted an important worldwide influence, an influence I recognize in the early work of Alfred Hitchcock (before 1940) and in that of the young Ingmar Bergman (in the period of his marital comedies before 1955).

Frank Capra, together with Leo McCarey, Lubitsch, and Preston Sturges, is one of the four masters of American film comedy. This Italian, with roots in Palermo, brought to Hollywood the secrets of the Commedia dell'Arte, and he knew, better than the other three, the art of involving his characters in profoundly desperate situations (I often cried while watching Capra's films) before righting events and creating the miracle that allowed us to leave the theater with an augmented love of life.

In recognizing the facts of human suffering, uncertainty, anxiety, the everyday struggles of life, Capra, with his unquenchable optimism, was a healing force. This good doctor, who was also a great director, became a restorer of men's spirits.

—Paris, France, June 7, 1974.
(Translated from the French by the authors.)

RELAXED DIRECTOR, Frank Capra, with foot on rope, discusses a scene in *Forbidden* with co-stars Barbara Stanwyck and Adolphe Menjou.

IN LOS ANGELES ICEHOUSE during a break in the filming of the plane crash scene in *Lost Horizon*, director Frank Capra, left, serves hot coffee to his star, Ronald Colman.

3

COMMITTED TO SENNETT'S LUNATIC
TOWER WITH GAG MAN FRANK CAPRA

by Tay Garnett

To the infant art form of motion pictures, Italy has given one of her rarest gifts—a giant who stands alone. No movie director has ever brought more joy to the laughter-hungry hearts of the world than Frank Capra. The quality that stands out like 3-D among my many fond personal memories of Frank, going back to the early Mack Sennett writing days —the thing which made him loom large among the rest of us Sennett slaves—was a quiet but dynamic determination to do everything he undertook better than it had ever been done before.

When we praised a story Frank had just written, he'd smile and say, "Yeah, I guess it's okay, but I'll do better next time. You can make book on it!" No arrogance in it; just a quiet conviction rooted in a prodigious, and as yet untapped, talent.

The picture business was *his* business, and he knew it. He also knew that inevitably, sooner or later, he'd make it *big*—and that meant *directing!*

Years later, after Frank had added still another to his covey of Oscars, when his friends at the Directors' Guild congratulated him, he'd shrug and say, "Look, fellows, we all know we haven't even started to make our best pictures yet." I've heard him say it a dozen times.

It was difficult to believe that such simple modesty and so vast a talent could have been spawned in the shrilling bedlam of the Sennett Tower.

The Tower!

The sound of it flushes a flock of nostalgic flashbacks. Among the more pleasant of these are those featuring that wise and wonderfully warm-hearted wop, Frank Capra. Who else?

The Tower itself, a three-story frame structure with a slight sacroiliac problem, was probably engineered by Rube Goldberg with a psychic nudge from the as-yet-unborn Dr. Seuss. It was a comic-book version of the Leaning Tower of Pisa.

The Old Ogre's offices monopolized the ground floor. The Payroll Pirates practiced their short-change techniques on the second.

From the first floor to the second, the building was completely dominated by convention, adhering rigidly to the perpendicular; but at the level where the stairway to the third floor began, the Tower shrugged off the yoke of conformity and took a suicidal lunge to port, toward a point of no return.

Articles

CAUGHT UNAWARES on the set of *State of the Union*, Spencer Tracy, right, adjusts his belt, while a pensive Katharine Hepburn looks elsewhere, and director Frank Capra looks bemused.

5

STILLS OF "YOU CAN'T TAKE IT WITH YOU" are checked by Frank Capra.

That it never quite made it was just one more of the mysteries with which the edifice was enshrouded.

Most of us accepted this bit of architectural lunacy as a simple Sennett eccentricity, but once I came upon Frank, standing outside, gaping incredulously at the building's flamboyant defiance of gravity. This was not Capra the gag man, but Frank Capra, B.S. Obviously, Cal Tech Engineering had failed to provide him with the means for rationalizing this outrage against scientific reason.

I said, "As an engineer, Frank, how do you explain it?"

He didn't miss a beat as he answered, "Ostrich's law, naturally."

I grunted, "Ostrich's law? Never heard of it."

Still deadpan, he said, "Oh, sure you have. Stick your head in the sand and hope it'll go away." He turned toward the building entrance as he added, "Shall we join the laddies in the Torture Chamber?"

Inside was the stairway, the only means of access to the Chamber—a narrow, uncarpeted, worn wooden staircase. Originally designed to function as a gymnasium, the third floor had now degenerated into a cage for gag men.

The Ogre had doped it out that confining the writers where he could keep an eye on them would increase the work yield importantly. The day after the Tower's conversion from gym to gag room, it became apparent that the Old Boy had goofed.

For working purposes, we inmates of the Sennett Asylum were divided into two-man teams. And who do you think was the guy that each of us wanted most to team up with? Who was the quiet gent who came up strong with the goodies when the going got tough? Shucks! You guessed it!

Usually, there were four or five yarns in the works at one time. That meant a pride of screeching paranoids each trying to outyell his partner in his excitement over a newly conceived comedy routine. Capra was the only one of us who chose the more conventional method of writing with a pencil, rather than conform to the Sennett style of creating with the vocal cords.

Capra was more serious minded than the rest of us and more wholly committed to his work. He seemed to know even then that he was composing the overture to a tremendous career. Undoubtedly, this sense of commitment was what persuaded the Old Man to call on Frank to "routine" gags. When one of us would give birth to a really funny one-time gag but fail to develop it into anything more, the gag would be turned over to Frank. On many occasions,

he came up with a running gag that numbered among the best of the outrageous Sennett routines.

In the Tower, the one peaceful spot was Capra's corner. He worked alone, untouched, while bedlam bedlamed. Each team was finding it almost impossible to come up funny for our story, with each of the other guys trying to yell loud enough to drown us all. Inevitably, we gave up and picked a subject of conversation in which we could all participate: booze, baseball, or broads. The only time we actually worked was when we heard Himself trying to sneak up those creaky stairs.

It was idyllic.

Utopia can seldom be regarded as a permanent address. The sly and suspicious Sennett started sneaking up on us shamelessly. He'd chosen a tough assignment, because of those old stairs—they were *his* stairs; yet they creaked with tattletale treachery. Despite his stealthiest efforts, he was unable to deny us the right of free speech. Invariably, by the time he'd reached the top of the stairs and squared off to glower at us murderously, we were divided into our designated teams, all yelling violently.

As I recall it (time has a way of shrinking with the years), only a day or so after Frank explained Ostrich's law to me, I arrived at the studio to find Frank standing outside the Tower looking up at it gloomily. I said, "Why don't you give up, Frank?" (I should have known better. The idea of giving up on anything had no place in Frank's makeup.) I went on blissfully, "You'll never figure the Tower out by anything remotely related to science, logic, or sanity."

Frank shook his head as he said mournfully, "I *knew* the old bastard would do something drastic."

At that moment, I saw a couple of workmen entering the building, carrying carpenters' tools. I asked, "Who are those guys?"

Frank said, "That's what I'm trying to tell you; the Ogre's tearing out the old stairs—gonna put in new ones that won't squeak. We'll be dead ducks."

"Of all the dirty, sneaking tricks . . . !" I stopped, as another thought occurred to me. "At least we'll get a day off while they tear the stairs out."

"Not a prayer," Frank said sorrowfully. "The Old Boy's covered all bases. He's got ladders in there for us to climb up on." He shook his head again. "No. Our only chance is that with the inside reinforcement of the stairway removed, the building will collapse."

With a sigh, he started toward the entrance. I followed dolefully. At the door, he stopped. "It's a crummy stunt, but don't worry, I'll think of something."

It was years later before I remembered that he'd said that.

The very next morning, Frank was waiting for all of us in the same place outside the Tower. He spoke cheerfully. "Morning, gang. Well, the new stairs are in, and there's not a squeak in a carload."

One of the guys said, "What are you so damned happy about? We've *really* got a problem now."

Frank said, "Could be, but I doubt it." At the door he said, "It'd be a good idea if all of us would go up the stairs one at a time, and count the steps as we go. Somebody goofed when they were putting in the new stairs. The seventh step is about a quarter of an inch higher than the others. If you don't count, you'll trip on it."

As we went up, each counted silently, giving a little added altitude to his foot in reaching for number seven. All but one, that is. Some gent at the rear was saying, "What difference can a lousy quarter of an inch—" He hadn't quite finished, when he reached that step, and *whamo!* He nearly fell on his face. He grumbled, "That stinkin' step's gonna be a damned nuisance." He was wrong about the nuisance part, but he never failed to count the steps after that.

That seventh step was a real lifesaver. Mack never did catch wise that he tripped over the same step every time he tried to do his hide-and-go-sneak bit up those silent new stairs. The racket he made—coughing, sputtering, and cursing each time he tripped—became our warning signal. By the time the Old Ogre reached our floor, sputtering, beet-faced, and puffing, we'd be well into our act.

On one occasion we failed to get started promptly enough after the warning sounded. The Blustering Harp arrived, to glare triumphantly around the silent room. Before he could get his attack off the launching pad, one of the boys turned on him accusingly. "Dammit, boss, look what you've done with your ad-lib yellin' and cursin'! You've clobbered our chains of thought. Can't you come up a little more quietly?"

The Old Man looked deeply hurt as he turned and went silently down the stairs.

Years later, when the Mack Sennett empire had collapsed, the Masquers' Club staged a stag dinner honoring the Old Boy. All the old-time Sennett directors and gag men who were still around, were invited. Capra and I were among them.

It was a pleasant evening, this renewing of old friendships. Ancient grudges were forgotten, for we all had one thing in common: The Old Man was in trouble, financially and professionally, and every one of us knew, deep in his heart, that for whatever any of us might have achieved professionally in the intervening years, Mack Sennett was in no small measure responsible. Frank Capra by that time was solidly established as one of the all-time, truly great directors of the world.

Then, dinner over, the speeches started. And what speeches! Warmed by good food and drink, soaring on a nostalgia kick, those guys really turned on the sentiment—rich and sometimes irreverent reminiscences.

I sat watching the Ogre. Then I looked at Frank, and suddenly, memories of the Tower came in a montage that danced through my brain like a Strauss waltz. I could see the Torture Chamber as though time and space had collapsed and I had never left there, and I saw superimposed flashes of those long-forgotten faces, so young, so animated as they reenacted a ballgame or dramatized the previous night's conquest. Then I heard the crunch of a heavy foot on a wooden stair, and the torrent of coughing, sputtering, and outraged cursing.

It ended as abruptly as it had started. I looked at Frank. In all these years, as far as I knew, not one of the old Tower gang had ever stopped to wonder about that trick step.

"That step couldn't have been higher than the rest by accident!" I could have sworn I heard it. "Some wise apple had to figure it out, stupe! Someone who knew what that added quarter of an inch would do."

I looked across the room at Capra—Frank Capra, B.S. of Cal Tech Engineering.

Then I looked at the Ogre. But I couldn't see him. All I could see was a weary old man. It had been a big evening for him, and he looked . . . tired.

In a delayed take, I zoomed back to Frank. I knew I'd missed something. Boy, had I missed something! Frank was watching the Old Man, and there was deep concern in his eyes—a tender concern mixed with an unmistakable affection.

I never saw Mack Sennett after that. I guess Frank knew then that none of us ever would. Yeah. It was always that way—wherever we were headed, Frank always got there miles ahead of the rest of us.

Godspeed, Frank.

—*Los Angeles, California*, August 5, 1974.

THIS IS FRANK CAPRA'S LIFE

by Ralph Edwards

Frank Capra's role as United States Ambassador of Goodwill to the world goes further than his films. It goes to the heart of the man himself. This was demonstrated when India asked Frank to return to the Film Festival in New Delhi. (He had originally gone to the Film Festival in India in 1952.)

The night in 1959 when we surprised Frank with his "life" on "This Is Your Life," Turner Shelton, Director of Motion Pictures for the United States Information Agency, said, "Because of his honor and humility . . . the Department of State asked Frank Capra to represent the movie industry at the Film Festival in India in 1952.

"This was a most important event for us, because we knew that there would be a large Communist representation at this . . . festival. And we knew that with Frank Capra, we could show the people of India that the men who make American movies are dignified, intelligent, creative people. Frank's impact on the festival was tremendous. On the night of the Soviets' biggest rally, word got out that Frank was going to speak about American pictures elsewhere, and the audience that had assembled for the rally left to hear Frank speak.

"Frank, we at the United States Information Agency believe that your life is a perfect demonstration of the magic of America—and it is because of men like you, dedicated to your work and to your country, that America has been and always will be free."

Frank Capra the man had something to say, and he said it in his films—and in his person. How lucky we are that what he had to say concerned a little man who overcomes the forces of evil around him.

We have surprised almost five hundred known and unknown Americans on "This Is Your Life." All these fine people enjoyed seeing their lives unfold before them, but I can't recall anyone who enjoyed this experience more than Frank Capra. From the time he realized that his personally conducted tour of the NBC studios by NBC vice-president John West was a fraud, and that the real reason for the tour was to guide him to me in the studio, Frank relaxed into the spirit of the show. He reveled in the surprise visits of people from his past, from Edward G. Robinson and Carolyn Jones to his brother Tony, who, when he was a boy, had sometimes faked fights with little brother Frank to enjoin sympathy from passersby. Frank told the onlookers he was being beaten because he had not sold all his newspapers. This usually brought on a quick sale of all remaining papers.

Frank was enthralled to see six actual members of his ukulele club from Manual Arts High School, Los Angeles, strumming on stage and equally excited to see Doctor Lee DuBridge, President of Cal Tech, formerly Throop College of Technology, from which Frank had graduated with a bachelor of science degree in 1918. Doctor DuBridge told how young Frank, an honor student, had worked for his tuition and meals throughout his college career.

Frank greeted Sam Briskin, then head of production for Columbia Pictures, where, in 1928, Frank Capra directed *Submarine*, the first sound picture ever made at Columbia.

Sam Briskin said of Frank's motion pictures: "The audiences loved them because Frank does everything with heart and humility. We could see ourselves in his characters—strong and weak, bad and good. Frank was, and is, the champion of the little man."

Part of the reason for the natural blend of Capra the man and Capra the filmmaker is Lucille—Lu, the perfect complement and aide to the artistry of her husband. Nowhere was the bond of love between man and wife more visible than that shown by Frank for his Lu. She told how Frank had proposed marriage by phone. Obviously, Frank had the right number.

Frank's ability to reach the so-called little man extended into the army. Brigadier General Lyman Munson explained how "Frank was given the task of organizing and bringing through production an intensive educational program of factual films dealing with the events leading up to the war, to show our troops why we were in this fight."

I rate Frank Capra's films as rewarding as a good church service. That's high for me. As for entertainment, I always had the same exhilaration stepping into a theater to see a Capra movie as I had in seeing my first vaudeville performance or my first stock-company production or the thrilling expectancy of my first view of Chautauqua.

Dear God, when do we get his kind of stuff again!

Hollywood, California, February 5, 1975.

DRAWN ESPECIALLY FOR THIS BOOK, 1974.

THE MOST INTERESTING MAN
I'VE EVER KNOWN

by Walter Lantz

Nothing suits me better than having the opportunity to say some nice things about my dear friend Frank Capra.

I first met Frank when I worked as gag man and animator at the Mack Sennett Studios. We both left Sennett. He went on to become one of our most famous directors, and I joined Universal Studios to produce the Oswald Rabbit cartoons in 1927.

Frank had a knack of producing and directing a motion picture that few directors have. First, he never directed a picture that didn't have a believable story and an opportunity for human-interest comedy.

9

He directed pictures to entertain worldwide audiences, not Hollywood.

I have spent many hours with Frank fishing on Silver Lake in the high Sierras and traveling over the back roads in a Jeep. He is the most interesting man I've ever known. No matter what I ask him, whether it is the species of a bird, the name of a tree, or why Mono Lake is salty, he gives me the answer. He is really a perfectionist in everything he does. That is why he produced such outstanding motion pictures.

Capra spends a good deal of his time lecturing at colleges all over the United States. He even went to Iran to lecture at a university. He shows one or two of his films, then conducts a question-and-answer session. I admire Frank for doing this, because he is getting a message over to the young people that good, clean, humorous comedies really pay off.

—*Hollywood, California*, August 20, 1974.

(*Opposite page*) CAMERAMAN JOSEPH WALKER, right, with Frank Capra, wrote to the authors of this book from Carlsbad, California on September 24, 1974: "I believe that Frank Capra, with his excellent technical education and deep understanding of human values, enthusiasm for life, and great sense of humor, would have been a success in any area. That he chose motion pictures for his field of endeavor was very fortunate for all of us who were associated with him. And very fortunate for Columbia Pictures, too! I am especially appreciative of Frank Capra's understanding and help on the technical problems of those early days."

CLOWNING for a publicity shot on the set of *Mr. Smith Goes to Washington*—left to right: Frank Capra, Jean Arthur and James Stewart.

FRANK CAPRA LISTENS as Frank Sinatra pointingly expresses his views about a scene to be filmed. (*A Hole in the Head*.)

DIRECTORS COMMENT

PETER BOGDANOVICH:

Frank Capra exemplifies his own artistic credo: one man, one film. No matter what the literary source, Capra's films are his. The same signature can be identified from *It Happened One Night* through *Mr. Deeds Goes to Town* and *Mr. Smith Goes to Washington* to *It's a Wonderful Life* and even the relative failure of *Pocketful of Miracles*. In these films we are in the presence of one man—his obsessions, fantasies, dreams.

The Capra hero—from his silent Harry Langdon comedies to his great later successes—is an innocent dreamer who comes up against hard reality, yet manages not only to keep his illusions but to triumph with them. Because this is the way Mr. Capra would like it to be.

—Edited for the authors by Peter Bogdanovich,
Beverly Hills, California, July 24, 1974,
from his PIECES OF TIME *(Arbor House, 1973).*

JOHN CROMWELL:

I hardly knew him while in Hollywood except to be an admirer of his work. Only after I read his magnificent book and saw many interviews relative to it did I come to "know" something about Frank and become able to appreciate how much his Hollywood experience had done to develop him as a person. I was also struck by the similarity of our mutual experiences as young men learning our professions, Frank in Hollywood and myself in the theater in New York. Further than that, each of us was helped (I could better say, enriched) by our close association with a prominent figure of the time: Harry Cohn in Frank's case and William A. Brady, by far the most colorful producer in New York, in mine.

I immediately became aware of (and fascinated by) the revelation of Frank as a man through the shape his reminiscences took. No wonder his book was so good! It was always so evident how much every experience had meant to him, and his conclusions were not in the rigid confines of his profession, but in the broader aspects of life, living, people, character. This makes up a sum of which Frank Capra can well be very proud.

—Letter to the authors from New York, New York,
July 8, 1974.

Comments on Frank Capra

ATTENTIVE ACTORS, Peter Falk, center, and Benny Rubin, right, listen as director Frank Capra explains how they should play their scene in *Pocketful of Miracles* for the most laughs.

13

DELMER DAVES:

Frank and I served many years together on the Board of Directors of the Directors Guild of America, so we were "tablemates" through many a year and many a session, especially during the strenuous contract-negotiations days. I felt Frank was surely the best of negotiators with the Producers Association when we spent our time on those duties; his background and eloquence were such that he was probably the most respected of all of us who served so long in those duties. He, of course, was the president of the Directors Guild for some time.

I have read his book—and found it so true to the man (as well as the occasional Sicilian temperament) that I rank it at the top of filmmakers' biographical works.

Communication was Frank's magic. Some directors work remotely, as a DeMille might with his staff and crew, but Frank worked "a la Italiana" (or Siciliana)—from the heart—and almost made blood brothers (as my Indian friends put it in the ten Westerns I made) of his actors and crew. I learned that this was the way for me, too. So Frank and I (with my Irish, I suppose) worked with our hearts, as well as our minds, and the actors and crew knew it. Because of Frank Capra, better, deeper, and more touchingly real films were born. So my gratitude toward Frank is for the key of communication he inspired. And we have been friends all these years.

—*Letter to the authors from Los Angeles, California,*
May 10, 1974.

ALLAN DWAN:

My personal acquaintance with Frank Capra was slight, but my admiration for his work is profound. With thousands of others, I miss his magic touch in today's market.

—*Letter to the authors from Van Nuys, California,*
July 10, 1974.

BLAKE EDWARDS:

Exemplification of a true genius is one who is gifted with extraordinary capacity for imaginative creation and original thought. In my opinion few men in film, past or present, qualify under this definition. Frank Capra is one of the few. He has made a fundamental contribution, and in so doing, he has been for those of us less talented, a guide and an inspiration. And there is another quality about

Frank Capra, perhaps even more unique than his genius—he is a very nice man.

—*Letter to the authors from London, England,*
January 25, 1975.

WILLIAM FRIEDKIN:

Like most filmmakers today, I admire Frank's work tremendously and have probably been influenced by many of his films. The most and the least I can say is that I'm a great admirer and have never ceased to take pleasure from Frank's pictures over and over again.

—*Letter to the authors from Burbank, California,*
July 19, 1974.

GARSON KANIN:

When I arrived in Hollywood in 1937, Capra was at his peak, and since he was always at work and not social, I did not encounter him for some time.

In the course of a discussion one evening, I am said to have said, "I'd rather be Capra than God—if there *is* a Capra."

—*Letter to the authors from Edgartown, Massachusetts,*
June 20, 1974, *with reference made to* HOLLYWOOD,
by Garson Kanin (The Viking Press, New York, 1974).

HENRY KING:

Time and space would not permit all my comments on this great man. He is the giant of the industry. His book, *The Name Above the Title,* is the only real story of Hollywood that has been written. One small film company rose to be one of the major studios on the films of Frank Capra. A Capra film is always a whole evening of entertainment—honest, clean, and wholesome. Frank has never had to turn to brutality, vulgarity, or profanity to tell the story. He is an artist and able to stimulate the audience's imagination and allow them to participate in the picture. We have a better world with Frank Capra films. It's a great loss that we do not have more.

—*Letter to the authors from North Hollywood,*
California, June 5, 1974.

STANLEY KUBRICK:

Frank Capra's films are an intimate part of the America in which I grew up. They were films that, in the main, encouraged one to believe the best of other people and, by so believing, to offer the earnest hope and fellowship many needed in those hard times. Capra's inclination was to take a generous view of people's natures, but at the same time not concealing society's ills. I have seen most of his films many times, and I consider him one of the world's most accomplished directors.

—Letter to the authors from Borehamwood, Hertfordshire, England, August 27, 1974.

FRITZ LANG:

Not knowing Mr. Capra personally but having seen his films, always with great pleasure, I feel that Mr. Capra is one of the very important contributors to the American cinema.

—Letter to the authors from Beverly Hills, California, May 11, 1974.

SAM PECKINPAH:

I remember Mr. Capra with gratitude. He had a way of combining beauty, warmth, imminent disaster, and heart. I loved his films, and I respect the man as a filmmaker of the first rank.

—Letter to the authors from Beverly Hills, California, August 5, 1974.

ARTHUR PENN:

I'm not much of a film buff, and I suffer from poor memory, but I can assure you that I remember the films of Frank Capra with delight, pleasure, and amazement at his inventiveness. They were the films of my youth, and they provided me with an outlook on the world considerably influenced by his good and memorable philosophy. He is indeed a gifted man.

—Letter to the authors from New York, New York, May 9, 1974.

OTTO PREMINGER:

It is not easy to say anything about Frank Capra in a few lines, because he represents to every director a giant of our profession. On the other hand, *giant* might be the wrong expression, because there is something very modest about his artistic and private personality. This modesty I think symbolizes better than anything how secure Capra was in everything he created.

—Letter to the authors from Nice, France, May 11, 1974.

MARTIN RITT:

The humanism of the films of Frank Capra will always be a source of great pleasure to me. I enjoy his films. Both as an audience and as a filmmaker, I feel indebted to him.

—Letter to the authors from La Jolla, California, August 30, 1974.

RAOUL WALSH:

Honesty has always been Frank Capra's trademark. It was stamped on his movies and on his life. It was all there without frills or furbelows.

—Letter to the authors from Simi Valley, California, May 4, 1974.

WILLIAM WYLER:

I know of no other director who in the relatively short period of ten or twelve years has given us such brilliant films, one after another, which were not only superbly entertaining, but richly thought provoking and making profound, astute, and courageous comments on the social and political life of the times. They are a lasting credit to Frank Capra and the whole American film industry.

—Letter to the authors from Beverly Hills, California, May 9, 1974.

FRED ZINNEMANN:

In the late 1930s there were four directors whose names were magic for the generation of young directors who were getting ready to start their careers: Frank Capra, John Ford, King Vidor, and George Stevens. This was so, not only because of the excellence and individuality of their work, but because they were practically the only men who had the courage to defy the "front office."

During the 1930s the studio executives were in almost total dominance of filmmaking ("product," they called it). Directors were employees and were expected to obey orders like everyone else. The orders were given courteously or bluntly, depending on the status of the director; but orders they were, and to defy them was close to blasphemy. An unofficial jungle telegraph existed among the companies; to be known as a troublemaker in one studio could make it very difficult for a man to get a job anywhere else. It was an era of despotism, sometimes benevolent, sometimes not, extending to all creative aspects of picture making—script, casting, sets, and especially editing. (At that time the studios insisted on "protection shots," that is, covering scenes with setups that the director considered unnecessary, so that the scenes could be recut by the studio to suit their own purposes.)

The only beacon of light and hope in this situation was the four men mentioned above. In his own way each of them managed to prevail against the system and to make his pictures exactly the way he saw them. In addition, Frank Capra, together with the others, was one of the founding fathers of the Directors Guild of America, established against the most strenuous objections of the studios. He was in the spearhead of the movement that finally brought the director back into focus and set us an example. And for that, my generation of directors will be forever grateful.

—Letter to the authors from London, England,
May 7, 1974.

WRITERS COMMENT

ART BUCHWALD:

Of course, I'm a great fan of Frank Capra's films.

I don't know what happened to the movie business, but nobody is making good comedies any more. The big question is, Why isn't there another Frank Capra? There should be. But for some reason the studios don't encourage this type of comedy.

It's trite to say Frank was a genius. I met him on a cruise a couple of years ago when he was lecturing to the Young Presidents Organization. I found him a delightful man. I asked him why he wasn't making movies, and he replied that he had done it all and there was nothing more he could do.

The world misses his movies very much.

—Letter to the authors from Washington, D.C.,
October 25, 1974.

JAMES GOULD COZZENS:

I wish I didn't have to admit that among my too many artistic deficiencies is incapacity to take in, understand and enjoy the art (I know it is) of the cinema. The most I can say is a poor indeed offer at compliment. I'm not sure I ever sat through a whole motion picture in my life, but of some I sat almost all the way through three (out of I'd guess four) were his. Opinion at any event allowed incompetent

is clearly no good and I'd not blame Mr. Capra for seeing it as insulting. I can only say that admiring, in my mind, is what it truly is, is truly meant to be.

—Letter to the authors from Stuart, Florida,
May 12, 1974.

PETER DE VRIES:

Not being one who is into films—I just go to the movies—there isn't much I have to say about Frank Capra's pictures except that I always enjoyed them (who didn't?) and still do, catching them whenever I can—in this day and age when the unhappy ending is as obligatory as the happy one was back then.

—Letter to the authors from Westport, Connecticut,
September 29, 1974.

ERNEST K. GANN:

For me Frank Capra has always represented true entertainment in the movies. Somehow, though, he managed to combine entertainment with something worth saying, as in *Mr. Smith Goes to Washington.*

Of all the directors, Capra seems to have been by far the most versatile, and I believe this would include contemporary directors.

It is a pity that Capra, Wellman, and their ilk are no longer making films. If they were, the magic of motion pictures might be known again, and all the world would become just a little more content.

With only a few exceptions, present-day directors seem lost in a messiah complex and have totally forgotten the motion pictures' prime reason for being.

Capra never did.

—Letter to the authors from Friday Harbor,
Washington, May 16, 1974.

HARRY GOLDEN:

I think Frank Capra is one of the most valuable citizens of America—a natural resource.

May he live to 120 like Moses.

—Letter to the authors from Charlotte, North Carolina,
August 6, 1974.

JAMES LEO HERLIHY:

No other movie maker, during my growing-up years, gave me more laughter, more tears, or more hope for America and the world, than Frank Capra.

—Letter to the authors from Hollywood, California,
January 29, 1975.

EVAN HUNTER:

I still remember feeling more "American" after seeing, especially, *Mr. Deeds Goes to Town, You Can't Take It with You, Mr. Smith Goes to Washington*, and *Meet John Doe*.

I shall never *ever* forget James Stewart's filibuster in *Mr. Smith Goes to Washington*. I would have been thirteen years old when I saw that film, and deeply involved in hoping to realize the American dream. Capra helped define it for me and many other young Americans, and for that alone his films would be important.

—*Letter to the authors from Sarasota, Florida*, February 18, 1975.

JAMES JONES:

I have always been an admirer of Frank Capra's work. And I think I can safely say that, along with the work of many others, Capra's films of the late thirties and the late forties influenced my life and my beliefs to a considerable extent. All these films may well have influenced the visual manner with which I have approached my own prose writing.

—*Letter to the authors from Paris, France*, March 29, 1974.

MACKINLAY KANTOR:

Capra was one of the truly deft, because obviously he liked what he was doing; and that's a glorious feeling forever and ever.

—*Letter to the authors from Sarasota, Florida*, May 22, 1974.

ERNEST LEHMAN:

If Frank Capra were active in filmmaking today, his pictures most probably would align perfectly with the current needs and demands of the public. Because what he would undoubtedly provide is an abundance of amused affection for humankind, a strong belief in the prevailing goodness of man, a contempt for despair, and a huge helping of meaningful entertainment. The guy would definitely get a G rating. For *Great!*

—*Letter to the authors from Los Angeles, California*, January 22, 1975.

MARY RENAULT:

I still remember *Lost Horizon* and *Mr. Deeds*, the latter for Gary Cooper, the former for a wonderful performance by Sam Jaffe as the bicentenarian High Lama.

—*Letter to the authors from Camps Bay, Cape Province, South Africa*, February 12, 1974.

IRWIN SHAW:

I have an affection for Frank Capra's films. They certainly were of a period that I'm afraid is gone forever. His pictures were indomitably optimistic and rich with faith in the essential goodness of America and its citizens. Scoundrels were included in the casts only to be confounded. I haven't seen any of the old pictures for a long time, and I'm afraid that if I did I'd mourn for a better and simpler time.

They were all the better because the best ones were done with rich humor, sometimes sly, sometimes gaggy, always based on character. You could feel a fresh breeze blowing through his comedies, cleansing and exhilarating. Behind them all was an innate sense of decency, respect for manner, but no pietistic false reverence.

He sure made us laugh!

—*Letter to the authors from Klosters, Switzerland*, March 23, 1974.

H. ALLEN SMITH:

Whenever I look at a list of Capra's films my moribund mind clouds up with wonderful memories. I think he was the greatest, with Leo McCarey running second, close up. Those Jimmy Stewart and Gary Cooper and Spencer Tracy and Cary Grant classics still stir my blood—even just thinking about them.

—*Letter to the authors from Alpine, Texas*, July 18, 1974.

MARY STEWART:

Nowadays the "director's film" or even the "cameraman's film" are commonplaces—and how commonplace, often, they are. To me both kinds are synonyms for boredom; gimmickry, symbolism that outweighs its meaning; irritation of the eye by angles and changed focus; dissatisfaction of the mind when problems are shown and then shelved without the courage of a decision, right or wrong.

In my teens, during the cinema's "golden age," I, like everyone else, followed the stars. One heard the names of the great directors, but to the average cinema-goer they mattered not at all beside the names of the star actors. Except for Frank Capra. Even then, one went to a "Capra film," and whatever else one felt about it, one was never bored.

What do I remember of the ones I saw? Warmth, drama; sentimentality that never repelled but, like it or not, got you by the throat; marvelous crowd scenes; gaiety and pathos and love, and above all a man's vision of how people *ought to be* and perhaps could be by the application of the few simple rules we lump together under the word *integrity*. You felt the better for going to a Capra film. I believe you were the better.

And over the years there are films one remembers. Ask me about Von Sternberg, and I think: "Dietrich, was it?" Ask me about Hitchcock, and I think: "Thrillers—oh, yes, *The Lady Vanishes*." And there was the director whose name I forget who always put his female stars in a bath. But ask me about Frank Capra, and I can still tell you all about *Mr. Deeds* and *Mr. Smith* and *Lost Horizon* and *You Can't Take It with You*.

The cinema of the seventies, heaven help the poor thing, could do with him.

—Letter to the authors from Edinburgh, Scotland,
October 28, 1974.

IRVING STONE:

I am not particularly a film buff, since I think the written word is still supreme, but I have seen most of Frank Capra's films. There is no question about their extremely high quality, not only cinematographically, but because each one makes a statement in its own field, whether it be politics, philosophy, or just plain love.

I met Frank Capra only once, and that was recently when we spoke together at a dinner for booksellers. We were both plugging our recently published books. Capra is a marvelous storyteller; he kept the audience enchanted for the better part of an hour.

—Letter to the authors from Beverly Hills, California,
May 29, 1974.

LEON URIS:

I've always been something of a super film buff, a natural-born truant who often escaped the Baltimore public school system by eight or ten straight hours in a moviehouse.

These days I'm married to a very young lady who has had formal film training. One of our greatest pleasures is a weekly screening of pictures she has obviously not seen, which I would like to see again, and I'm absolutely amazed at the scenes I can recite verbatim.

I suppose that watching all these films as a youngster made a serious impact on me and did much to fire up my own creative juices.

Nothing, but nothing, exerted greater influence than the Frank Capra masterpieces. I think he was so terribly important because he stood almost alone in an era when Hollywood went to great lengths to avoid a social commitment. I think he particularly appealed to that Jewish trait of always seeing the worst situation with a touch of humor.

Golly, there are just so many magnificent memories of so many scenes, I just couldn't list them all, and I find it impossible to pick out a favorite.

I hope I'm not redundant by saying they were vital to my formative years.

—Letter to the authors from Aspen, Colorado,
May 10, 1974.

ACTORS COMMENT

JACK BENNY:

About the only thing I can tell you about Frank Capra, since I was really never in contact with him, is that I know he made some great films, and I wish he had directed one of mine! One thing is for certain: If he had ever asked me to do a picture for him, I would have accepted it without even reading the script.

—Letter to the authors from Beverly Hills, California,
February 8, 1974.

JACKIE COOPER:

Everything I direct has me thinking of Frank Capra. I have always thought him to be the director I'd like to even half be!

—Letter to the authors from Beverly Hills, California,
September 14, 1974.

HENRY FONDA:

I have always regretted that I never had the opportunity to do a film for Frank Capra as did my friends Jimmy Stewart and Gary Cooper. I strongly admire the Capra work, and one of the main reasons I dislike one of my least-favorite films, *The Magnifi-*

cent Dope, is that I feel it was an attempt to rip off the Capra style without the Capra quality.

> —*Letter to the authors from New York, New York,*
> April 16. 1974.

LILLIAN GISH:

Frank Capra endeared himself to me by once saying publicly that "there has been nothing new since Griffith."

> —*Letter to the authors from New York, New York,*
> January 11, 1974.

GENE KELLY:

I certainly do have an opinion about Frank Capra's work and a very strong one at that, to wit: that it was of such generally high caliber, it seems difficult to overpraise him. *Mr. Smith* and *Mr. Deeds* taught all of us a lot who were growing up in the thirties—even though I guess we had much more fun roaring with glee at *It Happened One Night*. But the best of all Capra's work, I believe, is contained in *Lost Horizon*.

Count me in the list of his fans!

> —*Letter to the authors from Beverly Hills, California,*
> March 19, 1974.

LOTTE LENYA:

The word *genius* has been misused so very often, but in Mr. Capra's case it has found its full justification.

> —*Letter to the authors from New York, New York,*
> August 26, 1974.

VICTOR MATURE:

Certainly in my book, Frank Capra looms as a giant among the greatest directors of our industry.

I have never had the good fortune of working with Mr. Capra, but you can bet that I haven't missed any of his tremendous films. It would be difficult for me to single out any individual one for comment, but all of them bore his unmistakable stamp of genius and quality, a quality part humor and part sentimentality. You laughed and a lump came into your throat. You possibly shed a tear while you cheered his engrossing characters on.

People have told me that there were some among his unsympathetic critics (and they must have been a minute few) who labeled his incomparable touch as "Capracorn." To those cynics I can only say that life, then, must be corn, because it is full of the good people and the bad; the morals and the messages; the hangups and the happy endings that were part of the Capra magic. He is a short man in stature, but he towers among the tallest in our industry.

> —*Letter to the authors from Rancho Santa Fe,*
> *California*, April 25, 1974.

COLLEEN MOORE:

I am and have been an admirer of Frank Capra's talent since the early days when we worked at First National and he was directing Harry Langdon.

One of the great regrets of my life is that I was never able to work with Frank Capra. The proof of the greatness of his films is that today they are as good as when they were made. I think the reason is because he was always honest in his filmmaking and his motion pictures had something worthwhile to say. Frank said it with good taste in a manner that communicated with his audience. He made them think, gave them hope, melted them with tears, and entertained them—all at the same time. Quite a feat!

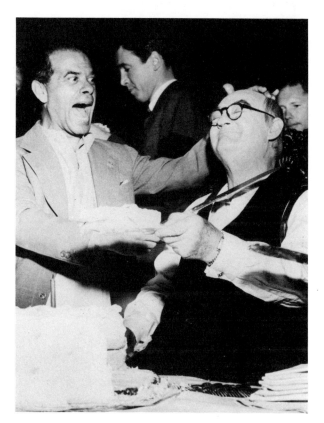

LIONEL BARRYMORE'S 68TH BIRTHDAY was celebrated on the set of *It's A Wonderful Life* by "cutup" Frank Capra, left. Between them, James Stewart is not to be distracted from eating his piece of cake.

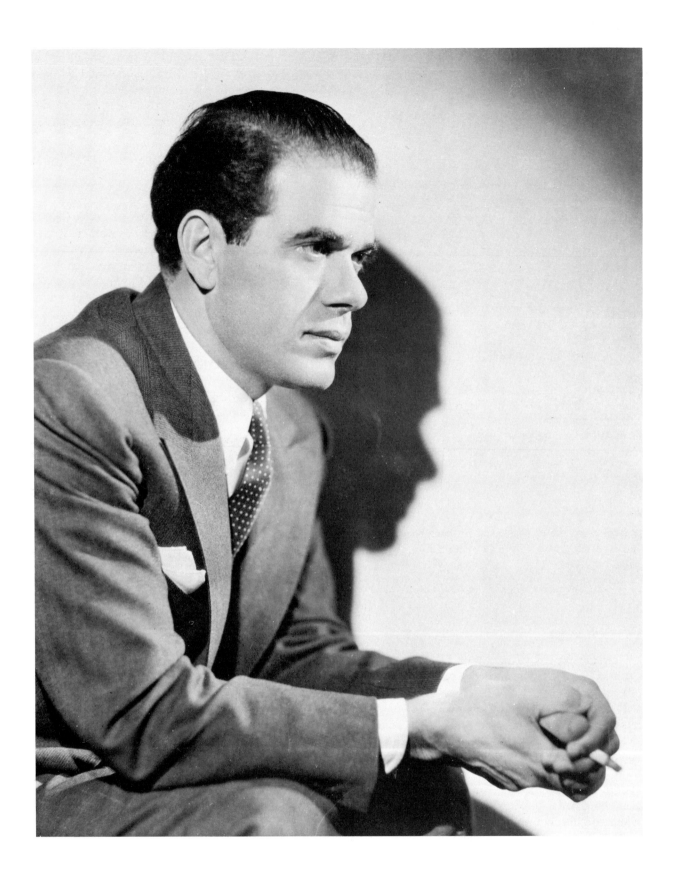

20

Capra films have an ageless quality, which is why they are studied today in all the film schools and treasured by his fans, of whom I am one.

—Letter to the authors from Templeton, California,
September 14, 1974.

GEORGE MURPHY:

I have known and respected Frank Capra for many years and am sorry that he is not still active in our industry. Had I been the head of a great studio, I most certainly would have insisted on retaining Frank Capra in some capacity and would thereby have guaranteed a high quality in the film product.

He was not only an outstanding filmmaker, but also a fine citizen, who by his personal deportment always provided a perfect example for citizens everywhere.

—Letter to the authors from Washington, D.C.,
May 20, 1974.

ROSALIND RUSSELL:

I very much regret never having made a Capra film. Mr. Capra was (and is) a genius with that gift of making both an amusing and a profound comment at the same time.

—Letter to the authors from Beverly Hills, California,
March 19, 1974.

JEAN STAPLETON:

I regret that I do not know Frank Capra personally and regret more that I have never worked under his direction. However, I have great memories of his work. His fine pictures are a rich part of my young years.

Lost Horizon was the most deeply affecting movie that I saw as a young person. I can still see vividly the High Lama scene—Margo shriveling up in the snow, Ronald Colman, who always captured my heart. The aura of enchantment that film produced on me will never fade.

I remember, too, the delicious delight of Gable and Colbert separated by the walls of Jericho. *Mr. Smith Goes to Washington* and *Mr. Deeds Goes to Town* were great favorites also.

—Letter to the authors from Los Angeles, California,
May 4, 1974.

HOW TO BAKE A SUNSHINE CAKE is demonstrated by director Frank Capra to his stars, Bing Crosby and Coleen Gray, while an almost hidden Clarence Muse, far right, observes. (*Riding High.*)

UKULELE CLUB at Manual Arts High School in Los Angeles. Frank Capra is fourth from right.

CAPPED AND GOWNED—Frank Capra, a 1918 graduate of the Throop Polytechnic Institute (later the California Institute of Technology).

22

CAPRA CHILDREN—Frank Capra, left, with a brother and sister, Tony and Ann.

Frank Capra was born in Bisaquino, Sicily, in 1897. Seventy-five years later the authors met him for the first time, summering in the High Sierras.

One minute before the hour set for our meeting, Mr. Capra telephoned the motel where he and his wife were picking us up to take us to dinner, to say that they would be ten minutes late. Nine minutes later his playfully rhythmic knock on the door announced their arrival.

The dinner, followed by an evening in the house at June Lake that *It's a Wonderful Life* built, sped by in seven hours; it included our dropping last names and Frank's farewell blessing of *"Vaya con Dios."* Since that time, the many-faceted aspects of our ever-growing friendship have been a constant joy!

Intelligently curious and widely read, this dynamic man of achievement possesses a dazzling range of interests—not in material things (aside from his original Audubons and a blue-and-white boat whose motor he cuts in midlake to watch the fish jump), but in facts, ideas, attitudes, persons.

That first evening there was talk of Homer and Eric Gill, of John Burroughs and Robert Ardrey. ("Writers are like gods to me!" he said.) There were warm memories of Edward Everett Horton's delightful Sunday parties and chilly observations on a weekend at San Simeon. We discovered that he hated the film *One Foot in Heaven* and thought *The Miracle of Morgan's Creek* the funniest film ever made. George Herriman, Will Rogers, and Mack Sennett sprang to life as he remembered them, and one could see Wallace Beery and Gregory La Cava, drunk and cursing, attempting to play Ping-Pong. The ecology of nearby Mono Lake, as he explained it, unfolded as an enthralling drama. Of his vocation, he confided, "When you handle film, it must be a sensuous experience—if it's not orgasmic, forget it!" Speaking of his own work, he added happily, "I can remember every frame—but not what I had for dinner last night."

Cicco (he was not called Frank until early in his school days) celebrated his sixth birthday in steerage en route to America with his parents and three of his six brothers and sisters. But he has told the story of his life in *The Name Above the Title* (The Macmillan Company, 1971), a book widely read and widely praised.

He sold newspapers on the Los Angeles streets as soon as he was able, and when he went to high school, he added three other part-time jobs—janitorial work at the school, guitar playing in a local bistro, and "stuffing" Sunday papers for the *Los*

Frank Capra's Wonderful Life

Angeles Times. His classmate of that time at Manual Arts High School, General James H. Doolittle, wrote to the authors from Los Angeles on August 14, 1974: "Frank Capra and I were in the same pyramid team some sixty years ago. My recollection is that Frank, who was the smallest of us, was often top man. He was rather heavy footed and, in climbing to the top spot, used to occasionally stomp our pyramid flat!"

At this time, doing acrobatics, Capra learned how to stand on his head. In later years, when, rarely, he was stuck for an appropriate verbal reply, it proved a perfect way to amaze and delight a large audience!

In 1918 Capra graduated from the Throop Polytechnic Institute (later the California Institute of Technology) with a degree in chemical engineering, and promptly enlisted in the army, where, to his disappointment, he was sidetracked from field soldiering into teaching ballistic mathematics to artillery officers.

After the war he spent several years bumming around the West. In Nevada, Arizona, Utah, and Oregon, he'd hang around hotels where traveling salesmen stayed and get invited into the game room where the guests played. Poker supported him in a fashion. Chemical-engineering jobs were nonexistent because of factory shutdowns after the war. Another job he took was house-to-house photo salesman for Hartsook's. "Six portraits for five dollars and only a dollar down," he recalls. But his fortunes sank pretty low.

Ending up in San Francisco, he followed a wild hunch as a long-shot player—and did it pay off! He read in a newspaper column that the old Jewish Gymnasium at Golden Gate Park was being turned into a movie studio. He presented himself to Mr. Walter Montague, and almost at once he was making his first picture, the one-reel *Fultah Fisher's Boarding House.* It was a success—and he had found his life's work.

He decided not to make another picture at once, however, but to spend a year in a San Francisco film laboratory where he could learn the technical roots of the business. Then, in Hollywood, he worked as prop man, film cutter, and gag writer for director Bob Eddy on two-reeler slapstick comedies. Progressing from there, he joined the Hal Roach Studio as a writer for the Our Gang series. Then he went to work for Mack Sennett as a gag writer. There, he later worked diligently with head writer Arthur Ripley and other writers to create material perfectly suited to the new screen comedian Harry Langdon.

Following several two-reelers at Sennett, which featured the "little boy" character, Langdon formed

his own corporation. Capra joined him, working with director Harry Edwards on Langdon's first feature-length film, *Tramp, Tramp, Tramp,* which co-starred the very young Joan Crawford. Crawford wrote to the authors from New York City on April 1, 1974:

Tramp, Tramp, Tramp was very early in my career, and right after that film, I realized I was in a very special business and had better learn my craft.

I'm sure Frank Capra taught me more than I ever realized. Being so young, I didn't know who taught me what, but being so eager to learn, I absorbed their knowledge of our craft.

Capra always has been, and is still, a beautiful man —full of knowledge, humor, and good taste in everything he does. I wish I had worked with him later when I had learned more.

Capra went on to personally direct Langdon in his next two feature-length films, *The Strong Man* and *Long Pants.* When the teaming of Capra and Langdon ended, acrimoniously on the star's side, Capra left California and went to New York to make *For the Love of Mike,* which was not a success. So in 1927, at thirty, he was out of work and again single. (While working for Eddy, he had married Helen Howell, who had played small parts in Eddy comedies, but the marriage ended in 1927.)

Mack Sennett came to the rescue, employing him as a gag writer once again. After three months, Harry Cohn, head of an almost unknown Poverty Row studio (Columbia Pictures), picked Capra's name from a list of unemployed directors—on a hunch. Capra responded to the call, admiring another hunch player like himself. It was the beginning of a great chapter in movie history. Recently, on "The Merv Griffin Show," Capra said, "I liked Cohn. We feuded, sure, but that was his challenge. He had no use for you if you didn't fight with him. If he could bully you, he didn't want you around. He was a great showman—and he backed his hunches."

In 1927, *The Jazz Singer* burst upon the world, and sound had arrived. Frank Capra, with his scientific education and grassroots knowledge of film-making, was an astounding asset to his new employer. "Gimme that science crap about sound again, will ya, Frank!" was the bewildered demand of a wary but impressed Harry Cohn.

In 1929, Frank Capra met Lucille Reyburn, petite, charming, vivacious, beautiful, and "for real," a descendant of Horatio, Lord Nelson. In 1932 they were married, and the romance continues to this day. They spent their honeymoon at Lake Placid. Benny Rubin, writing to the authors from Hollywood on March 21, 1974, shares this recollection:

In 1932, after an appendectomy, I got on a train that was headed for Lake Placid and the winter Olympics. I paid cash for my fare but did not have any sleeping accommodations. Ted Husing and Damon Runyon had the conductor get me a blanket and fix a "lounge" chair for me to sleep on. I just about got settled, when who should come walking thru the car? My old friends Frank and Lu on their honeymoon. *Punch line!* They took me to their drawing room and let me sleep on the couch! I was at every kid's christening and every kid's wedding since.

An amusing vignette of Frank and Lu Capra can be enjoyed in a memory sent to the authors from Los Angeles on September 17, 1974, by Regis Toomey:

The following is a fish story—a true fish story, an anecdote that may amuse. Back around 1935, before I made *Meet John Doe* with Frank Capra, I was doing a lot of fishing with Tay Garnett off Catalina Island. Tay and I spent every weekend possible trying to land a marlin, but we had no luck whatever.

Tay had a beautiful 108-foot boat that had been built on the East Coast at the turn of the century. And he had a dinghy with an inboard motor designed for marlin fishing. It was part of our routine, after breakfast, to take off for the dock, where one of us would buy the bait and the other would go up to the nearby market to get a box of green figs, for which Catalina is famous.

This particular morning I got the bait and was putting it away when Tay came back with the figs. I saw him coming down from the dock and he was shaking his head and laughing. He came aboard and sat down. "Guess who I just saw up there," he said. "The little dago and his wife. And do you know what? They told me they just dropped over to catch a *couple* marlin!"

I asked Tay if Capra had ever fished for marlin, and he said he never knew he had ever fished for *anything.* Well, it was funny, all right: A guy who has never fished for marlin casually says that he and his wife are going to catch a *couple.* And we'd been fishing for weeks without catching *one!*

Well, we got out to sea and were ready to start fishing. Tay was baiting his hook. He started to laugh and said, "What do you want to bet that the little dago *won't* catch a marlin?" I told him no, I wouldn't bet against Capra if he figured there were two marlin in the ocean intended for him. We came in several hours later, without having caught a marlin, and tied up at the dock before going aboard Tay's yacht. There were two marlin hung on the dock—*beauties!*—and each

26

ON THE BEACH, director Frank Capra, seated right, wearing white cap, discusses romantic scene with Jack Holt and Fay Wray during the filming of *Dirigible*. Joseph Walker is behind the camera.

AUTHOR OF NOVEL on which *The Bitter Tea of General Yen* was based, Grace Zaring Stone, center, visits Frank Capra and Barbara Stanwyck during filming.

THE TWO MEN who built Columbia Pictures and made movie history—Harry Cohn, left, and Frank Capra with the Oscar Capra was awarded as Best Director for *You Can't Take It With You*. The film itself won an Academy Award as Best Motion Picture of 1938.

MAKERS OF "LOST HORIZON" and visitors to the set—Left to right: Thomas Mitchell, William Perlberg, Rosalind Russell, Jack Holt, Ronald Colman, Frank Capra, Isabel Jewell, Robert Riskin, Jane Wyatt and Harry Cohn.

PLAYBACK—Delighted Frank Capra and Jean Arthur listen to new, improved recording made during the filming of *You Can't Take It With You.*

SPECIAL OSCAR was presented to pioneer film maker D. W. Griffith at the eighth annual Academy Awards ceremony in 1935. Left to right: Frank Capra, President of the Academy; D. W. Griffith, Jean Hersholt, H. B. Walthall, Frank Lloyd, C. B. DeMille, Donald Crisp.

one had a tag attached. On one tag it said, "Frank Capra—185 lbs." On the other it said, "Mrs. Frank Capra—225 lbs."

We asked where the Capras were. We were told they had gone back on a chartered boat several hours ago. "Well, how long did it take them to land these fish?" we asked. We were told that they had chartered a fishing boat, gone out, and come back in less than an hour with the two beautiful marlin.

Tay and I got into the dinghy, chugged out to the *Athene*, went aboard, and settled down to some serious imbibing. In fact, we both got plastered!

In 1939, after winning five Academy Awards (one more was yet to come), Capra left Columbia Pictures for total independence as a filmmaker. Then from 1942 through 1945, he served the people of the United States in a very special way, by making orientation films for the armed forces. His success won him the respect of Franklin D. Roosevelt, Winston Churchill, even of Marshal Stalin—and, more importantly for him, the friendship of a great American, General George C. Marshall.

Capra returned to a changed Hollywood, made several estimable pictures, including his own all-time favorite, *It's a Wonderful Life*, four science films for television, and a film for New York's 1964-65 World's Fair, and then retired. Retired? Not quite. He wrote his autobiography and now fills his days attending showings of his films and answering questions about their making—all over the world! Chiefly, he enjoys spreading the doctrine of optimism to American college students; but in Canada, Britain, France, India, Iran—everywhere!—he answers the call of young people, of film festivals, of the State Department. An ambassador of American verve and a symbol of the American dream come true, Frank Capra continues to serve his nation and his art.

This, then, is the record of the work of a man who felt that no two pictures were alike, that each was a living part of his perception. He was insepa-

HAPPY TRIO on the set of *Mr. Smith Goes to Washington*—left to right: James Stewart, Guy Kibbee and Frank Capra.

THREE CAMERA "SET-UP"—Confrontation scene between James Stewart, far left, and white-haired Claude Rains, standing under light, is presided over by Frank Capra, on stepladder. Harry Carey, far right, is at the rostrum. Capra shot many scenes with multiple cameras, each shooting different people during the same scene.

AT 1953 ACADEMY AWARD CEREMONIES—Frank and Lu Capra are accompanied by their son Frank, and their daughter, Lulu.

DISTINGUISHED SERVICE MEDAL AWARDED—General of the Army George C. Marshall, Chief of Staff, presents the Distinguished Service Medal to Colonel Frank Capra, Assistant Chief, Army Pictorial Service, in the Pentagon Building on June 15, 1945.

IMPRESSIVE MEETING—Frank Capra, left, and Prime Minister Winston Churchill, on whose recommendation Capra was awarded the Order of The British Empire for his World War II documentary films.

RARE PHOTO of two great American film directors—Frank Capra, left, and John Ford—taken at a testimonial dinner for Frank Capra, given by the Los Angeles Chamber of Commerce and the Directors Guild on May 12, 1962, a date designated as "Frank Capra Day" in Los Angeles. John Ford had stated that Frank Capra could direct standing on his head —and Capra showed how he would do it!

WILLIAM WYLER, left, is presented a Golden Globe, the Hollywood Foreign Press Association Award, for Best Direction (*Ben-Hur*, 1959) by Frank Capra.

rably bound to the world celluloid made possible, and he could function best in the vortex that is directing —a general in charge of a technical army that assisted him in creating a unique result. He sought the right themes: "Drama has to do with a man striving to make a choice. Which way will it go? When we want to know that," he said to the authors, "we're involved."

He added, "And actors are the only way directors can communicate with the audience. I remember countless inspired moments when an actor's character would really come alive because the actor added that extra something a director couldn't foresee. I *loved* them for that!"

HAROLD ROSS AND DAVE CHASEN, left and center, famed editor of *The New Yorker* and Hollywood restaurateur, respectively, with Frank Capra and a string of trout the trio caught at Silver Lake in the high Sierras.

Edward L. Bernds, sound engineer for all Capra's major Columbia films, recounted, with the help of his diary of those years, the following revealing incident:

If an actor was tense or tended to blow his lines, Capra would laugh easily and be more relaxed than ever. If an actor was really in trouble he would ask Joe Walker to relight the set, for example, or complain that the back wall was too hot—all this to give the actor time to collect himself.

I've heard him cut a scene and blame an imaginary noise, and on one occasion when an actor was really struggling, he backed away from the set a little bit, behind everyone (except me, I was sitting back at my control panel), picked up a nail from the floor, and tossed it over his shoulder. It made a fearsome clatter in that quiet sound stage, and he immediately demanded to know the culprit who made the noise. In the storm of this outside activity, the actor pulled himself together and, as I recall, did very well.

Frank Capra, a widower for several years, died on September 3, 1991, at the age of ninety-four in La Quinta, California, where he had lived for many years and early in his career had used as a retreat to work on screenplays for his films.

WE REMEMBER...

when we first met Frank Capra in 1972. We were in Palm Springs vacationing and had just finished reading Frank's autobiography, *The Name Above the Title*. In appreciation of his book, we sent him a book we had just coauthored, *Affectionately, T. S. Eliot (The Story of a Friendship: 1947–1965)*. Frank wrote to say that he and his wife, Lu, had just left La Quinta for their summer home at June Lake in the High Sierras and regretted not having a chance to meet us. We immediately phoned him and he invited us to June Lake. We became instant and longtime friends.

He and Lu visited us in Vermont and we traveled together to Brown University where Frank's movies were shown and where he spoke to students. He told one group of them, "I don't see any mavericks among you!" We went to New York and saw the Broadway production of *Jesus Christ, Superstar*. On another occasion, he and Lu came to be with us in Vermont for a Frank Capra Film Festival, which included Frank's personal favorite, *It's a Wonderful Life*. He told us, "Everything I ever wanted to say is in that movie."

Frank had a wonderful and unpredictable sense of humor. Once, when visiting Frank and Lu at their

THE MERV GRIFFIN SHOW—Frank Capra, left, appearing on television with Merv Griffin, August 14, 1973.

home in La Quinta, we were swimming in the long lap pool while our hosts sat at the far end, with Frank observing us and Lu working on her needlepoint. Knowing that we were later to have cocktails, dinner, and a showing of a film, one of Frank's naturally (it turned out to be *Arsenic and Old Lace*), we asked him, "What time do we have to get out of the pool?" Frank looked around and replied, "Why? Is there another shift coming in?"

Back in June Lake one summer, we said to Frank, "You know, Citadel Press puts out a series of books entitled 'The Films of...' Would you be interested in having us do *The Films of Frank Capra*, which would be a definitive record of your career?" Having written his own highly successful autobiography, Frank did not seem interested in the idea, so we dropped the matter.

Shortly after returning to Vermont, we received a phone call from Frank. He asked, "How's the book coming along?" We replied, "What book?" He said, "THE book, OUR book—*The Films of Frank Capra!* I just want you to know that I'll help in any way." The next day, in New York, Citadel Press agreed to publish the book.

Doing research, we quickly discovered how many friends Frank Capra had. We received over one hundred twenty-five responses from stars, support-ing players, directors, and others who had worked with Frank or simply admired him. We found out what a profound effect his life and his movies had had on people, and the people wrote lovingly of him. We sent each of the contributors a three-pound wheel of Vermont Cheddar cheese in appreciation, and Frank wrote each and every one of them to thank them for their contribution.

Frank bought tons of the book to send to friends, and he carried it around with him to the various colleges and universities where he spoke.

After we had moved to California in 1977, the year the book came out, we saw Frank and Lu often, and rekindled friendships with his "Capra people," as we called them.

We brought Beulah Bondi to La Quinta for a visit with the Capras, and when Beulah died, Frank, upon our request, graciously spoke at her memorial service at the Motion Picture Country Home and Hospital. Then he returned to our home for lunch with many of the actors who had worked in his films. Also there were Ann Doran, who was the supporting actress used most often by Frank, and Mary Treen from *It's a Wonderful Life*, who said her dream was always to be in a Capra film, and she finally made it! Jane Wyatt recalled working on *Lost Horizon* and Fritz Feld spoke of being in Frank's last film, *A Pocketful of Miracles*. We all remembered lovely Beulah Bondi, James Stewart's mother in *It's a Wonderful Life*, and also a featured player in *Mr. Smith Goes to Washington*.

With Frank's passing, Citadel decided to reissue the book with a slightly revised title, *The Complete Films of Frank Capra*. Frank was justifiably proud of his work and the book's second life proves that the Capra films will never die. He who had a wonderful life shared it with friends personally—and on film with a worldwide audience.

Our farewell blessing to Frank is what he said to us after our first meeting, "Vaya Con Dios."

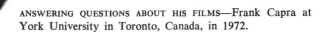

ANSWERING QUESTIONS ABOUT HIS FILMS—Frank Capra at York University in Toronto, Canada, in 1972.

A DANCE by Anne of Austria to herald her arrival at the saloon of Fultah Fisher's Boarding House.

SINISTER LUZ, knocked down by Hans, harbors a grudge.

JOVIAL HANS, the blue-eyed Dane, introduced in the film at the bar of Fultah Fisher's Boarding House. The bartender is "Honest" Jack who sold slops and harvested the sailors' pay.

A Fireside Production, released by Pathé. Produced by G. F. Harris and David Supple at Montague Studios, San Francisco, California. Directed by Frank R. Capra. Based on the poem *The Ballad of Fisher's Boarding-House*, by Rudyard Kipling. Photographed by Roy Wiggins. Running time: 12 minutes.

CAST:

Anne of Austria, Mildred Owens; *Hans*, Olaf Skavlan; *Salem Hardieker*, Ethan Allen; *British Sailor*, Gerald Griffin; *Luz*, Oreste Seragnoli.

The lure of reading is shown in the opening scene. A portly, middle-aged man is settled in an upholstered armchair before an ornate fireplace, opening a book. At once the scene dissolves to the setting he is reading about: an exotically foreign-looking, disreputable smoke-filled saloon crowded with boisterously rough types.

The first stanza of a poem is superimposed on that scene, as, throughout the movie, other stanzas (or an individual line or lines) will also be used, as titles. When these titles, which precede the scenes that illustrate them, are on screen, the action is slowed almost to a standstill—an effective device that allows the audience to read without distraction; yet the characters in the background are not rendered lifeless, and the resumption of their story becomes merely a quickening of pace.

Before the plot begins, Capra, like Kipling, introduces the characters, a motley crew.

The normal activity in the saloon "where sailormen reside" is telling tall stories and raucous bragging, punctuated by banging fists upon the table. Luz, the sinister, more violent than the others, starts an argument and is good-naturedly knocked down by Hans the blue-eyed Dane, who wears a "little silver crucifix that keeps a man from harm." Luz is obviously resentful of the Dane.

Then the notorious whore Anne of Austria, who came "To eat the bread of infamy and take the wage of shame," enters at the top of the stairs and joins Salem Hardieker, "a lean Bostonian," at his table. But her eye immediately roves—to Hans. He politely rejects her attentions, being true to port law that made her—temporarily—Salem's girl.

Spurned, she becomes Hans's accuser—"He called me names!"—and a fight between Salem and Hans begins.

Hans is stabbed by revengeful Luz—"A knife-thrust unawares"—who sneaks up the stairs and out.

Fultah Fisher's Boarding House

1922 (Silent)

ANNE OF AUSTRIA flirts with Hans, who wears a silver crucifix "that keeps a man from harm."

A THREAT in picture and line of title.

FIGHT AND THE MURDER OF HANS by third party Luz, dramatically filmed in shadows.

Hans is cradled in Anne's arms. He dies, and she cries hysterically.

Anne, having found the crucifix on Hans's dead body and meditated upon it, runs to the stairs, pulls off her ostentatious jewelry, in favor of the crucifix, rejects all approaches to her by the men, and retreats up the same dark stairway by which she had entered so lightheartedly just a short time ago.

The scene dissolves to the reader by his comfortable fireside. He closes his book.

Capra omitted two stanzas and transposed one from Kipling's poem. From the very first, Capra's personal and dramatic view of life was at work. As written by Kipling, Salem Hardieker, the impulsive, stabbed his rival in anger. Young Frank Capra saw a more potent strength in having Luz, Fate's pawn, fell Hans, the blue-eyed Dane, "Hans the mighty." Two honest men fight, but one is doomed by circumstance. Capra, like Thomas Hardy, allowed Fate her cruel triumphs.

Irony is stressed in the refrain

> The little silver crucifix
> That kept a man from harm.

However, here young Capra expressed an opposite view. Anne of Austria does not, true to her character and Kipling's words, steal the silver crucifix. She is transformed by its power, and insofar as such a recounting of sordid lives can have an upbeat ending, Frank Capra has provided it. Anne's reformation is a ray of light that cuts through the smoke-filled pessimism of the original ballad.

Capra was twenty-five years old and penniless when he was hired to make this one-reel movie. Totally without film experience but with daring imagination, he decided to light his saloon set realistically, from a single source, making use of shadows. "I'll copy Rembrandt, paint with light as Rembrandt had with pigment," he wrote in his autobiography. And he cast the film realistically with authentic colorful types (nonactors) from the San Francisco waterfront, "smelly and filthy"—except for a professional chorus girl who played Anne of Austria (a real Barbary Coast whore wouldn't act in the movie for ten bucks a day because, as she told Capra, she could make that much in an hour at her chosen profession).

Capra's dictum, as related in his autobiography, was: "The riffraff in Kipling's bar has got to *reek* of sweat and grog and vileness." He used no makeup, no wigs, and no phony beards. He now thinks that his "actors" used fictitious names. Even he added a middle initial, *R.*, to his name. He told the authors, "I didn't have a middle name or a middle initial. But in those days I thought it was very high class to have a middle initial, so I invented one! Frank *R.* Capra sounded much better to me than just plain Frank Capra, which I thought had no ring. I remember a story about an uneducated man who couldn't read or write but became a millionaire. When he went to the bank, he signed his checks with two *X*s. One day he signed three *X*s, and the bank president told him that he had made an error. No, came the reply, he hadn't made a mistake. He had recently moved to Park Avenue and taken on a middle initial! So my middle initial stood for Park Avenue. I used it for a few pictures, inconsistently, and then finally dropped it."

(This rare film resides in the collections of Frank Capra and the Library of Congress. Stills for this book were taken from the frames of the film, with the kind permission of Mr. Capra.)

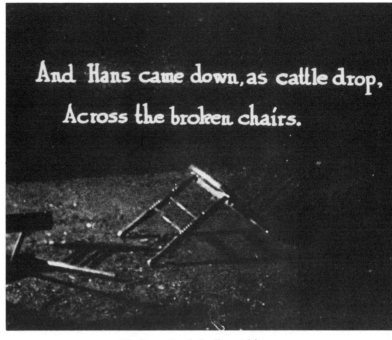

SILENT FILM TITLE graphically and artistically used by young Frank Capra.

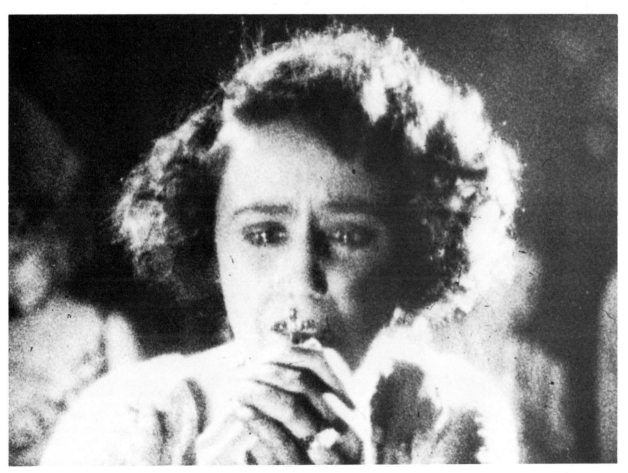

MOMENT OF CONVERSION—With the death of Hans and the possession of his silver crucifix, Anne of Austria finds faith and vows to reform.

MISPLACED BY FATE, Paul Bergot (Harry Langdon) in No Man's Land, trying to master the machine gun—before he is picked up and carried off by a German.

38

A First National Picture. Produced by Harry Langdon Corporation. Directed by Frank Capra. Screenplay by Arthur Ripley, Frank Capra, Hal Conklin, and Robert Eddy. Comedy Construction by Clarence Hennecke. Photographed by Elgin Lessley and Glenn Kershner. Edited by Harold Young. Running time: 75 minutes.

CAST:

Paul Bergot, Harry Langdon; *Mary Brown,* Priscilla Bonner; *"Gold Tooth,"* Gertrude Astor; *Parson Brown,* William V. Mong; *Roy McDevitt,* Robert McKim; *Zandow the Great,* Arthur Thalasso; *Bus Passenger,* Brooks Benedict.

GERTRUDE ASTOR:

I remember so well the fancy taffeta dress with beautiful French lace that I bought for the part. I thought the studio clothes were impossible, but although what I paid four hundred dollars for was fun to wear and so becoming, I realize now that it was not right for my part. I should have been shabby—but gaudy!

Harry Langdon was a funny little wordless man. He would never sit near anyone on the set; indeed, he would wander a block away and sit alone on a bench until Frank Capra needed him for a scene. Although a star, he acted like a nonentity. I sauntered over once and asked him why he sat alone. "Oh, I like it. I don't like people. I like to be alone and think." He said this in his quiet voice, a voice difficult to hear, actually.

It was a contrast: Frank Capra so young and so serious, and Harry looking at you, blinking those pale blue eyes, and then glancing over his shoulder to make sure you weren't following him into his private world of silence.

—Told to the authors on the telephone from Hollywood, California, July 21, 1976.

In *The Strong Man,* as the unwarlike Belgian soldier Paul Bergot, Harry Langdon is captured by a huge German (Arthur Thalasso) in no-man's-land and brought to postwar America as part of the German's weightlifting act, the Great Zandow & Co.

In New York, Paul searches the city streets for Mary Brown (Priscilla Bonner), an American girl who had written to him during the war. "Gold Tooth" (Gertrude Astor), a woman being trailed by a detective, slips a roll of bills into Paul's coat pocket; a little later, when she tries to retrieve the

GERTRUDE ASTOR, who plays "Gold Tooth" in *The Strong Man.*

The Strong Man

1926 (Silent)

ARRIVAL IN AMERICA and off on tour: The Great Zandow (Arthur Thalasso) and his "captured" assistant, Paul Bergot (Harry Langdon).

money, she discovers it has fallen into the lining of his coat. She decides to lure him up to her apartment by telling him that she's "little Mary." He believes this until she lights a cigarette. He attempts to leave, but she engages him in a tug-of-war, and finally, she pretends to faint. The doorman at her apartment house needs help getting her in, adding indignantly to Paul, "You can't leave your woman lying around like this!"

Because of her weight, Paul carries her, with her beads dangling, up a great marble staircase by sitting on the stairs with her on his lap and pushing himself up step by step.

In her room, she attempts to undress him in order to get her money out of his coat, and we see him prone (from an overhead shot). Thinking that he's being seduced, he shakes his finger at her. She finally retrieves the money and gives him the key by which she had locked him in the room. Paul, with his finger to his mouth, has the exit line: "Don't let this leak out."

On tour, the Great Zandow & Co. head for Cloverdale, a once peaceful town, now overrun by a bootlegger element that has corrupted many with the Palace Music Hall—a place of hula dancing, beer drinking, gambling, and loose women—much to the dismay of Parson Brown (William V. Mong) and his daughter, Paul's Mary. She (a title informs us) "looked at the world through the eyes of optimism —perhaps because she was blind."

En route to the town on a crowded bus, Paul, who has a bad cold, is sneezing over a man next to him and taking spoonfuls of Smith Bros. cough medicine. "One more germ out of you, and the Smith brothers lose a good customer," the man tells him.

Soon Paul unties his tie and scratches at a chest plaster, which he then tears off, deciding to rub in camphor, but accidentally taking hold of a jar of limburger cheese and applying it. Everyone on the bus is outraged when Paul announces, "My head's clear. I'm beginning to smell!"

40

"Throw him out!" shout the passengers—and they do! But a hairpin turn in the road results in his falling down the hillside right back into the bus—through the roof!

Paul and Mary discover each other. A perfect pair, they fall touchingly in love, like the innocent children they are.

Paul, taking the drunken Zandow's place in the act, routs the Cloverdale bullies by firing a cannon in the midst of his performance. An innocent Joshua, he causes the walls of corruption to fall as he presides over a visual feast of destruction.

At film's end, Cloverdale is restored to the rule of justice and decency, protected by the majesty of the law—with Paul as the town policeman!

DAZED BUT UNHURT, Paul, Bergot (Harry Langdon), having plummeted through the roof, is back in the bus from which fellow passengers had ejected him shortly before.

SHOWING OFF HIS NEW LONG PANTS and bicycle, The Boy (Harry Langdon) seeks to impress The Vamp.

A First National Picture. Produced by Harry Langdon Corporation. Directed by Frank Capra. Story by Arthur Ripley, adapted by Robert Eddy. Comedy Construction by Clarence Hennecke. Photographed by Elgin Lessley and Glenn Kershner. Running time: 60 minutes.

CAST:

The Boy, Harry Shelby, Harry Langdon; *His Mother,* Gladys Brockwell; *His Father,* Alan Roscoe; *His Bride, Priscilla,* Priscilla Bonner; *His Downfall, the Vamp, Bebe Blair,* Alma Bennett; *His Finish,* Betty Francisco.

The Boy, Harry Shelby (Harry Langdon), a romantic-minded reader of love stories, is given the long pants he has always coveted. The father (Alan Roscoe) fears he'll go wild when he sees them and get into trouble on the streets, but his mother (Gladys Brockwell) solemnly and humorlessly declares, "These pants will never go to his head."

But go to his head they do! On his bicycle, he rides past the Vamp, Bebe Blair (Alma Bennett), whose luxurious chauffeur-driven car is immobilized by a flat tire. She is the epitome of his idea of a princess of romance, although we learn that she is involved in snow (dope) smuggling. He approaches the car, showing off his bike, his long pants, and his stunt riding. A top shot shows him rhythmically circling the car, all aflutter.

Back at the Boy's home, Priscilla (Priscilla Bonner) telephones, and the Boy is summoned from his ride to receive the call. When he returns, his dream girl is gone. He looks all around for her at the site of their meeting—on tiptoes, a magnificent use of body language! Then he finds a note she has dropped, which he misinterprets as revealing the Vamp's love for him.

He skips home and tells his parents, "Don't be surprised if I get married soon!" Naturally, they think he means to marry Priscilla. But a newspaper's front page reveals that Bebe Blair is in jail—on a frameup—and the Boy tells his father to give the presents back: he's not going to marry "other women" when his sweetheart is in distress.

The Boy reaches the city with flowers for the Vamp, who escapes from jail. Now her true character becomes apparent to the Boy: She drinks! This knowledge renders the Boy speechless. She has a knock-down, drag-out fight with her rival in a night-club dressing room, while the Boy sits watching, immobilized and transfixed.

Long Pants

1927 (Silent)

AT THE VAMP'S CAR, baby-faced Harry Langdon as The Boy, gazes languidly at the girl who is the ideal of all the princesses he's dreamed about.

Finally, he comments, "Why, I'm *surprised*. My goodness. I'm sorry, but we must part. I'm through."

The Boy finally returns home, as his father had sagely predicted, to find his parents and Priscilla waiting for him. Happily, exotic romance and adventure seem far behind him now.

THE VAMP (Alma Bennett) in her touring car, is momentarily intrigued by the antics of The Boy (Harry Langdon).

44

AS THE FIGHT BEGINS between The Vamp (Alma Bennett), left, and nightclub dancer, His Finish (Betty Francisco), The Boy (Harry Langdon), realizes he's in the wrong place.

45

A First National Picture. Produced by Robert Kane. Directed by Frank Capra. Production Manager and Scenario Writer: Leland Hayward. Screenplay by J. Clarkson Miller, based on the story "Hell's Kitchen," by John Moroso. Photographed by Ernest Haller. Assistant Director: Joe Boyle. Running time: 75 minutes.

CAST:

Mike, Ben Lyon; *Abraham Katz*, George Sidney; *Herman Schultz*, Ford Sterling; *Mary*, Claudette Colbert; *Patrick O'Malley*, Hugh Cameron; *"Coxey" Pendleton*, Richard "Skeets" Gallagher; *Henry Sharp*, Rudolph Cameron; *Evelyn Joyce*, Mabel Swor.

BEN LYON:

Frank Capra was a joy to work for, being sympathetic, understanding, helpful, and inspiring. In his autobiography he stated that *For the Love of Mike* was his first failure. I'll admit it wasn't an important film, but it was entertaining.

—*Letter to the authors from Los Angeles, California,*
September 11, 1974.

BENNY RUBIN:

In 1927, in New York, I was a vaudevillian between bookings. Frank came there to make a movie titled *For the Love of Mike*. The leading lady was a kid called Claudette Colbert. Frank gave her her first movie job. He gave me the job of finding, or topping, better comedy than was in the script—I was the gag man. He saw to it that I was paid two hundred and fifty dollars a week for two weeks—which was more than he got for directing the picture, because the producer *never* paid him!

—*Letter to the authors from Hollywood, California,*
March 21, 1974.

On location shooting, Frank Capra used the actual regatta in Connecticut, in which Yale was a participant, as background for the big race that climaxes the film. He told the authors that he shot the race from a train following the shells and that he also placed a camera at the periscope's eyepiece on a submarine from the nearby submarine base.

In the film, three bachelors—Herman Schultz (Ford Sterling), a delicatessen owner; Abraham Katz (George Sidney), a tailor; and Patrick O'Malley (Hugh Cameron), a street cleaner—adopt an abandoned baby boy and call him Mike. They send him

For the Love of Mike

1927 (Silent)

AN ABANDONED BABY is adopted by, left to right, Patrick O'Malley (Hugh Cameron), Abraham Katz (George Sidney) and Herman Schultz (Ford Sterling).

through school, and with the encouragement of a neighbor, Mary (Claudette Colbert), he attends Yale and becomes stroke on the varsity crew.

For his twenty-first birthday his three "fathers" sponsor a banquet to introduce him to their business associates, but Mike arrives drunk and insults the guests. Chagrined, Mike returns to college, gambles compulsively, and falls into the clutches of professional gamblers who demand that he throw a crew race. Mike refuses, wins for Yale, and gains Mary's love. Once again, the three "fathers" are proud of their "son."

CLAUDETTE COLBERT, making her movie debut as Mary in *For the Love of Mike*, plays a neighbor of her boy friend's two "fathers" —Abraham Katz (George Sidney) left, and Herman Schultz (Ford Sterling).

BEN LYON, as the drunken Mike at his twenty-first birthday party, offends his three "fathers"—left to right: Abraham Katz (George Sidney), Herman Schultz (Ford Sterling), Patrick O'Malley (Hugh Cameron)—and his girl friend Mary (Claudette Colbert).

AFTER WINNING THE ROWING RACE, Mike (Ben Lyon), holding the oar, is greeted by two of his "fathers," Patrick O'Malley (Hugh Cameron), left, Abraham Katz (George Sidney) and his girl friend, Mary (Claudette Colbert).

AT WORK BEHIND HER CIGAR COUNTER at the Stratford Hotel, Molly Kelly (Viola Dana) is on the lookout for a millionaire to marry.

MOLLY BUMPS INTO A MILLIONAIRE—Andy B. Charles, Jr. (Ralph Graves): "I hope you don't feel hurt." Molly Kelly (Viola Dana): "Why don't you blow your horn when you come to a crossing?"

A Columbia Picture. Produced by Harry Cohn. Directed by Frank R. Capra. Story by Elmer Harris, with titles by Al Boasberg. Photographed by Joseph Walker. Art Director: Robert E. Lee. Edited by Arthur Roberts. Assistant Director: Eugene De Rue. Running time: 69 minutes.

CAST:

Molly Kelly, Viola Dana; *Andy B. Charles, Jr.*, Ralph Graves; *A. B. Charles, Sr.*, Burr McIntosh; *Mrs. Maggie Kelly*, Aggie Herring; *Secretary Brooks*, Carl Gerard; *Valet*, Sydney Crossley.

The title of Frank Capra's first Columbia Picture, *That Certain Thing*, was a popular expression in 1928. Capra told the authors that it was highly complimentary to say that someone had "that certain thing."

The story of this film is simple: Molly Kelly (Viola Dana) has her dream come true when she marries a millionaire, Andy B. Charles, Jr. (Ralph Graves), but his father, A. B. Charles, Sr. (Burr McIntosh), immediately disinherits him because he believes his daughter-in-law is nothing but a gold digger. The couple, although penniless, stays together, and they end up establishing a successful box-lunch business that offers lively competition to the father's chain of restaurants. There is a reconciliation since the father respects his daughter-in-law for her business expertise.

This lively film contains many funny moments.

Of Molly's mother, Mrs. Maggie Kelly (Aggie Herring), a title reads that she always told her husband where to go, and one day he went there, leaving her a widow.

At the opening of the film, Molly is washing her two brothers in a tub filled to overflowing with soap bubbles. The battling kids splash water in her face, and she dries her face with a pair of bloomers hanging on a line in the bathroom. Then, with both children out of the tub, she rinses them off with a sprinkling can. As Molly leaves the bathroom, the boys jump back into the tub. It overflows and drips down to the apartment below, where a returning lady chides her dog, who is lying innocently beside the puddle.

A streetcar conductor tells Molly, "I'm crazy about you."

"Well," she retorts, "when I go crazy, too, we'll get married."

That Certain Thing

1928 (Silent)

HONEYMOON IS INTERRUPTED when a store representative comes to repossess all the gifts Andy B. Charles, Jr. (Ralph Graves) has given his new bride, Molly (Viola Dana), telling him that his father will disinherit him if he doesn't get rid of his gold digger wife.

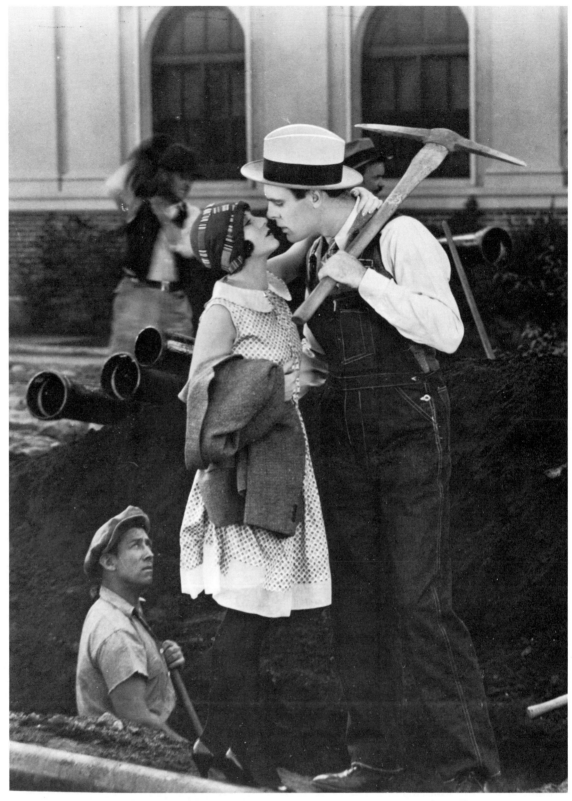

A JOB FOR A MILLIONAIRE'S SON—Andy B. Charles, Jr. (Ralph Graves) kisses his new wife, Molly (Viola Dana), before starting his first day of work.

Of the millionaire son, a title tells us that he "loved his father so dearly he was always drinking to his health."

Molly's millionaire husband gets a job digging ditches. Unfortunately, he immediately breaks a water main, soaking his boss. He is fired, and he tells his wife that he's quit because the boss is all wet! They are fortunate indeed that Molly is inspired to go into the box-lunch business!

THE SANDWICH WITH A SECRET ("Cut the ham thick!") is sampled by Andy B. Charles, Jr. (Ralph Graves). His wife, Molly (Viola Dana) holds one of her popular box lunches, while her mother, Maggie Kelly (Aggie Herring), employed in the factory, shows the successful business operation to A. B. Charles, Sr. (Burr McIntosh) in this posed still.

CHALLENGED BY A BULLY—"Spike" Mullins (Johnnie Walker) bullies sensitive Jerry McGuire (Buster Collier) while Hilda Jenson (Shirley Mason) tries to restrain the prize fighter.

NEW CLOTHES are designed and fitted by Jerry McGuire (Buster Collier) for Hilda Jenson (Shirley Mason).

54   VICTIMIZED by prize fighter bully "Spike" Mullins (Johnnie Walker), left, Jerry McGuire (Buster Collier) vows that he'll get even with him, while Hilda Jenson (Shirley Mason) realizes that she is the cause of all the trouble.

A Columbia Picture. Produced by Harry Cohn. Directed by Frank Capra. Story by Norman Springer, adapted by Elmer Harris. Continuity by Rex Taylor. Photographed by Ray June. Art direction by Robert E. Lee. Edited by Arthur Roberts. Assistant Director: Eugene De Rue. Running time: 60 minutes.

CAST:

Hilda Jenson, Shirley Mason; *Jerry McGuire*, Buster Collier; *"Spike" Mullins*, Johnnie Walker; *"Flash" Tracy*, Ernie Adams; *Otto*, Carl Gerard; *"Maison" Katz*, William H. Strauss; *Mary Malone*, Jean Laverty.

Jerry McGuire (Buster Collier), a designer for a Greenwich Village dress shop, is in love with Hilda Jenson (Shirley Mason), who works in a delicatessen across the street. She, however, is infatuated with prize fighter Spike Mullins (Johnnie Walker), and to attract his attention she has Jerry design enticing clothes for her. The plot works: Spike falls for her; but he runs roughshod over Jerry in a brutal way that turns Hilda's love for him sour. Jerry secretly goes into training and, when the opportunity comes, meets Spike in the ring. To help Jerry, Hilda sabotages Spike's stomach by overfeeding the champ. Concerning this scene, *Variety* reported in its May 2, 1928, issue, "Some of the funniest work is accomplished by Shirley Mason when she feeds the champ on everything she has in the store before he meets her boy friend." With this advantage, Jerry wins the fight and the girl.

So This Is Love

1928 (Silent)

WINNER in the ring and in love, Jerry McGuire (Buster Collier) is embraced by Hilda Jenson (Shirley Mason).

TENT SHOW—Ginger Bolivar (Bessie Love), selling tickets, mistakes Don Wilson (Johnnie Walker) for an aspiring actor come to audition, while her father, Col. Jaspar Bolivar (Lionel Belmore), delivers a barker's spiel to would-be theatre patrons.

THE BOLIVAR STOCK COMPANY in performance. The Confederate soldier is J. Madison Wilberforce (Sidney D'Albrook); Don Wilson (Johnnie Walker) is holding the flag, while Ginger Bolivar (Bessie Love) proudly salutes, and Eric Barrymaine (David Mir) stands by bravely with drawn sword.

56

BACKSTAGE ANTICS between Don Wilson (Johnnie Walker), newly cast in a Bolivar Stock Company melodrama, and Ginger Bolivar (Bessie Love), who plays the ingenue in the melodrama.

A Columbia Picture. Produced by Harry Cohn. Directed by Frank R. Capra. Adapted by Elmer Harris from the story "Come Back to Aaron" by Robert Lord and Ernest S. Pagano. Continuity by Peter Milne. Photographed by Philip Tannura. Art direction by Robert E. Lee. Edited by Arthur Roberts. Assistant Director: Eugene De Rue. Running time: 66 minutes.

CAST:

Ginger Bolivar, Bessie Love; *Don Wilson, Harry Mann*, Johnnie Walker; *Col. Jasper Bolivar*, Lionel Belmore; *Wingate*, Ernest Hilliard; *J. Madison Wilberforce*, Sidney D'Albrook; *Eric Barrymaine*, David Mir.

BESSIE LOVE:

In that long ago time of Frank Capra's comedy *The Matinee Idol*, Frank was a good workman and expected everyone else to be so. I cannot imagine him going over the budget in time or money. If your call was nine o'clock, the assistant would see that you were on the set and starting to rehearse at nine. This, in a day when directors were off in a huddle with the writer and supervisor somewhere until almost noon, whatever time the company call, trying to agree on how the sequence should be shot. The actors and crew sat around and waited.

One morning I was late. It must have been the first morning, because I was amazed when told that Frank was waiting and that he never waited for anybody. I knew I was wrong. I should have allowed an extra hour for the glamorous "actress" make-up —false eyelashes which were new then, stagey hairdress and costume. I wanted all this to be extra right, different from the sweater-and-skirt girl I was playing when "off-stage." Frank was fit to be tied, but there was nothing I could do except be as quick as I could and slither onto the set. Which I did!

Frank's idealism as a filmmaker was unknown to me then, if I remember correctly. I thought of his pictures as only good commercial successes.

Not long ago Frank gave an illustrated lecture at the National Film Theatre here in London, where I now live. He spoke simply and quietly about America—our country, its problems. And a rich country can have problems. More wealth than the ancients could comfortably house can be amassed in one generation if you are willing to work. And quicker than that if you are ruthless. The byproducts of greed—callousness and selfishness—are not surprising.

The Matinee Idol

1928 (Silent)

IN BLACKFACE DISGUISE, Don Wilson (Johnnie Walker) shows off for his manager-producer Wingate (Ernest Hilliard), left of Ginger Bolivar (Bessie Love), and, continuing left to right, other members of The Bolivar Stock Company, played by: David Mir, Sidney D'Albrook and Lionel Belmore.

AFTER MASQUERADE PARTY, Ginger Bolivar (Bessie Love) tells Don Wilson (Johnnie Walker), center, that she has just met the star of their Broadway show. Her boy friend, J. Madison Wilberforce (Sidney D'Albrook) stands behind her, and, on the left, listening, are Col. Jaspar Bolivar (Lionel Belmore) and Eric Barrymaine (David Mir).

That day at the National, Frank talked about how, during the intervening years, he had wanted to help the nation out of a few of the quagmires we were in. And he'd seen that he could do it with his films. My eyes grew wide at this new Capra vista. And my ears *must* have been flapping. It was the quiet, gentle, conversational tone that Abraham Lincoln might have used. It was so casual that you felt you could go right out of that theater and do something of the kind yourself. And you were a mug if you didn't at least have a go.

There should be more Frank Capras around.

—Letter to the authors from London, England,
May 6, 1974.

BENNY RUBIN:

Re *The Matinee Idol.* I visited Frank on the set while I was playing the Orpheum Theatre in Hollywood. While he was explaining the plot, he spoke of being in a hell of a spot. *How* and *what* could Johnnie Walker do that would say (in pantomime, without using titles) that he was a Broadway star? Here is what we did. The cameras were waiting for

me at 8:00 A.M. It took me five minutes to put on the blackface (I brought the stuff with me) and another ten to have them adjust Walker's clothes to fit me (he was four inches taller); then I danced five different routines. On the screen you saw long shots of me doing intricate steps; then Frank would cut to Johnnie's face. The shots of my hands and feet were intercut with more head shots of Johnnie.

In a photo of me taken at the time with Bessie Love, Frank Capra, and Johnnie Walker, I was wearing a Russian costume. I had to have it with me, because when the last shot was made, Harry Cohn had a police escort drive me to my matinee— and I just made it!

—Letter to the authors from Hollywood, California,
July 6, 1974.

Don Wilson (Johnnie Walker), outstanding blackface comedian, temporarily stranded in upstate New York, finds himself caught up in the fun of trying out for a tent melodrama produced by the Great Bolivar Stock Company. He is auditioned by the show's owner's daughter, Ginger Bolivar (Bessie Love), who is unaware that he is a Broadway star.

58

ACTOR HIRED AND MATCH MADE—Don Wilson (Johnnie Walker) returns to The Bolivar Stock Company to apply for the position of actor and husband for Ginger Bolivar (Bessie Love).

She gives him a part in their current play, a Civil War drama.

Don's producer-friend, Wingate (Ernest Hilliard), having been stranded too, is in the audience. He sees the unintentionally hilarious result when Don appears onstage in the ludicrous play and decides to put the melodramatic scene in his new Broadway revue—for laughs.

Don reluctantly agrees. Later, during rehearsals, the star falls in love with Ginger, and his misgivings grow, especially since he has changed his name and has to play a dual role with her (as the aspiring actor she's hired and, in blackface, the star of the show).

Humiliated by the sophisticated New York reception of their scene, Ginger runs out of the theater. Don pursues her in blackface in the rain, and his deception is revealed when his makeup is washed off. He is dragged back to the theater to finish his performance, and Ginger returns to upstate New York. Later Don follows her and auditions again—this time for the real-life part of her husband.

BENNY RUBIN, left, in Russian costume for his matinee performance at the Orpheum Theatre in Hollywood, after doing the stand-in dancing for Johnnie Walker in *The Matinee Idol*. Others are, from left to right: Bessie Love, Frank Capra and Johnnie Walker.

HANDSOME WILLIAMS (Mitchell Lewis) carries the blind street violinist, Nora (Alice Day), to his cafe after a rival gangster in a speeding car has shot at him and caused her to faint. Marie (Margaret Livingston), a spy for the rival gang, observes Williams' regard for the girl.

DECEPTION—Nora (Alice Day), blind, "sees" Dan (Theodor von Eltz) by touch, but has been deceived into believing he is Handsome Williams (Mitchell Lewis), right.

VILLIANOUS MARIE (Margaret Livingston), as a member of a rival gang, spies on Handsome Williams (Mitchell Lewis).

THE KIDNAPPING OF NORA (Alice Day) is carried out by Tiger Louie (William Norton Bailey) and Marie (Margaret Livingston).

A Columbia Picture. Produced by Harry Cohn. Directed by Frank Capra. Screenplay by William Counselman. Continuity by Peter Milne. Photographed by Ben Reynolds. Running time: 61 minutes.

CAST:

Handsome Williams, Mitchell Lewis; *Nora*, Alice Day; *Marie*, Margaret Livingston; *Dan*, Theodor von Eltz; *Tiger Louie*, William Norton Bailey.

MARGARET LIVINGSTON:

I shall never forget Frank Capra. As the kids today would say, he's a living doll! And he was a great director!

—*Letter to the authors from New Hope, Pennsylvania,*
June 16, 1974.

Handsome Williams (Mitchell Lewis), so nicknamed because he's ugly, heads a gang of hijackers who prey on truckloads of liquor transported by bootlegger Tiger Louie (William Norton Bailey).

Handsome runs a café, decorated without mirrors so he will not have to see himself. Dan (Theodor von Eltz), a truly handsome man, is the piano player at the café. Nora (Alice Day) is a blind street violinist who plays outside Handsome's café.

One night, a car of the enemy gang whizzes by and opens fire on the café. Handsome manages to duck just in time. Nora faints; Handsome carries her into his café and offers her a job.

When Nora asks Handsome what he looks like, he misleads her by having Dan put his face forward for her to "see" by touching.

Marie (Margaret Livingston), Tiger Louie's mistress, is spying on Handsome. Aware of the advantage it will give him, Louie kidnaps Nora and holds her as a hostage to ensure the safe delivery of his truckloads of liquor, but an enamored Handsome rushes to her rescue with a truckload of men, and a gun battle ensues. Dan, who has fallen in love with Nora, arrives in his roadster and gets her safely out of the beleaguered house. He then returns to rescue Handsome, and all three get away in Dan's car.

In reaching out to touch Handsome's face when he puts his arms around her, Nora discovers the truth and involuntarily shrinks from his ugliness.

The police are in pursuit. Realizing the folly of the deception he has been practicing, Handsome stops the car and has the two lovers get out, making it possible for them to escape.

The Way of the Strong

1928 (Silent)

SACRIFICE is made by Handsome Williams Mitchell Lewis), right, as he tells Dan (Theodor von Eltz) to leave with Nora (Alice Day).

A REVENGEFUL GOLD DIGGER, Irene Gordon (Margaret Livingston), left, disrupts the home life of John Caswell (Francis X. Bushman), left, and his wife, Helen (Helene Chadwick), when his son, Doug (Arthur Rankin), brings her home as his bride-to-be.

SHE'S A FEMME FATALE, but Doug Caswell (Arthur Rankin) can't resist the charms of Irene Gordon (Margaret Livingston).

MARGARET LIVINGSTON:
"What could be more exciting than a handsome man with a check book in his hand and dollar signs flying all over?"
—*Letter to the authors from New Hope, Pennsylvania October 29, 1974*

A Columbia Picture. A Frank Capra Production. Produced by Harry Cohn. Directed by Frank Capra. Story by Frank Capra and Peter Milne. Continuity by Dorothy Howell. Photographed by Joe Walker. Art direction by Harrison Wiley. Edited by Arthur Roberts. Assistant Director: Joe Nadel. Running time: 70 minutes.

CAST:

Helen Caswell, Helene Chadwick; *John Caswell*, Francis X. Bushman; *Irene Gordon*, Margaret Livingston; *Doug Caswell*, Arthur Rankin; *Marie Caswell*, June Nash; *Mitchell*, Alphonz Ethier; *Maid*, Edna Mae Cooper.

John Caswell (Francis X. Bushman), a wealthy banker, decides to settle down in marriage once again for the benefit of his motherless son. Therefore, he terminates his relationship with glamorous gold digger Irene Gordon (Margaret Livingston).

Caswell marries Helen (Helene Chadwick), a woman of his own social class. After some time, his son, young Doug Caswell (Arthur Rankin), now attending college, brings home a girl who turns out to be Irene, seeking revenge.

Caswell tells Doug that Irene had been his mistress. The young man insists upon confronting her with this fact. The father follows him to Irene's apartment, where he finds her shot dead. A revolver lies nearby. To protect his son, Caswell resets the scene to make the death look like a suicide.

Detective Mitchell (Alphonz Ethier) traces the fur-greedy adventuress's newest fur coat, a sable, to Doug, who confusedly confesses to the murder under the pressure of questioning. However, Mitchell doesn't believe him. He had found an earring clutched in the victim's hand and discovers its mate among Helen Caswell's jewels. Mrs. Caswell offers her version, suggesting that an unidentified woman might have committed the crime unintentionally, going to Irene Gordon's apartment in order to frighten her into giving up love letters that could ruin a young man's life. The revolver might have gone off accidentally, accounting for what appeared to be a murder.

Mitchell rejects the theory as improbable and states that he is now convinced that it was suicide. Before leaving the Caswell residence (furnished in traditional taste, in contrast to Irene Gordon's modernistic decor—a relatively new development, designing sets to reflect the personality of the occupant), Mitchell places the two earrings side by side on Mrs. Caswell's vanity, thus telling her that he knows the true facts. But he has closed the case.

Say It With Sables

1928 (Silent)

ELUCIDATION OF THE MYSTERY—Helen Caswell (Helene Chadwick) tells detective Mitchell (Alphonz Ethier) her version of how Irene Gordon might have been killed.

YOUNG LOVERS—Jane Atwill (Jobyna Ralston) and Clem Rogers (Douglas Fairbanks, Jr.).

BIG CITY NEWSPAPER OFFICE—City editor (Robert Edeson), center, with newspaper in hand. Left, cub reporter Clem Rogers (Douglas Fairbanks, Jr.), and, right, reporter Johnson (Del Henderson).

A Columbia Picture. A Frank Capra Production. Produced by Jack Cohn. Directed by Frank Capra. Story by Frederick A. Thompson. Adaptation and continuity by Sonya Levien. Photographed by Chet Lyons. Art direction by Harrison Wiley. Edited by Frank Atkinson. Assistant Director: Buddy Coleman. Running time: 62 minutes.

CAST:

Clem Rogers, Douglas Fairbanks, Jr.; *Jane Atwill*, Jobyna Ralston; *Marie*, Mildred Harris; *Blake*, Philo McCullough; *Van*, Wheeler Oakman; *City Editor*, Robert Edeson; *Mr. Atwill*, Edwards Davis; *Johnson*, Del Henderson; *District Attorney*, Charles Clary.

DOUGLAS FAIRBANKS, JR.:

I am not only an old friend of Mr. Capra's, but I yield to none in my respect and admiration for his matchless gifts. *The Power of the Press* was so long ago, I can't even recall the plot. I don't even remember who else was in it. The fact that it is lost *may* be a thinly disguised blessing! I have a suspicion that were it still in existence, it might compromise whatever "artistic" reputation either Mr. Capra or I may have. Even though details of my one and only professional experience with Mr. Capra have receded in my memory, I do have the proud statistic of having worked in a Capra film to keep me warm—and we've remained friends, even though our paths have not crossed in far too long. I heartily agree with and applaud every honor that has so deservedly come his way since.

—*Letter to the authors from New York, New York,*
May 1, 1974.

When the experienced reporters on a big-city newspaper are out on other assignments, Clem Rogers (Douglas Fairbanks, Jr.), cub reporter, is sent to cover the murder of the district attorney (Charles Clary) in the midst of a political campaign.

Going to the DA's house, he sees a beautiful woman, Jane Atwill (Jobyna Ralston), leaving by the window, and her lost handbag reveals that she is the daughter of the reform candidate for mayor.

Cocksure, Clem writes an accusatory story, but Jane convinces him of her innocence.

A mysterious girl, Marie (Mildred Harris), connected to Blake (Philo McCullough), the rival candidate, is the clue to the fatal shooting, and Clem searches her out and secures her statement clearing

The Power of the Press

1928 (Silent)

DECEPTIVE PHONE CALL is made by Clem Rogers (Douglas Fairbanks, Jr.) with the encouragement of Jane Atwill (Jobyna Ralston), in order to locate an important missing person connected with the murder of the District Attorney.

Jane and implicating Blake's henchman Van (Wheeler Oakman).

Surprised by Van in Marie's hideaway, Clem is temporarily captured, only to turn the tables on the gunman and bring him to the newspaper office.

The resultant headlines win the election for Atwill (Edwards Davis) and Atwill's daughter for Clem.

MURDERER CAPTURED—Clem Rogers (Douglas Fairbanks, Jr.), left, and Marie (Mildred Harris) struggle to tie up murderer Van (Wheeler Oakman).

MURDERER NAMED by a pointing Marie (Mildred Harris). City Editor (Robert Edeson) is sitting on desk. To the right of him, wearing hat, is Johnson (Del Henderson)—and the couple who broke the case: Jane Atwill (Jobyna Ralston) and Clem Rogers (Douglas Fairbanks, Jr.)

CONFESSION is obtained from Van (Wheeler Oakman) by Clem Rogers (Douglas Fairbanks, Jr.), right, city editor (Robert Edeson), left, and Jane Atwill (Jobyna Ralston).

CONGRATULATIONS—City editor (Robert Edeson) shakes the hand of Clem Rogers (Douglas Fairbanks, Jr.). Between them are Jane Atwill (Jobyna Ralston) and Johnson (Del Henderson).

NAVY BUDDIES—Bob Mason (Ralph Graves), left, Jack Reagon (Jack Holt), and parrot.

ACE DEEP-SEA DIVER Jack Reagon (Jack Holt) prepares to submerge, with the help of Bob Mason (Ralph Graves).

68

A Columbia Picture. An Irvin Willat Production. Produced by Harry Cohn. Directed by Frank Capra. Scenario by Winifred Dunn. Photographed by Joe Walker. Art direction by Harrison Wiley. Edited by Ben Pivar. Assistant Director: Buddy Coleman. Running time: 93 minutes.

CAST:

Jack Reagon, Jack Holt; *Bessie*, Dorothy Revier; *Bob Mason*, Ralph Graves; *Submarine Commander*, Clarence Burton.

Submarine was Columbia's first big A picture. Budgeted at two hundred fifty thousand dollars, several times the cost of an average Columbia film, it was the most ambitious movie Columbia had attempted. Harry Cohn chose Capra to take over the film's direction from the respected Irvin Willat, an expert on sea pictures noted for his underwater photography, because Cohn wasn't satisfied with Willat's work. Afraid the project would not be successful, Cohn turned to Capra, whom he trusted because Capra had proved himself successful, directing five "quickie" cheap films for Columbia in the preceding seven months that had been hits. So, ten months after Capra had joined Columbia, he took the giant step from quickies to A pictures.

Capra insisted on reshooting everything, starting from scratch, and Cohn let him have his way. There was location shooting at San Pedro in Los Angeles Harbor, and Capra used a hundred extras from the Navy.

Striving for realism, he insisted that Jack Holt and Ralph Graves wear no makeup. Holt was opposed to the idea at first, but Capra, cajoling with charm and flattery, convinced Holt by telling him (as recorded in Capra's autobiography): "I took this assignment, Mr. Holt, in the hope that I could make you look like *real* navy—without greasepaint, no hairpieces, no pressed uniforms—but with a wad of tobacco in that hard cheek and the love and hates of a champion in that diver's heart."

Holt was won over. Capra gave him licorice to chew, to simulate a wad of tobacco, and he gave Graves some BB shots to spit through his teeth at Holt's neck in a scene that took place in a shore boat, deviating from the script to inject comedy touches that would relieve the melodrama.

Capra had worked with Graves before, in Capra's first Columbia film, *That Certain Thing*, and he had written for him at Sennett prior to that. However,

Submarine

1928 (Silent with added sound effects)

MISPLACED AFFECTION is offered to Bessie, a dance hall girl (Dorothy Revier), by Jack Reagon (Jack Holt) when he is drunk and lightheaded.

NEW WIFE, Bessie (Dorothy Revier), is ill-suited to marriage bonds. Her departing sailor-husband is Jack Reagon (Jack Holt).

LOVERS—Bessie (Dorothy Revier) and Bob Mason (Ralph Graves).

70

he had never directed Holt before. The trio was so successful with *Submarine* that the team was to make two more films together (*Flight* and *Dirigible*) with basically the same story: two servicemen on adventurous duty (one saving the other's life at film's end) and both involved with the same girl.

Submarine was Columbia's first venture into sound. The early sound films used only sound sequences and effects, and one effect in *Submarine* was startlingly used. Jack Holt, a deep-sea diver, taps on the side of a sunken submarine to determine if anyone inside is alive. After a long wait, a faint tap-tap-tap is heard. The audiences were thrilled. Sound had arrived!

For long shots of the underwater rescue, Capra, using his ingenuity and his knowledge as a chemical engineer, put a toy submarine on the sandy bottom of a four-foot-square-by-three-foot-high aquarium, filled it with water, turned on the lights, which generated convection currents, and photographed a toy diver lowered with air hoses and lifelines. He had put sodium in the diver's helmet to produce bubbles, and he shot the action in ultraslow motion. The special effect was brilliantly accomplished. As Capra recalls in his autobiography, it "produced an

unearthly illusion of eeriness—the lonely mysterious murky depths of the restless sea." Capra had found the aquarium in Columbia's prop room, bought the toy submarine for fifty cents in a corner drugstore, and acquired the toy diver in a nickel "claw machine." He proved himself a movie magician.

Billed as "A Mighty Drama of the Sea," *Submarine* was a solid hit, the biggest moneymaker Columbia had ever had. It enjoyed extensive runs in first-run theaters.

Cohn tore up Capra's unfinished one-year contract at five hundred dollars per week and offered a straight three-year contract at fifteen hundred dollars per week. Capra signed without reading the contract. As he wrote in his autobiography, "When you've got a good thing going, why fool around with it?"

The story of *Submarine* concerns two Navy buddies, Jack Reagon (Jack Holt) and Bob Mason (Ralph Graves), who fall afoul of each other over an irresponsible dance-hall girl, Bessie (Dorothy Revier). But a desperate crisis (Mason trapped in a submerged submarine) causes Bessie to confess her duplicity and Mason's innocence. This leads to Mason's dramatic rescue by Reagon.

71

JEAN HERSHOLT

RICARDO CORTEZ

LINA BASQUETTE

A Columbia Picture. A Frank R. Capra Production. Produced by Jack Cohn. Directed by Frank R. Capra. Screenplay by Sonya Levien, based on the play *It Is to Laugh,* by Fannie Hurst. Dialogue by Howard J. Green. Photographed by Ted Tetzlaff. Sound Cameraman: Ben Reynolds. Art direction by Harrison Wiley. Edited by Arthur Roberts. Production Manager: Joe Cooke. Technical Director: Edward Shulter. Assistant Director: Tinny Wright. Recorded by Western Electric with Columbia Symphony Orchestra. Music Conductor: Bakaleinikoff. Running time: 75 minutes.

CAST:

Julius (Pa) Goldfish, Jean Hersholt; *Birdie Goldfish,* Lina Basquette; *Morris Goldfish,* Ricardo Cortez; *Eddie Lesser,* Rex Lease; *Tilda (Ma) Goldfish,* Rosa Rosanova; *Butler,* Sid Crossley; *Mrs. Lesser,* Martha Franklin; *Irma Striker,* Julanne Johnston; *Pinsky,* Jack Raymond; *Tradesman,* Otto Fries; *Mrs. Striker,* Julia Swayne Gordon.

JEAN HERSHOLT (in 1929):

This man, Frank Capra, will emerge as a giant amongst the pygmy minds of Hollywood.

—Quoted to the authors by Lina Basquette from Chalfont, Pennsylvania, March 12, 1974.

LINA BASQUETTE:

It has become almost a cliché to say, "Frank Capra is a genius"—or "one of the finest men who ever made films"—but these things are true and should be constantly repeated.

Here is an excerpt from my autobiography, *Virtue Is a Dirty Word,* which I am just completing:

In an office that looked more like a prison cell, I met Frank Capra—a dark, fiery young man as attractively Italian as spumoni, short and sparse in build with expressive small hands. He did not belong on Gower Street but to the cobbled streets of Genoa. It was hard to believe that this man who exuded sensitivity and artistry had recently been a "gag writer" for Hal Roach comedies.

After five minutes with Frank Capra, I was aware that he was a creative dynamo of potential greatness; unquestionably another one of Harry Cohn's incredible "kidnappings" from a competitor's lack of foresight that would pay off phenomenal dividends for Columbia.

—Letter to the authors from Chalfont, Pennsylvania, March 12, 1974.

The Younger Generation

1929 (Silent with talking sequences)

FLEE FROM POLICE—Eddie Lesser (Rex Lease), falsely accused of being an accomplice to a stickup, is helped to flee from the police by his girl friend, Birdie Goldfish (Lina Basquette). Later they marry and agree that Eddie should give himself up. He goes to jail and, while waiting for him, Birdie has his child.

RICARDO CORTEZ:

I thoroughly enjoyed working with Frank Capra. He is and was a warm, friendly man and a very fine director. I never heard him raise his voice to anyone. He is an actor's director. We need more of his kind.

—*Letter to the authors from New York, New York, April 22, 1974.*

The Younger Generation was Capra's and Columbia's first partly talking picture. With the advent of sound, there simply weren't enough sound stages or enough sound equipment to go around. Both were at a premium. As Capra told the authors, "We couldn't rent a sound stage for a long duration of time, both because of the great demand and for economic reasons. So for *The Younger Generation*

all the silent scenes were shot at one time and all the sound scenes at another time. Later they were intermixed. The script was not shot in continuity, and no decision was made about which scenes would be talking and which silent."

Unexpectedly, viewing the film today, one is not unduly disconcerted by the scenes alternating between sound and silent—surely a compliment to its absorbing quality.

The Younger Generation tells the story of a ruthless social climber, Morris Goldfish, later Maurice Fish (Ricardo Cortez), who turns his back on the Jewishness of his parents and his ghetto origins.

He is now an "importer," having risen above, first, "second-hand furniture," and then "antiques," and lives in a palatial Fifth Avenue apartment, attempting to make his father, Julius (Jean Hersholt), his mother, Tilda (Rosa Rosanova), and his viva-

74

cious sister, Birdie (Lina Basquette), conform to the cold formality he believes correct for his social position.

Birdie aligns herself with her father, saying that they're a "couple of Goldfishes, but we're in the wrong bowl!"

The father, sitting in front of the enormous fireplace with a shawl around his shoulders, says, in this elegant but inhospitable setting, "I haven't been warm since we left Delancey Street."

Birdie is in love with her childhood sweetheart, Eddie Lesser (Rex Lease), a songwriter who is unwittingly used as a decoy by a gang of crooks. Undaunted, Birdie marries him, visits him at the jail to which he has been sent, bears him a baby, and sells his songs to music publishers. Dreading scandal, which would be a threat to his social aspirations,

Maurice intercepts letters from Birdie to their parents. Papa Julius is distraught by her apparent neglect. Finally, through Lesser's mother, he learns that he and his wife are grandparents.

Maurice disowns his parents in a climactic scene of uninhibited snobbery. Julius, fleeing the house, is made ill and dies, and the mother, refusing a trip to Paris offered by Maurice, goes to live with Birdie, her grandchild, and her now-released son-in-law, Eddie.

In a superb final silent scene, Maurice Fish is left alone with the butler. He lights the fire and sits before the huge carved-stone fireplace. The butler lowers the Venetian blinds and the prisonlike bars of light and dark recall Papa Julius's loneliness. The son shivers, lifts a throw lying at hand, and wraps it shawl-like around his shoulders.

IN BED WITH PRODUCER AND STAR, Frank Capra, right, looks over *The Younger Generation* script with, left to right, Jack Cohn (older brother of Harry Cohn and co-founder of Columbia Pictures) and Jean Hersholt.

YOUNG LOVERS—David Cornish (William Collier, Jr.) and Jean Rankin (Dorothy Revier).

HOLDING MURDER WEAPON (a carving knife) in a handkerchief, Inspector Killian (Jack Holt) questions Captain Peter Rankin (Alphonse Ethier).

A Columbia Picture. A Frank R. Capra Production. Produced by Harry Cohn. Directed by Frank R. Capra. Screen dialogue by Howard J. Green. Continuity by Dorothy Howell. Based on the play *The Donovan Affair*, by Owen Davis. Photographed by Teddy Tetzlaff. Art direction by Harrison Wiley. Edited by Arthur Roberts. Assistant Director: Tenny Wright. Running time: 83 minutes.

CAST:

Inspector Killian, Jack Holt; *Jean Rankin*, Dorothy Revier; *Cornish*, William Collier, Jr., *Lydia Rankin*, Agnes Ayres; *Jack Donovan*, John Roche; *Carney*, Fred Kelsey; *Dr. Lindsey*, Hank Mann; *Porter*, Wheeler Oakman; *Mary Mills*, Virginia Brown Faire; *Captain Peter Rankin*, Alphonse Ethier; *Nelson*, Edward Hearn; *Mrs. Lindsey*, Ethel Wales; *Dobbs*, John Wallace.

The Donovan Affair was Frank Capra's and Columbia Pictures' first "100% Talking Picture"—featuring a "Great Talking Cast!" A silent version was also made for theaters not yet equipped to handle sound, a practice that continued for several years.

This complicated whodunit is set in a country house, a fact permitted by the plot but, more importantly, necessitated by the need to use the new sound cameras, which were enclosed in fixed booths, in a rental sound studio containing only interior sets.

Jack Donovan (John Roche), gambler and ladies' man, is murdered. A continually disappearing cat's eye ring is a major clue to the stabbing murders that take place in a repeatedly darkened room in the presence of all.

Inspector Killian (Jack Holt) systematically follows every lead. Suspicion falls at one point on a malingering gardener, who has a wooden leg, but in the end we learn that the *butler* did it!

The Donovan Affair

1929

YOUNG FRANK CAPRA, in chair, surrounded by crew, directs, left to right, Agnes Ayres and Dorothy Revier in this publicity shot.

POSED STILL of lovers Elinor (Lila Lee) and "Lefty" Phelps (Ralph Graves).

RECRUITS LINED UP FOR INSPECTION—Marine Instructor "Panama" Williams (Jack Holt), left, and new recruits, second and third from left in line: Steve Roberts (Harold Goodwin) and "Lefty" Phelps (Ralph Graves) in the scene with the ad-lib that might have caused censorship problems.

A Columbia Picture. A Frank R. Capra Production. Produced by Harry Cohn. Directed by Frank R. Capra. Story by Ralph Graves. Dialogue by Frank R. Capra. Photographed by Joe Walker. Assistant Cameramen: Elmer Dyer and Paul Perry. Art direction by Harrison Wiley. Edited by Ben Pivar, Maurice Wright, and Gene Milford. Technical Sound Engineer: John Lividary. Sound-mixing Engineer: Harry Blanchard. Sound Recorders: Dean Daly and Eddy Hahn. Sound-equipment Supervisor: Ellis Gray. Assistant Director: Buddy Coleman. Running time: 110 minutes.

CAST:

"Panama" Williams, Jack Holt; *Elinor*, Lila Lee; *"Lefty" Phelps*, Ralph Graves; *Major*, Alan Roscoe; *Steve Roberts*, Harold Goodwin; *Lobo*, Jimmy De La Cruze.

HAROLD GOODWIN:

The first day on *Flight* I found out a lot of things about Frank, all favorable. He was loose, unhurried, confident, and jovial. During the rehearsal of my first scene, I threw in an ad-lib that made Ralph Graves laugh at a very serious time. Ralph and I were playing the parts of recruits, lined up for inspection, when Jack Holt told Ralph to wipe the smile off his face. The ad-lib I threw in was, "He's nuts about you."

Frank asked what I had said, and I repeated the line. I thought I was in for a dressdown. Now, talkies were in their infancy, and dialogue was watched carefully. The word *nuts* was considered a little risqué, and we were afraid someone (Harry Cohn) might object, but Frank thought for a second, then laughed and said, "Great, leave it in!"

Another incident I'll always remember was my death scene in *Flight*. I had a line, "Don't let the ants eat me." The prop man, Art Black, had got a whole colony of red ants. They were kept in a glass box, and from time to time someone would throw a piece of bread and butter or something in the box. In a short time there would be nothing left. A frog was thrown to them, and he was gone in no time!

There was to be a close shot of these ants crawling on me. Art, the prop man, assured me that he had a repellent lotion he would put on me. When it came time for the shot, I asked Art to apply some of the lotion to the back of his hand and introduce a couple of ants to the stuff just to see what they would do. He complied, and when the ants pene-

Flight

1929

ANSWER TO REQUEST FOR DATE is spelled out by bewitching Elinor (Lila Lee) to "Lefty" Phelps.

WATCHING SOLO FLIGHT of "Lefty" Phelps are, left to right: the Major (Alan Roscoe), Elinor (Lila Lee) and "Panama" Williams (Jack Holt).

trated the hair on his hand, they took hold, and he yelled and yelled, all the time trying to get rid of the ants.

Frank witnessed the demonstration and changed the shot.

—Letter to the authors from Woodland Hills, California, August 28, 1974.

"The first all-talking drama of the air will thrill you!" read the ad for *Flight* in *Liberty* magazine.

The story, on which Frank Capra and Ralph Graves had been working, took a new twist when, on New Year's Day 1929, Capra and Harry Cohn went to the Rose Bowl game and saw Roy Riegles of the California team score the winning play by running the wrong way and giving the game to Georgia Tech!

The idea of this notorious game was used as the opening of the film. "Lefty" Phelps (Ralph Graves, playing the part patterned after Roy Riegles), escapes into the anonymity of the Pensacola U.S. Naval Air Station. "Panama" Williams (Jack Holt), who saw the disastrous run take place, becomes his marine instructor, and his sympathy for "Lefty" creates a friendly bond between them.

Both men fall in love with the same girl, Elinor (Lila Lee), a nurse, which leads to a breach between the two friends when they're on a rescue mission of U.S. Marines ambushed in Nicaragua.

After winning the girl, "Lefty" crash-lands in enemy territory, and Elinor pleads with a jealous "Panama" to find him. He does, but is injured in the process, and "Lefty," in turn, rescues him. Their friendship is more solidly based than ever, after serious, moving, funny, dramatic scenes that justify the contemporary ads: "See Columbia Pictures for better entertainment."

80

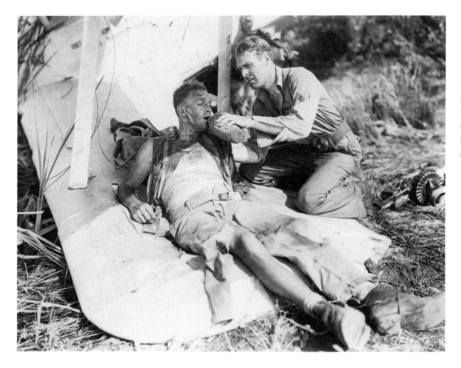

HAROLD GOODWIN as Steve Roberts is cared for by "Lefty" Phelps (Ralph Graves), who struggles to keep ants off him and finally cremates his body in the wrecked plane before bandits arrive.

PLEA—Elinor (Lila Lee) pleads with "Panama" Williams (Jack Holt) to rescue rival "Lefty" Phelps (Ralph Graves).

BODY PAINTING by Bill Standish (Lowell Sherman) at wild party which opens *Ladies of Leisure*.

"TAKE A GOOD LOOK, IT'S FREE," Kay Arnold (Barbara Stanwyck), left, a party girl currently working as a model for artist Jerry Strong (Ralph Graves), right, says to philanderer Bill Standish (Lowell Sherman), while society fiancee of Jerry, Claire Collins (Juliette Compton), looks on disapprovingly.

A Columbia Picture. A Frank R. Capra Production. Produced by Harry Cohn. Directed by Frank R. Capra. Adaptation and dialogue by Joe Swerling. Based on the David Belasco stage play *Ladies of the Evening*, by Milton Herbert Gropper. Titles by Dudley Early. Photographed by Joseph Walker. At direction by Harrison Wiley. Edited by Maurice Wright. Chief Sound Engineer: John P. Livadary. Sound-mixing Engineer: Harry Blanchard. Assistant Director: David Selman. Running time: 98 minutes.

CAST:

Kay Arnold, Barbara Stanwyck; *Bill Standish*, Lowell Sherman; *Jerry Strong*, Ralph Graves; *Dot Lamar*, Marie Prevost; *Mrs. Strong*, Nance O'Neil; *Mr. Strong*, George Fawcett; *Claire Collins*, Juliette Compton; *Charlie*, Johnnie Walker; *Party Guest*, Charles Butterworth.

EDWARD BERNDS:

I had come from working at United Artists with Doug Fairbanks and Mary Pickford, even D. W. Griffith—having rubbed elbows with the real giants of the industry—so I wasn't prepared to be overly impressed by a young director whose name I thought was Capper. I was asked to fill in as sound man on location shooting for *Ladies of Leisure* (at Malibu Lake), and Capra liked my work so well he decided to keep me on for the whole picture. From then on I was the sound man on every one of his pictures at Columbia.

—*Told to the authors on tape from Van Nuys, California*, September 23, 1974.

Ladies of Leisure

1930

WEARING NEW DRESS, Kay Arnold (Barbara Stanwyck) is complimented on it by morning drunk Bill Standish (Lowell Sherman), right, at door of the studio apartment of Jerry Strong (Ralph Graves), left, where he has come for a bottle of brandy. "I think I'll go in for art too, and open a pretty little studio," he says, and invites Kay to sail with him to Havana as his drinking and love-making companion.

"BE YOURSELF," Jerry Strong (Ralph Graves) tells Kay Arnold (Barbara Stanwyck). "That first night when you were asleep on my shoulder—I saw hope—you were yourself." The bed in this still is where Kay spends the night in the studio, and the large window next to it is where we see the relentless rain in Capra's stirring love scene.

Ladies of Leisure made Barbara Stanwyck a star. Capra was to cast her as the feminine lead in four more films, making her the actress who starred most often in his films. As Ella Smith wrote in her study of Stanwyck's career, *Starring Miss Barbara Stanwyck* (Crown Publishers, Inc., New York, 1974), "Stanwyck's work in *Ladies of Leisure* is perfection. If she had never made another film, she would be remembered for this one."

Stanwyck was twenty-two, and despite the Broadway success of *Burlesque*, her film reputation was nonexistent, her three appearances on celluloid having been disasters. Then Capra saw her emotional intensity in the first thirty seconds of a three-minute screen test, and a major screen actress's brilliant career was launched in *Ladies of Leisure*.

The story begins at a wild New York penthouse party whose rhythm is summed up in the perpetual movement of the cocktail shaker.

Jerry Strong (Ralph Graves) leaves the party disappointed by the shallowness of his fiancée, Claire Collins (Juliette Compton). Shortly, his car is disabled by a flat tire, and he meets Kay Arnold (Barbara Stanwyck), who is likewise fleeing a party —this one aboard a yacht from which she has rowed ashore.

Struck by her beauty, Jerry tells Kay he wants to paint her portrait. He is the artist son of wealthy parents; she, a party girl.

In a sequence at night in Jerry's studio penthouse, Capra creates a highly romantic scene. Kay and Jerry are on the terrace, the stars are out, lights shine through a myriad of tiny apartment windows. "Look at them twinkle," says he; she agrees, but is looking down. He says, "Look up." She says the stars are too far away. He tells her, as her face is seen breathtakingly framed against the blackness, that she could reach for them if she only tried. Then, seeing hope in her expression, he rushes her inside and begins to paint, working on her portrait late into the night. Then he suggests she stay the night.

She turns out the light and, in a daring scene of great sensitivity, undresses in silhouette before the large studio window. The firelight flickers on her face.

He undresses in his room. The camera alternates between them. She is photographed through the window, through the rain. She, in love with him, is perplexed and unhappy. Unable to sleep, she looks to his doorknob; the rain beats against the window;

IRATE FATHER, Mr. Strong (George Fawcett), right, tells his son Jerry (Ralph Graves) that he disapproves of his relationship with Kay Arnold (Barbara Stanwyck).

COMFORTING HER ROOMMATE, Dot Lamar (Marie Prevost) advises Kay Arnold (Barbara Stanwyck), "Don't let that dame get you down, honey," referring to Mrs. Strong who has just paid a visit. Kay confides, "I love him . . . his mother's right . . . I must give him up."

she closes her eyes; she hears him walking to her bed; he gently puts an additional blanket over her, certainly not what she expects. She pretends to be asleep; then, alone and happy, she draws the blanket up and bites it in an unrestrained moment of emotional release.

Concerning his use of rain, Capra wrote in his autobiography: "In practically every picture I've ever made there are scenes in the rain—especially love scenes. It's a personal touch. Rain, for me, is an exciting stimulant, an aphrodisiac."

In the morning, her vulnerability and his tension lead first to argument, but then to a mutual acknowledgment of love.

Intervention by Jerry's family almost thwarts the lovers' future together, but a dramatic rescue of Kay after her attempted suicide leads to a convincing happy ending.

Capra and Stanwyck were to have a future together in what Ella Smith, in *Starring Miss Barbara Stanwyck*, calls "one of the most exciting director-actress combinations ever to hit the screen." One reason for this was Capra's almost immediate recognition that her first take was always her best performance. Despite the technical difficulties, Capra, by using multiple cameras, successfully dealt with this new directional challenge.

CIRCUS FINANCES are looked over by Mary Rainey (Joan Peers), owner of the circus, and her manager, Smiley Johnson (Joe Cook).

A Columbia Picture. A Frank Capra Production. Produced by Harry Cohn. Directed by Frank Capra. Book by James Gleason and Maurice Marks. Dialogue and continuity by Dorothy Howell and Jo Swerling. Based on the play by James Gleason. Photographed by Joe Walker. Art direction by Harrison Wiley. Edited by Maurice Wright. Chief Sound Engineer: John P. Livadary. Sound-mixing Engineer: E. L. Bernds. Music by Bakaleinikoff. Assistant Director: Sam Nelson. Running time: 87 minutes.

CAST:

Smiley Johnson, Joe Cook; *Frankie (The "Princess"),* Louise Fazenda; *Mary Rainey,* Joan Peers; *Bud Conway,* William Collier, Jr.; *Amos K. Shrewsberry,* Tom Howard; *Dave,* Dave Chasen; *Dalton, the ringmaster,* Alan Roscoe; *Foltz, the lion tamer,* Adolph Milar; *Nero,* Clarence Muse; *Mr. Conway,* Ed Martindale; *Grace Conway,* Nora Lane; *Lord Gwynne,* Tyrrell Davis.

CLARENCE MUSE:

Once I asked Frank Capra, "Do you remember when we made that circus picture, *Rain or Shine,* with Joe Cook several years ago? We planned that fake rainstorm, but the boys put it on so heavy the wagons turned over, an elephant ran away, and for a while there was general pandemonium."

Capra answered, smiling, "Well, we got out of it all right, didn't we?"

"Certainly! We always seem to when you are at the helm. I never did see such a man for standing by and smoking his cigarette when everything goes wrong about him."

"Hysterics don't get you anywhere, Clarence."

—*Letter to the authors from Muse-A-While Ranch,
Perris, California, September 3, 1974.*

EDWARD BERNDS:

Working with Frank Capra, I soon realized what a wealth of guts and daring he had! In *Rain or Shine,* for instance, he very casually burned down an entire circus! It was a one-shot thing. He just put enough cameras on to cover everything he wanted, and he burned the whole thing down. He shot it with, as I recall, about a dozen cameras. He had guts and originality!

—*Told to the authors on tape from Van Nuys,
California, September 23, 1974.*

Rain or Shine

1930

LOUISE FAZENDA as the "Princess," the "beautiful Oriental dancer," kicks A. K. Shrewsberry (Tom Howard) out of her trailer when he makes advances. His rejoinder, "Well, you gotta find those things out!"

Turning to Broadway's wild, far-out comedy star Joe Cook, Capra filmed the comedian's successful musical *Rain or Shine* without the music (Harry Cohn's budget wouldn't allow for that) but with increased emphasis on the madcap shenanigans of the show's original cast: Joe Cook, Tom Howard, and Dave Chasen. The movie turned into a shindig of hilarious proportions.

The story tells of the attempts of Mary Rainey (Joan Peers) to run her late father's financially troubled circus with the help of her manager, Smiley Jones (Joe Cook).

Rain or Shine (the title comes from the slogan that the circus has two big shows daily, rain or shine) is consistently rapid-fire funny, thanks to Cook's extraordinary talent and Capra's comedic sense.

Smiley's response to a request to be seen alone is, "Impossible. I'll be with you!"

A prospective investor, Amos K. Shrewsberry

JUVENILE AND INGENUE: Bud Conway (William Collier, Jr.) and Mary Rainey (Joan Peers). He has just interrupted her bareback riding rehearsal.

"THAT'S SOME SPAGHETTI! That's enough!" says A. K. Shrewsberry (Tom Howard), left, to Smiley Johnson (Joe Cook), who is mixing the dish and who replies, "Finish that up and I'll give you some more!" Looking on are Dave (Dave Chasen) and the "Princess" (Louise Fazenda).

88

(Tom Howard), says, "Call me A. K." Naturally, Smiley retorts, "Okay, A. K."

Reading A. K.'s palm, Smiley tells him that he'll live to be thirty-two. A. K. says, "But I'm forty now." Smiley shrugs and comments, "Well, we can't do anything about that."

The "Princess" (Louise Fazenda), an Oriental dancer in the circus, is touted as having won three Miss America cups. With perfect timing she adds, "And the saucers, too!"

Smiley and Dave (Dave Chasen) work together flawlessly: Smiley explains that Dave's hot-dog concession is a great moneymaker, practically all profit. The rolls are on the level, the mustard is on the level, but Dave's finger, painted with iodine, is slipped out of the roll once the customer buys the hot dog. When a boy complains, his mother accuses him of swallowing the hot dog whole! A. K. Shrewsberry was taken in too: "I bought eighteen of those things—there's no nourishment in them."

At a formal dinner party, Dave arrives wearing a hanger in his coat, and we hear: "What kind of tea is this?"

"Cocoa."

"My cocoa is cold."

"Well, put on your hat!"

Smiley suggests, "Try some unborn French peas," and an empty plate is passed.

In the spectacular fire that ends the film, Smiley wets himself down, climbs to the top of the tent from the outside, and cuts through the canvas to reach Mary, who has been trapped inside. The flames lick after them as he carries her on his back and rides a rope down to safety just as the whole structure collapses. There is a return to humor, however, as an elephant douses Smiley's burning clothes, and the exuberant comic returns to patter. Left amid the smoldering ruins, he ruefully contends that he now owns the show. "I'm just waiting for it to cool off so I can pick it up."

HOT DOG SCENE in which Dave (Dave Chasen), left, uses his iodine-coated finger as a wiener. Smiley Johnson (Joe Cook), center, explains the deception to A. K. Shrewsberry (Tom Howard).

ONE-MAN SHOW performed by Smiley Johnson (Joe Cook), watched and assisted by Dave (Dave Chasen), left, and Mary Rainey (Joan Peers).

GORILLA GETS INTO THE ACT—Left to right, Mary Rainey (Joan Peers), Smiley Johnson (Joe Cook), Bud Conway (William Collier, Jr.) and Dave (Dave Chasen) restrain a gorilla that has gotten loose. Everyone repeats the line, "Mike let him out," until the gorilla himself says, *Charlie let me out.*

HUSBAND AND WIFE, "Frisky" and Helen Pierce (Ralph Graves and Fay Wray). She pleads with him to stop his grandstand globe-trotting and stay at home with her.

LIKE THREADING A NEEDLE—Jack Bradon (Jack Holt) explains to "Frisky" Pierce (Ralph Graves) how Pierce's plane will have to hook onto his dirigible.

SOUTH POLE DESCRIBED by Louis Rondelle (Hobart Bosworth), left, as "center of a great ice cap, huge, that rises almost abruptly ten thousand feet above the Antarctic continent." Interested Clarence (Clarence Muse), standing, later volunteers to go on the expedition as a cook. Listening, left to right, are: Jack Bradon (Jack Holt) and "Frisky" Pierce (Ralph Graves).

A Columbia Picture. A Frank R. Capra Production. Produced by Harry Cohn. Directed by Frank R. Capra. Story by Commander Frank Wilber Wead, USN. Adaptation and dialogue by Jo Swerling. Continuity by Dorothy Howell. Photographed by Joseph Walker. Aerial photography by Elmer Dyer. Edited by Maurice Wright. Sound Engineer: E. L. Bernds. Technical effects: Ned Mann and W. J. Butler. Assistant Director: Sam Nelson. Running time: 100 minutes.

CAST:

Jack Bradon, Jack Holt; *Frisky Pierce*, Ralph Graves; *Helen Pierce*, Fay Wray; *Louis Rondelle*, Hobart Bosworth; *Sock McGuire*, Roscoe Karns; *Hansen*, Harold Goodwin; *Clarence*, Clarence Muse; *Admiral Martin*, Emmet Corrigan; *Commander of U.S.S. Lexington*, Al Roscoe; *Lieutenant Rowland*, Selmer Jackson.

HAROLD GOODWIN:

You know the old adage, if it's a bathing-suit picture, we'll shoot it in January; if it's a snow picture, we'll shoot it in September. Well, that is exactly what happened on *Dirigible*. Where Santa Anita race track is now, there once was a balloon school, a sort of lighter-than-air base. It was abandoned, and that's where our sets for the Arctic region were built. We wore fur parkas and had wind machines blowing bleached corn flakes in our faces in ninety-degree weather. Sometimes it was almost unbearable.

On top of that, we had let our beards grow, and to give the look of frost, the prop man put heated paraffin on our faces. He would paint it on with a brush. It worked fine and looked great, but after a while it would start to pull and itch. Between scenes, we would frantically pull the stuff off with a few patches of beard, only to have our faces repainted. Frank called it "frost in the puss."

—*Letter to the authors from Woodland Hills, California*, August 28, 1974.

CLARENCE MUSE:

Once, I reminded Frank Capra of an incident that happened while filming *Dirigible*: The wind machines were turned on to stir up the fake snow, and one of the airplanes blew away! I told him that I remembered he remained unconcerned, grinning and smoking a little cigarette.

Capra replied, "What was the difference, Clar-

Dirigible

1931

IN ANTARCTIC, Louis Rondelle (Hobart Bosworth), left, and "Frisky" Pierce (Ralph Graves), right, prepare to fly on to the South Pole.

"WHAT ARE YOU DREAMING ABOUT, snow and ice?" Jack Bradon (Jack Holt) asks Helen Pierce (Fay Wray). Her reply, "I'd like to swim to Paris." "Why Paris?" "That's where they go to get divorces, isn't it?"

ence? We've always come out on top. The gods have simply been good to us."

—*Letter to the authors from Muse-A-While Ranch, Perris, California*, September 3, 1974.

EDWARD BERNDS:

Here's an example of the way Capra could handle his actors. Jack Holt was a drinker, and he was good and drunk when we were to shoot the big hangar scene, which included practically the entire personnel of Lakehurst Naval Air Station. So to punish Holt and teach him a lesson, Capra allowed Holt, in his drunken condition, to play the scene, in which he addressed hundreds of sailors he had lined up, explaining the expedition they were about to go on. He weaved about and slurred his words, which he just managed to get out.

Capra had the scene printed and showed it to Holt. After that, there was no trouble in reshooting

the scene, with Holt sober, as it finally appears in the film! And Holt was never drunk again—on the set.

We filmed the South Pole scenes in Arcadia, California, in the San Gabriel Valley, at a balloon-school airfield. It was hot there that summer. Assistant Director Sam Nelson would yell, "All the men in furs!" and there would be a groan from all the actors as they put on their heavy parkas.

The miniatures were made in the hangar. I remember a little muscular grip named Harry was killed there. He was on a couple of planks high up in the rafters pulling up a heavy weight of some kind, when a knot gave way and he went over backward and was killed.

—*Told to the authors on tape from Van Nuys, California*, September 23, 1974.

Dirigible was Capra's and Columbia's first film to open at the prestigious Grauman's Chinese Theatre. As the audience applauded, Harry Cohn exuberantly signaled victory to his director with raised clasped hands; Capra reciprocated the triumphant greeting—they had made the first step up from poverty row to the big time. Audiences were drawn

RADIO NEWS of the perilous flight to the South Pole by "Frisky" Pierce (Ralph Graves) is heard by Jack Bradon (Jack Holt) and Helen Pierce (Fay Wray).

THE CRASH at the South Pole. Louis Rondelle (Hobart Bosworth), in foreground, suffers a broken leg as a result of the crash.

THE DEATH of Louis Rondelle (Hobart Bosworth) is discovered in the morning by, left to right, Sock McGuire (Roscoe Karns), "Frisky" Pierce (Ralph Graves) and Hansen (Harold Goodwin).

to the exciting new subject matter—only two years earlier the *Graf Zeppelin* had sailed twenty thousand miles around the world to universal acclaim.

Jack Bradon (Jack Holt), dirigible commander, and flying ace "Frisky" Pierce (Ralph Graves) are fast friends, but Helen (Fay Wray), Pierce's wife of two years, tiring of marriage to a man always absent on headline-making exploits, is increasingly attracted to the more stable Bradon.

During one flight, the airship, an awesome sight, majestically sails out over Manhattan, but the next day it breaks up in a great electrical storm, the tail half falling off, then the front half crashing into the rough sea. Bradon, who had ordered the crew to the nose just in time, cuts his way out of the dirigible's top and assembles the men at the tip. The sight and sound of the airship cracking apart in the air is shot with great pace and visual excitement; then the raging storm and the waves all but engulf the men. Pierce, in a scout plane, is the first to sight the ill-fated dirigible and directs an aircraft carrier to the successful rescue.

A scientific mission to the Antarctic climaxes the film, with close-up scenes of heroic exploits and vast distance shots of rescue operations.

Pierce, who has suffered much, having been lost in the wasteland of the Antarctic, returns to his wife to satisfy her reawakened love and accept his responsibility as her husband.

ON THE SET for one of the last scenes in *Dirigible*, Frank Capra, center, goes over the script with Ralph Graves, left, and Jack Holt.

IN LION'S CAGE, evangelist Florence Fallon (Barbara Stanwyck) tells John Carson (David Manners), a blind volunteer from the audience: "You have shown faith, and you will see again."

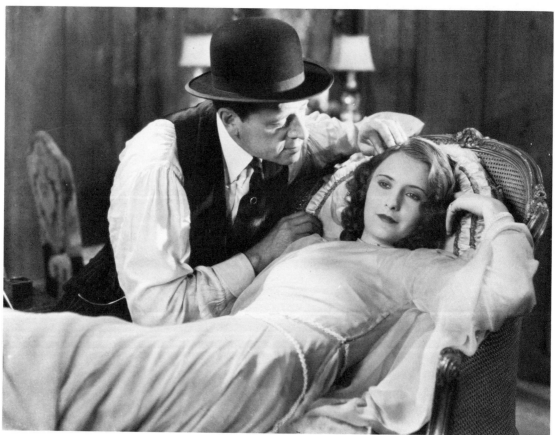

PROMOTER Hornsby (Sam Hardy) tells an exhausted Florence Fallon (Barbara Stanywck) after her "performance:" "You've been giving those apple knockers too much for their money."

A Columbia Picture. A Frank R. Capra Production. Produced by Harry Cohn. Directed by Frank R. Capra. Screenplay and dialogue by Jo Swerling, based on the play *Bless You, Sister,* by John Meehan and Robert Riskin. Continuity by Dorothy Howell. Photographed by Joseph Walker. Edited by Maurice Wright. Sound Engineer: Glenn Rominger. Running time: 87 minutes.

CAST:

Florence Fallon, Barbara Stanwyck; *John Carson,* David Manners; *Hornsby,* Sam Hardy; *Mrs. Higgins,* Beryl Mercer; *Dan Welford,* Russell Hopton; *Simpson,* Charles Middleton; *Collins,* Eddie Boland; *Gussie,* Thelma Hill; *Violet,* Aileen Carlyle; *Brown,* Al Stewart; *Briggs,* Harry Todd.

DAVID MANNERS:

I have the finest regard for Frank Capra as the best director I had the honor of working with.

—*Letter to the authors from Pacific Palisades, California,* February 21, 1974.

Fiery young Florence Fallon (Barbara Stanwyck) is disillusioned by her preacher father's death. She attributes it in large part to the congregation, which has turned a house of God into a "meeting place for hypocrites."

Wily promoter Hornsby (Sam Hardy), in town between trains, tells her that because she knows the Bible almost by heart, she can get even. His motto is, "Religion is great if you can sell it; no good if you give it away."

On an "evangelistic" tour, her broadcast words prevent blind John Carson (David Manners) from committing suicide. His landlady, Mrs. Higgins (Beryl Mercer), takes him to the fairgrounds where Florence Fallon is appearing, and he volunteers to enter the lion cage with Sister Fallon as a test of his faith. The two become friends and then fall in love. Fallon is happy with Carson, away from the world of Hornsby's racket religion, for which she is the front.

As a consequence, Fallon confesses her fakery to Carson, but he tells her that she isn't a fake to him. He decides to stage his own "miracle"—regained eyesight—to give her confidence in herself. She is not fooled by the act but is inspired to proclaim, "You've made *me* see."

Fallon heads for the platform of the tabernacle to tell the truth about herself. A grand ovation greets

The Miracle Woman

1931

BLIND JOHN CARSON (David Manners), having forgotten to turn on the lights in his apartment for his guest, Florence Fallon (Barbara Stanwyck), who is wearing his hat and coat for protection against the rain, says: "Excuse me, I might give you a little light!"

BUST OF EVANGELIST Florence Fallon is delivered to blind John Carson (David Manners) by his landlady, Mrs. Higgins (Beryl Mercer). Florence Fallon (Barbara Stanwyck), disapproving of the sale of such likenesses, asks Carson why he bought it. His reply: "I want to know what you look like."

FAKE CRIPPLE, demonstrating for Hornsby (Sam Hardy) at a party with carnival people, says: "Get this for a miracle. See, I come up to the Sister like this. She lays on the healing mits and I sees the light and wham—hallelulah!" Florence Fallon (Barbara Stanwyck) is disgusted by the shills used as part of her "act."

her, and flowers are thrown. As she is about to speak, Hornsby orders the lights cut off. The electrical equipment short circuits and creates a fire. The fire is an accident, not, as erroneously reported in other sources, purposely set by Hornsby—and he is *not* killed in it.

Sister Fallon averts a panic and is rescued by Carson, whom she will later marry.

In the final scene, Hornsby is crossing a busy street, when he sees Sister Fallon marching with the Salvation Army. He comments to a sidekick, "And she gave up a million bucks for that! The poor sap!"

As the Salvation Army band plays "Battle Hymn of the Republic," the camera closes in on the serene face of a transformed Florence Fallon, radiant with humility and love.

THREATENING EXPOSURE, Florence Fallon (Barbara Stanwyck) tells Hornsby (Sam Hardy): "I'm going up there on that platform to tell the people the truth. To tell what a liar and cheat I've been and neither you nor anybody else is going to stop me." John Carson (David Manners) moves to restrain angry Hornsby.

96

TABERNACLE FIRE during which Florence Fallon (Barbara Stanwyck) remains on a burning stage urging the congregation to sing "Onward Christian Soldiers" while they calmly march out, averting a panic.

MAKE-UP FOR FIRE SCENE is applied to Barbara Stanwyck under the supervision of Frank Capra (at head of stretcher), while co-star David Manners (with torn trouser leg) waits to play his final scene in the film.

REPORTER BARRED from the Schuyler mansion by butler Smythe (Halliwell Hobbes), who tells Ann (Jean Harlow): "Mrs. Schuyler left orders, Miss, that if this person came again I was to call the police." Stew Smith (Robert Williams) is the *person*.

TWO CLASSES MEET—Stew Smith, an uncouth newspaperman (Robert Williams), left, is introduced by Ann Schuyler (Jean Harlow) to, left to right: her snooty mother, Mrs. Schuyler (Louise Closser Hale), the officious family lawyer, Dexter Grayson (Reginald Owen), and her troublesome brother, Michael Schuyler (Donald Dillaway).

98

"SOMETHING TELLS ME I BETTER LEAVE," Stew Smith (Robert Williams) says to Ann Schuyler (Jean Harlow) when he sees her formidable mother, Mrs. Schuyler (Louise Closser Hale).

A Columbia Picture. A Frank R. Capra Production. Produced by Harry Cohn. Directed by Frank R. Capra. Story by Harry E. Chandler and Douglas W. Churchill. Dialogue by Robert Riskin. Adapted by Jo Swerling. Continuity by Dorothy Howell. Photographed by Joseph Walker. Art direction by Steve Gooson. Edited by Gene Milford. Sound Engineer: Edward Bernds. Technical Director: Edward Shulter. Assistant Director: C. C. Coleman. Running time: 82 minutes.

CAST:

Gallagher, Loretta Young; *Stew Smith*, Robert Williams; *Ann Schuyler*, Jean Harlow; *Smythe, the butler*, Halliwell Hobbes; *Dexter Grayson*, Reginald Owen; *Conroy, the editor*, Edmund Breese; *Michael Schuyler*, Donald Dillaway; *Bingy Baker*, Walter Catlett; *Dawson, the valet*, Claude Allister; *Mrs. Schuyler*, Louise Closser Hale; *Dinner Guest*, Bill Elliot; *Waiter*, Harry Semels; *Radcliffe*, Olaf Hytten; *Reporters*: Tom London, Hal Price, Eddy Chandler, Charles Jordan; *Speakeasy proprietor*, Dick Cramer; *Butler*, Wilson Benge.

Platinum Blonde and Jean Harlow became synonymous, and now Harlow, whose acting was never thought adequate before, finally began her spectacular climb to stardom. Frank Capra has admitted to the authors that the movie was entirely a commercial venture, to make money for Columbia Pictures, especially after *The Miracle Woman*, which was not a box-office hit.

When asked about the common criticism that he had miscast Harlow as a socialite, Capra responded with a chuckle: "I had the darnedest time getting her to pronounce library correctly. She would say 'liberry.' But she certainly was one of the most hardworking and unaffected actresses I have ever worked with. She would even be on the set when she didn't have to be because she was so eager to learn. She wasn't popular with the other actors, however, because they were jealous of her. Her photo was on every movie-magazine cover, and the other actors resented that. But she was an unaffected, sweet, dear lady whom I had nothing but total respect for."

Theater owners wired Columbia to say that *Platinum Blonde* was the best title to come along all year. The plot switch, with Harlow not getting the hero, was appreciated by women (Loretta Young was obviously no threat to them), and men didn't care because all they cared about was seeing gorgeous Harlow, appropriately dressed.

As a result of the film, Platinum Blonde clubs were founded in at least a hundred cities, and beauty

Platinum Blonde

1931

AT JOE'S SPEAKEASY, newspaper editor Conroy (Edmund Breese), left, having learned of Smith's marriage to Ann Schuyler, confronts him with, "Stew Smith is dead and buried. From now on you'll be Ann Schuyler's husband." Loretta Young plays Gallagher, fellow newspaper worker and Smith's "Pal."

PHONE CALL TO NEW HUSBAND—Ann Schuyler (Jean Harlow) reminds Stew Smith (Robert Williams): "It's nearly six o'clock and you know how long it takes you to dress. The Ambassador's coming at eight and you've got to be ready before he gets here."

NEWSPAPER HEADLINE, "Cinderella Man Grows Hair On Chest; Attacks Reporter In Schuyler Home," is read by, left to right: Dexter Grayson (Reginald Owen), Mrs. Schuyler (Louise Closser Hale) and Ann Schuyler (Jean Harlow). Mrs. Schuyler remarks, "A cheap common brawl in my house," and when further reading in the paper that Smith is quoted as saying, "I wear the pants," her shocked reaction is: "Pants! Not even trousers!"

parlors had to stock a good supply of bleach. Even Harlow's dress, makeup, and speech were widely copied.

Writer Robert Riskin joined Capra to make *Platinum Blonde*, and they were to become an incomparable team, making together most of the Capra films that are best remembered today.

The story moves back and forth between the worlds of high society (the Schuylers) and newspaper people.

Reporter Stew Smith is played by Robert Williams, a promising comedian who died of peritonitis the week the film was released. Frank Capra sadly told the authors that Williams never saw the picture and that Capra believed Williams would have become a great star.

Smith, in covering a breach-of-promise suit involving Michael Schuyler (Donald Dillaway), falls in love with radiantly beautiful Ann Schuyler (Jean Harlow), whom he marries, ignoring the fact that fellow reporter Gallagher (Loretta Young) loves him. His editor calls him "a rich wife's magnolia— a boid in a gilded cage." And so, indeed, it turns out. Bored with the mansion setting and not wanting

FED UP with society wife Ann Schuyler (Jean Harlow), right, Stew Smith (Robert Williams) asserts his independence by packing up and leaving the Schuyler mansion with Gallagher (Loretta Young).

DRUNKEN BRAWL at the Schuyler mansion (whose participants include butler Smythe (Halliwell Hobbes), left, and Bingy Baker (Walter Catlett), on banister) is discovered by, left to right: Mrs. Schuyler (Louise Closser Hale), Dexter Grayson (Reginald Owen) and Ann Schuyler (Jean Harlow).

FAREWELL TO MOTHER-IN-LAW—Mrs. Schuyler (Louise Closser Hale), left, is told off by Stew Smith (Robert Williams): "You can take your red room, your green room, your left wing, your right wing—and you know what you can do with them!" He leaves with Gallagher (Loretta Young).

to go out with Ann's society friends, Stew, remaining home to work on a play, is lonely. In a scene that is visually a perfect analogy to his ennui, he plays hopscotch on the black and white squares of the fabulous marble floor.

When the Schuylers are offended by Stew's uncouth cronies and shocked to find Gallagher in the house working with him on the play, he moves out of his gilded cage to a divorce and into the arms of an appreciative Gallagher.

ALIMONY IS OFFERED by lawyer Dexter Grayson (Reginald Owen), left, to Stew Smith (Robert Williams). Gallagher (Loretta Young) is unable to restrain insulted Smith who punches Grayson and throws him out.

MISTAKEN STATEROOM — Bob Grover (Adolphe Menjou) explains to Lulu Smith (Barbara Stanwyck) that he ended up in her stateroom by mistake, having, in his drunken condition, misread the number 66 upside down as 99.

HALLOWEEN MASKS enliven a very original love scene between Bob Grover (Adolphe Menjou) and Lulu Smith (Barbara Stanwyck).

ILLEGITIMATE CHILD—Two-year-old Roberta (Myrna Fresholt) is cared for by her devoted mother, Lulu Smith (Barbara Stanwyck).

A Columbia Picture. A Frank R. Capra Production. Produced by Harry Cohn. Directed by Frank R. Capra. Story by Frank Capra. Adaptation and Dialogue by Jo Swerling. Photographed by Joseph Walker. Edited by Maurice Wright. Sound Engineer: Edward Bernds. Running time: 83 minutes.

CAST:

Lulu Smith, Barbara Stanwyck; *Bob Grover*, Adolphe Menjou; *Al Holland*, Ralph Bellamy; *Helen*, Dorothy Peterson; *Wilkinson*, Thomas Jefferson; *Roberta (age two)*, Myrna Fresholt; *Roberta (age eighteen)*, Charlotte V. Henry; *Briggs*, Oliver Eckhardt; *Florist*, Halliwell Hobbes; *Mrs. Smith*, Flo Wix; *Mr. Jones*, Claude King; *Mr. Eckner*, Robert Graves; *Advice-to-the-lovelorn Columnist*, Harry Holman.

RALPH BELLAMY:

Forbidden was the fourth of my ninety-six feature pictures to date, and that was more than forty years ago. It's still one of my most pleasant memories. Barbara Stanwyck had just become a star of magnitude and a dream to work with. And Frank was just beginning to be recognized as the great director he became.

The picture wasn't a classic, but it was a great part and fun to do. Incidentally, that word *fun* has almost disappeared from the picture-making procedures as we know them today. It didn't imply comedy, or even humor necessarily. It was a rapport with each other—cast and crew, writers, director, and producer. It was a companionship relation that I believe even photographed in some mystic way. We had it then. . . .

It wasn't that good a picture, but Capra was a delight for an actor. He respected the actor's talent and contribution, allowing him in rehearsal before each scene to have fairly free reign. Then he'd pull it all together, leaving the actor with a feeling of having contributed and achieved something. There was only one Frank Capra. There should be a hundred more. It would be a better business.

—*Letter to the authors from Los Angeles, California,* April 16, 1974.

EDWARD BERNDS:

Concerning the care needed to shoot Barbara Stanwyck and others perfectly on the first take, Capra enunciated his edict clearly to the sound crew

Forbidden

1932

RECONCILIATION IN RAIN—Bob Grover (Adolphe Menjou) pleads with Lulu Smith (Barbara Stanwyck) not to leave him, even though he cannot marry her.

ADVICE TO THE LOVELORN columnist, played by Harry Holman, seated, is replaced by city editor Al Holland (Ralph Bellamy) with new employee Lulu Smith (Barbara Stanwyck).

AGING EDITOR AND COLUMNIST: Al Holland (Ralph Bellamy) and Lulu Smith (Barbara Stanwyck). She tells him that she'd like a couple of days off to attend the convention at which Bob Grover will be nominated Governor.

and the camera crew: "You guys are working for the actors; they're not working for you!"

—*Told to the authors on tape from Van Nuys, California*, September 23, 1974.

In writing *Forbidden*, Capra admits that he borrowed from the immensely popular and intriguing *Back Street* by Fannie Hurst.

Small-town spinsterish librarian Lulu Smith (Barbara Stanwyck) decides, on a beckoning spring day, to take her savings out of the bank and see life aboard a romantic cruise ship bound for Havana.

She meets Bob Grover (Adolphe Menjou), with whom she becomes romantically involved, and after the trip she settles in the city where he lives in order to be near him. Working as a newspaperwoman, she attracts the attention of newsman Al Holland (Ralph Bellamy).

A memorable scene reveals her place in Grover's life. She is cooking dinner; Bob is stopping in a florist shop en route; it's Halloween. Her doorbell rings, and when she opens a square panel in the door, a long-nosed masked head pops in, announcing "I'm the census taker," to which Lulu replies, "Oh, I lost my senses long ago."

Bob has bought her a mask too. She dons it, and they engage in a mock romantic dialogue of playful intimacy. He opens the dumbwaiter door, takes out the roses he bought, and gives them to her.

She tells him she's happy when she's with him, but, like Cinderella, she worries about midnight: "It's never going to strike twelve for us, is it, Bob?"

At that juncture, Holland telephones to ask her to marry him. Bob, pensive and disturbed, puts his mask back on.

After the phone conversation, Bob tells Lulu he loves her—but he is married, and his wife is an invalid. "I'll keep on loving you no matter what happens," is Lulu's immediate and convincing response. To save her from ruining her life, he tells her he can't accept the sacrifice. She misunderstands his motives, thinking he is rejecting her, and orders him out. So ends this remarkable masking scene, one of laughter and tears incongruously intermingled.

Two years of separation pass. Lulu has borne Bob's child, and he has become district attorney and a candidate for mayor. He finds her after a long search, and they resume their fated relationship. Complications arise, unhappily forcing Lulu to have her daughter adopted by Bob and his wife.

Bob's political success over the years brings him a nomination for the governorship, but he is weary of a double life and is about to expose himself, when Lulu—for their daughter's sake—marries the long patient Holland. Holland, however, on the very eve of the election, uncovers the truth, and after a violent struggle between husband and wife, Lulu shoots and kills him.

As Governor, Bob pardons Lulu within a year and, dying, acknowledges their relationship in his will and leaves her half of his estate.

Walking in the crowded street, Lulu tears up the only copy of the will and throws it into a trash can. Around her, newsboys are shouting the "extras" of the governor's death. Lulu walks sadly away, and the camera does not follow her as she is swallowed up in the throng of passersby.

TORMENTOR Al Holland (Ralph Bellamy), right, tells Bob Grover (Adolphe Menjou) at the convention: "Nomination's in the bag. I made a special request to be seated behind you. I wanted to see how a fourflusher behaves when he has a full house."

TO PROTECT HER LOVER, Lulu (Barbara Stanwyck) threatens to kill her husband, Al Holland (Ralph Bellamy), if he reveals her past relationship with gubernatorial candidate Bob Grover.

DIRECTOR FRANK CAPRA, with Barbara Stanwyck in his arms, demonstrates to Adolphe Menjou how a love scene should be played.

"IT'S OBVIOUSLY A RUN ON A BANK," wrote Constance Cummings from London to the authors of this book on June 6, 1974, when she saw this posed still featuring herself and Walter Huston. Although admitting to an "appalling" memory, she did say, "I *do* remember when the banks closed and panics ensued. What strikes me most about the photo is all those hats! That puts it back in time. No one wears hats now—or very few. What a *dear* man Walter Huston was."

THE BANK VAULT, an important character in *American Madness,* as shown in this dramatically posed publicity still depicting bank president Thomas Dickson (Walter Huston) attempting to restrain depositors from creating a "run."

106

A Columbia Picture. A Frank Capra Production. Produced by Harry Cohn. Directed by Frank R. Capra. Story and dialogue by Robert Riskin. Photographed by Joseph Walker. Art direction by Stephen Goosson. Edited by Maurice Wright. Sound: Edward Bernds. Assistant Director: Buddy Coleman. Running time: 75 minutes.

CAST:

Thomas Dickson, Walter Huston; *Matt Brown*, Pat O'Brien; *Phyllis Dickson*, Kay Johnson; *Helen*, Constance Cummings; *Cyril Cluett*, Gavin Gordon; *Ives, Inspector*, Arthur Hoyt; *Inspector*, Robert E. O'Conner; *Dude Finlay*, Robert Ellis; *Clark*, Edwin Maxwell; *Ames*, Edward Martindale; *O'Brien*, Berton Churchill; *Judge*, Ralph Lewis; *Doctor Strong*, Pat O'Malley; *Cluett's secretary*, Jeanne Sorel; *Schultz*, Walter Walker; *Charlie*, Anderson Lawlor; *Oscar*, Sterling Holloway.

CONSTANCE CUMMINGS:

Frank Capra was one of the first really important directors I ever worked with. And I remember with gratitude how gentle and helpful he was to me, a beginner in films. But I do not claim any personal credit for this. Indeed, Frank was always kindly and good-natured, as highly talented people so often are, and he was both respected as one of Hollywood's leading talents and regarded as a personal friend by everyone in the studio from the highest to the lowest! Everyone liked Frank very much, and I never heard him raise his voice or be cross or even abrupt with anyone.

—Letter to the authors from London, England,
March 6, 1974.

GAVIN GORDON:

American Madness—oh Lord, 40 years ago—was my first picture with Frank Capra. It was apparent to all in a very short matter of hours that a man of authority was in charge. I remember from the first day with him, we began to *move*. Things that come back to me are not so much of specific incidents as an overall impression of a man in command, cerebrating constantly in deep, serious concentration, knowing what he wanted, planning for it, and patiently trying to get it. He was the first picture director I'd worked with who seemed instinctively to know how to direct and get results from an actor tied in knots by a strange medium. He had a freshness, an enthusiasm, and a bright curiosity for ex-

American Madness

1932

BANK EMPLOYEES, left to right: Oscar (Sterling Holloway), Helen (Constance Cummings) and Matt Brown (Pat O'Brien).

107

BANK PRESIDENT, Thomas Dickson (Walter Huston), greets his secretary, Helen (Constance Cummings), with a cheerful: "Helen, you're becoming more beautiful every day. What are we going to do about it?"

periment. Frank not only demanded naturalness, but knew how to achieve it. He knew how to cajole an actor into giving as *easy* a performance as possible—natural and *effortless*.

In retrospect, I think Frank and Hitchcock, for whom I also have unstinting respect and admiration, both have the most controlled concentration on a set. They seemed deep in thought into which the pleasant chitchat of the hour never really penetrated. Only the rare ones have this. And in both these remarkable men, I found the same qualities of kindness, infinite patience, great good humor, and sure technique in handling human beings. It is doubly remarkable that so *very few* have this empathy—or even care to have it, so wrapped up are they in their own greatness.

—*Letter to the authors from Tarzana, California,*
August 18, 1974.

EDWARD BERNDS:

Exposition is necessary in every picture, and it can be as dull as dishwater, but it never was in a Capra picture. Capra once told me, "When you

have exposition, when you have to tell the audience something, be sure you make it as *entertaining* as possible!" To him that meant throwing in comedy bits or other bits of business, which also helped to establish characterization. For instance, in *American Madness*, to liven up an exposition speech of Walter Huston's, he had Huston putt a golf ball around the office as he spoke. It made him more human and gave the audience something to look at as well as listen to.

—*Told to the authors on tape from Van Nuys, California,* September 23, 1974.

Apppropriately, this topical depths-of-the-Depression story of a run on a bank has as its silent star the Union National Bank. A compelling authenticity of atmosphere is established at the beginning as we are shown the marvelous workings of the great vault.

Bank president Thomas Dickson (Walter Huston) believes in the character of the persons he lends money to and is criticized by the bank's board of directors, who think, not of the people, but of merging with a bigger bank. The directors also disagree

108

with Dickson's philosophy that to meet a depression, banks must change and "get money back into circulation before we'll get back to prosperity."

Simultaneously, Cyril Cluett (Gavin Gordon), the bank's vice-president, cooperates with plans to rob the bank, to get the cash to pay off his heavy gambling debts. He throws the suspicion on chief teller Matt Brown (Pat O'Brien), and he maneuvers Phyllis Dickson, Thomas Dickson's wife (Kay Johnson), into becoming his alibi. Matt intervenes to protect the honor of his employer's wife. Alert police eventually entrap Cluett.

Nevertheless, rumor exaggerates the extent of the robbery loss, and a run starts. Those whom Dickson goes to for help turn a deaf ear. But Matt and Dickson's faithful secretary, Helen (Constance Cum-

GAVIN GORDON, as bank Vice-President Cyril Cluett, is caught in the act of forcing his attentions on the bank president's wife, Phyllis Dickson (Kay Johnson), by Chief Teller Matt Brown (Pat O'Brien).

DECEIVED HUSBAND, Thomas Dickson (Walter Huston), right, is angry with his employee Matt Brown (Pat O'Brien) for having concealed the truth about his wife's involvement with Cyril Cluett.

mings), in whom Matt is romantically interested, mobilize the many beneficiaries of Dickson's former goodwill.

The camera climbs to the ceiling of the Union National Bank to show us, between marble pillars, the tops of the heads of the surging mass of panic-stricken depositors. Just as the faith of one man in the character of his fellowmen is about to be totally destroyed, the first of his "men of character" arrives to make a deposit. He is followed by others, and the tide begins to turn.

Some commentators find faith in men, and men's response to that faith, a sentimental Capra solution. And indeed, for copyright purposes, the temporary title for this film was *Faith*. Yet the year after this film was released, Franklin Delano Roosevelt, as the newly elected president of a desperate people, proclaimed, "The only thing we have to fear is fear itself"—a statement of faith that invigorated the nation and defeated circumstances—but then he, too, believed that men can control their destinies.

YOUNG MISSIONARIES, Dr. Robert Strike (Gavin Gordon) and Megan Davis (Barbara Stanwyck), in each other's arms before their marriage plans are interrupted. In the scene are fellow missionaries Mr. & Mrs. Jackson (Lucien Littlefield and Clara Blandick).

CIVIL WAR IN CHINA—Megan Davis (Barbara Stanwyck) and Dr. Robert Strike (Gavin Gordon) are stopped by bandits when they attempt to transport children from an orphanage.

110

A Columbia Picture. A Frank Capra Production. Produced by Walter Wanger. Directed by Frank R. Capra. Screenplay by Edward Paramore, based on the novel *The Bitter Tea of General Yen,* by Grace Zaring Stone. Photographed by Joseph Walker. Edited by Edward Curtis. Musical score by W. Frank Harling. Sound Engineer: E. L. Bernds. Assistant Director: C. C. Coleman. Running time: 88 minutes.

CAST:

Megan Davis, Barbara Stanwyck; *General Yen,* Nils Asther; *Mah-Li,* Toshia Mori; *Jones,* Walter Connolly; *Doctor Robert Strike,* Gavin Gordon; *Mr. Jackson,* Lucien Littlefield; *Captain Li,* Richard Loo; *Miss Reed,* Helen Jerome Eddy; *Bishop Harkness,* Emmett Corrigan; *Mrs. Jackson,* Clara Blandick; *Doctor Lin,* Moy Ming; *Reverend Bostwick,* Robert Wayne; *Doctor Hansen,* Knute Erickson; *Mrs. Hansen,* Ella Hall; *Mr. Pettis,* Arthur Millette; *Miss Avery,* Martha Mattox; *Mrs. Blake,* Jessie Arnold; *Engineer,* Ray Young; *Missionaries*: Lillianne Leighton, Harriet Lorraine, Nora Cecil, Robert Bolder; *Doctor Mott,* Miller Newman; *Doctor Shuler,* Arthur Johnson; *Mrs. Bowman,* Adda Gleason; *Mrs. Warden,* Daisy Robinson; *Mrs. Meigs,* Doris Louellyn. Willie Fung, Jessie Perry, Milton Lee.

GAVIN GORDON:

When I went into *Bitter Tea* as the young missionary opposite Barbara Stanwyck, Frank told me that I was being mishandled in pictures. He said, "You're no heavy, you're a leading man." I couldn't have agreed with him more. That's all I'd ever been in the theater, and in much lighter roles than the constipated things I was then being thrown—and was later to be tossed, *ad nauseam.* Barbara Stanwyck has always seemed to me an extraordinarily good actress. Wonderful to work with. I enjoyed this picture. I never saw Frank blow up, lose his temper, or act other than with perfect self-control. He is, and to my knowledge has always been, a very well-disciplined man.

—*Letter to the authors from Tarzana, California,*
August 18, 1974.

The Bitter Tea of General Yen opened New York City's Radio City Music Hall.

A turbulent oriental score ushers in the credits, a relief map of China, and the opening scene of the burning of a city near Shanghai. Against the background of distant flames, hordes of refugees fill the screen and, with the immediacy of a newsreel, plunge us into the devastation of civil war.

ON PRIVATE TRAIN, Megan Davis (Barbara Stanwyck) regains consciousness to find herself being cared for by General Yen (Nils Asther) and Mah-Li (Toshia Mori).

The Bitter Tea of General Yen

1933

CAPTIVE Megan Davis (Barbara Stanwyck) is appalled by the executions she has witnessed through her bedroom window. General Yen (Nils Asther) tells her that it is more humane to shoot his prisoners than to have them starve to death.

112

Islanded in the midst of this chaos, in the home of two elderly American missionaries, young Bob Strike (Gavin Gordon) and Megan Davis (Barbara Stanwyck), childhood sweethearts who haven't seen each other for three years, are about to be married. They, too, are missionaries and plan to work for the welfare of China like "persistent ants trying to move a great mountain" (in the words of an experienced churchman who is present). But before the ceremony can take place, the two rush out to rescue children at an orphanage, and in the bombing and machine gunning that follows, they are separated.

Megan regains consciousness aboard the private train of General Yen (Nils Asther). The warlord, making himself responsible for her safety, takes her to his summer palace. A most comfortable prisoner,

Megan nevertheless, at first, refuses to join fellow American Jones (Walter Connolly), business advisor to the general, at the general's table.

The clash between Yen's realistic view of the Chinese and her idealism, based on ignorance of these people, leads to her unwittingly betraying him to his enemies, as she aids servant Mah-Li (Toshia Mori) and Mah-Li's supposed lover, Captain Li (Richard Loo). She tries to win the insinuatingly attractive Yen to the Christian concept of giving love without its being merited, rather than compelling loyalty from his followers. He calls her bluff by asking if she will die for her beliefs as Christ did. Ignorant of what Jones calls the "fifty centuries of authority" that Yen represents, she accepts the unequal challenge.

"SEND ME BACK TO SHANGHAI," Megan Davis (Barbara Stanwyck), center, orders General Yen (Nils Asther), while holding onto the servant girl Mah-Li (Toshia Mori) for security.

When the time comes for Megan to forfeit her life, the gallant, defeated Yen refuses to hold her to her bargain. He tells her to return to Bob, who speaks the same meaningless words as herself.

Alone, General Yen rings, but no servant comes; he, for whom palace doors had previously opened as if by magic at his approach, has none left to attend him.

Megan, in her room, dresses in the gorgeous gown he had earlier provided, applies makeup, and returns to him, just as he has prepared poisoned tea for himself. As a servant would have, she puts a cushion behind his back and a costly robe over his knees. "I had to come back," she tells him. "I couldn't leave. I'll never leave you." He dries her tears. He drinks the tea. She holds his hand, not knowing that he is dying.

In the final scene, Megan and Jones are aboard ship one hour from Shanghai. They talk of the general, of all he lost. But his fate is true to the time-transcending triumph of the tragic hero who, in Yen's words, can "crowd life into an hour."

DREAM—Megan Davis (Barbara Stanwyck) dreams of being attacked by General Yen (Nils Asther), whose appearance is sinisterly distorted.

AT DINNER, Megan Davis (Barbara Stanwyck), as guest of General Yen (Nils Asther), second from left, joins Captain Li (Richard Loo), right, and Jones (Walter Connolly), left, the American financial advisor to General Yen.

SUICIDE SCENE—Megan Davis (Barbara Stanwyck) admits her love for General Yen (Nils Asther), who is about to drink poison tea.

BIRTHDAY of Barbara Stanwyck is celebrated on the set by the cast and crew of *The Bitter Tea of General Yen*. Director Frank Capra is to the right of Stanwyck.

WONDERFUL CAST of *Lady for a Day*—left to right: Jean Parker, May Robson, Warren William, Guy Kibbee and Glenda Farrell.

"YOU TOOK A NOSEDIVE, LADY," one of the people on the street says to Apple Annie (May Robson) and another comments, "That's what cheap gin'll do," after a crowd of people has helped her up. Annie's response: "Lemme alone! I'm all right. Scat outta here! Beat it! Amscray!"

116

A Columbia Picture. Directed by Frank Capra. Screenplay by Robert Riskin, based on the short story "Madame La Gimp," by Damon Runyon. Photographed by Joseph Walker. Art direction by Stephen Goosson. Edited by Gene Havlick. Musical Director: Bakaleinikoff. Costumes by Robert Kalloch. Sound Engineer: E. L. Bernds. Assistant Director: Charles C. Coleman. Running time: 88 minutes.

CAST:

Dave the Dude, Warren William; *Apple Annie/"Mrs. E. Worthington Manville,"* May Robson; *"Judge" Blake,* Guy Kibbee; *Missouri Martin,* Glenda Farrell; *Happy McGuire,* Ned Sparks; *Louise,* Jean Parker; *Count Romero,* Walter Connolly; *Carlos,* Barry Norton; *Shakespeare,* Nat Pendleton; *Governor,* Hobart Bosworth; *Commissioner,* Wallis Clark; *Inspector,* Robert E. O'Connor; *Butler,* Halliwell Hobbes; *Mayor,* Samuel S. Hinds; *Dupe,* Irving Bacon; *Blind Man,* Dad Mills.

Damon Runyon's "Madame La Gimp" is one of the earliest short stories populated with the Broadway characters that were to make Runyon famous. It is a New York fairy tale about a filthy, gin-sodden "old haybag" (the phrase is Runyon's) who is transformed into a society matron.

While Runyon's hag begged by selling out-of-date newspapers and wilted flowers, her screen counterpart sells apples—a perfect Depression symbol not found in the original story, which predated the crash.

Apple Annie (May Robson) also shakes down the beggars who work what she considers her territory. She uses the proceeds to provide a convent education for a daughter in Spain, and she dubs her willing victims godparents! Her illegitimate daughter, Louise (Jean Parker), now eighteen, has written that she plans to marry Carlos (Barry Norton), the son of a Spanish nobleman, Count Romero (Walter Connolly), and the three are sailing at once for New York so that they can meet her mother.

Annie has told her daughter that she is married to a wealthy man, E. Worthington Manville, and is part of New York society. She has accomplished this deception by having the employee of a swank hotel steal its stationery for her to write on, and smuggle to her the daughter's replies.

The imaginary world Annie has created for her daughter is now about to be destroyed. But Dave the Dude (Warren William), gambler and petty mobster, who considers Annie's apples good-luck charms, steps in with the help of his girlfriend, night-

Lady for a Day

1933

HUSBAND FOR A DAY, "Judge" Blake (Guy Kibbee), kisses the hand of dolled-up Apple Annie (May Robson), now "Mrs. E. Worthington Manville," while Dave the Dude (Warren William) looks on approvingly.

VISITORS FROM SPAIN ARE GREETED—Left to right: "Judge" Blake (Guy Kibbee), Carlos (Barry Norton), Count Romero (Walter Connolly), Louise (Jean Parker), "Mrs. E. Worthington Manville" (May Robson), Dave the Dude (Warren William) and Happy McGuire (Ned Sparks).

club owner Missouri Martin (Glenda Farrell), to engineer the fantastic hoax of transforming Annie into "Mrs. E. Worthington Manville."

Dave the Dude procures for Annie's use the luxurious quarters of a rich bachelor friend who is out of town. He gets "Judge" Blake (Guy Kibbee), a pool shark with courtly manners and educated speech, to pose as her distinguished husband. Missouri Martin takes charge of Annie's physical transformation with elegant hair styling, makeup, and clothes. Missouri trains her nightclub gals and Dave the Dude his mugs to act out their roles as Annie's society friends.

As Runyon's narrator says in the original story: "It is commencing to sound to me like a movie such as a guy is apt to see at a midnight show."

The deception succeeds, as "Mrs. E. Worthington

Manville" is reunited with her daughter and the evening of the big social reception (so carefully rehearsed) approaches.

To climax his picture, Capra has the real governor (Hobart Bosworth), mayor (Samuel S. Hinds), and other important people, all formally dressed and with their wives, attend Annie's party.

The reception is a brilliant success. The ship sails for Spain and Louise and Carlos's wedding, it being understood in true fairy-tale parlance that the young lovers will "live happily ever after." The lady for a day will "join them later."

Lady for a Day was a huge success, and Capra, May Robson, *Lady for a Day*, and Robert Riskin were all nominated for Academy Awards. It was the first time a Columbia picture, or anyone connected with a Columbia picture, had ever been nominated.

118

MOMENT OF CONCERN by Dave the Dude (Warren William) and "Mrs. E. Worthington Manville" (May Robson) over whether their scheme will work.

REAL GOVERNOR ARRIVES AT PARTY—The Governor (Hobart Bosworth) takes the hand of "Mrs. E. Worthington Manville" (May Robson) while Carlos (Barry Norton) and Count Romeo (Walter Connolly) look on with satisfaction.

APPLE EATERS, Frank Capra (with baggy socks) and Warren William, clown for a publicity photo with nightclub chorus girls in *Lady for a Day*.

120

ROBERT RISKIN, second from left, who wrote *Lady for a Day*, on the set with Frank Capra, left, and stars Warren William, standing, and May Robson.

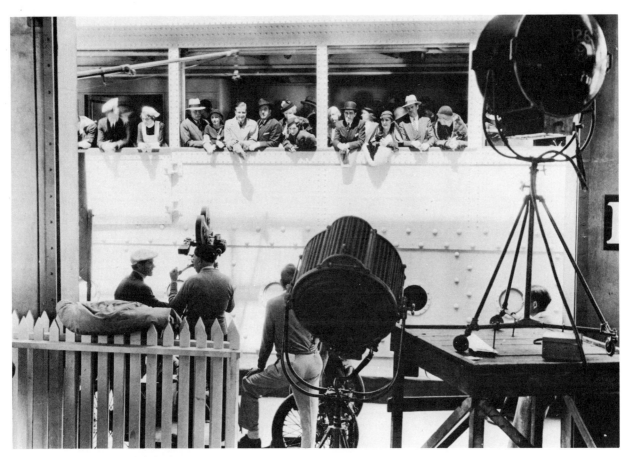

BEHIND THE SCENES view of shipboard sequence in *Lady for a Day* about to be shot by Frank Capra, left of camera. At the ship's railing, under microphone, wearing white coat, is Barry Norton, and next to him is Walter Connolly.

122

A Columbia Picture. A Frank Capra Production. Produced by Harry Cohn. Directed by Frank Capra. Screenplay by Robert Riskin, based on the *Cosmopolitan* magazine short story "Night Bus," by Samuel Hopkins Adams. Photographed by Joseph Walker. Art direction by Stephen Goosson. Edited by Gene Havlick. Musical Director: Louis Silvers. Costumes: Robert Kalloch. Sound: E. L. Bernds. Assistant Director: C. C. Coleman. Running time: 105 minutes.

CAST:

Peter Warne, Clark Gable; *Ellie Andrews*, Claudette Colbert; *Alexander Andrews*, Walter Connolly; *Oscar Shapeley*, Roscoe Karns; *King Westley*, Jameson Thomas; *Bus Drivers*: Ward Bond, Eddy Chandler; *Danker*, Alan Hale; *Zeke*, Arthur Hoyt; *Zeke's wife*, Blanche Frederici; *Joe Gordon*, Charles C. Wilson; *Lovington*, Wallis Clark; *Henderson*, Harry C. Bradley; *Auto Camp Manager*, Harry Holman; *Manager's Wife*, Maidel Turner; *Station Attendant*, Irving Bacon; *Reporters*: Charles D. Brown, Hal Price; *Flag Man*, Harry Todd; *Tony*, Frank Yaconelli; *Drunken Boy*, Henry Wadsworth; *Mother*, Claire McDowell; *Detectives*: Ky Robinson, Frank Holliday, James Burke, Joseph Crehan; *Drunk*, Milton Kibbee; *Vendor*, Mickey Daniels; *Dykes*, Oliver Eckhardt; *Boy*, George Breakston; *Secretary*, Bess Flowers; *Minister*, Rev. Neal Dodd; *Best Man*, Edmund Burns; *Maid of Honor*, Ethel Sykes; *Prissy Old Man*, Tom Ricketts; *Radio Announcer*, Eddie Kane; *Society Woman*, Eva Dennison; *Butler*, Fred Walton; *Newsboy*, Matty Rupert; *Policemen*: Earl Pingree, Harry Hume.

It Happened One Night

1934

EDWARD BERNDS:

We all knew we were making a fine picture. We had no doubt about it! The famous hitchhiking scene was not in the original script. Capra wrote it the night before we shot it. He told it to the cameraman, Joe Walker, and me and a couple of other people in the studio car going to the location in the morning.

—*Told to the authors on tape from Van Nuys, California*, September 23, 1974.

JOE PASTERNAK:

I'd like to say a lot of things about Frank Capra and his pictures, and about him as a man, but I can sum it up in one sentence: He was the "daddy" of good taste in making motion pictures. I loved all his pictures, but the one that stands out in my mind is *It Happened One Night*. It's a picture I have seen

ON A HUNGER STRIKE, Ellie Andrews (Claudette Colbert), being held against her will aboard the yacht of her wealthy father, Alexander Andrews (Walter Connolly), left, threateningly addresses stewards: "I thought I told you not to bring any food in here!"

MIAMI-TO-NEW YORK BUS on which Peter Warne and Ellie Andrews (Clark Gable and Claudette Colbert), left, begin their adventures. The bus driver in this posed still is Ward Bond. Much of the film was shot on location—at bus stops and at the newly established auto camps (later to be called motels).

124

MASHER EVICTED—Aboard bus, Peter (Clark Gable), left, rescues Ellie (Claudette Colbert) from wolfish Oscar Shapeley (Roscoe Karns) by lying to him that Ellie is his wife and that he'd like to sit next to her, "if you don't mind."

dozens of times, and I will continue seeing it every time I have a chance.

—Letter to the authors from Hollywood, California,
June 14, 1974.

It Happened One Night won five Academy Awards—for Best Picture, Best Director, Best Actor (Clark Gable), Best Actress (Claudette Colbert), and Best Screenplay, the first time any movie captured all the major awards—and this record remained unbroken for forty-one years!

In the first scene, rich, spoiled Ellie Andrews (Claudette Colbert) dives off the palatial yacht of her father, Alexander Andrews (Walter Connolly), where she has been held against her will because he objects to her marriage to a playboy aviator, King Westley (Jameson Thomas).

She swims to shore and thus begins her freewheeling trip from Miami to New York. She is joined by newspaperman Peter Warne (Clark Gable), whom she meets at once aboard a bus. Recognizing Ellie (her picture is in the papers), Peter offers to help her reach her destination undetected in return for a day-to-day story of her "mad flight to happiness."

NO UNDERSHIRT WORN by Clark Gable as Peter Warne caused many men throughout the country to stop wearing them, and the undershirt business suffered as a result. Here, Peter teasingly gives virginal Ellie (Claudette Colbert) a lesson in how a man undresses.

125

WALLS OF JERICHO SCENE—Wearing an extra pair of pajamas belonging to Peter (Clark Gable), Ellie (Claudette Colbert) prepares for bed on her side of the walls of Jericho which Peter has erected to protect her from "the big bad wolf." Capra's rain, seen through the window, makes the confining room cozily romantic.

WAITING IN LINE FOR SHOWER— Sent to the end of the line after having innocently tried to buck it, Ellie (Claudette Colbert) is laughed at by Capra's funny-looking character types at the auto camp. Traces of the prior night's rain is shown by the puddles and boards covering them.

LESSON IN DONUT DUNKING is given by Peter (Clark Gable) to Ellie (Claudette Colbert): "Say, where'd you learn to dunk, in finishing school? Twenty million dollars and you don't know how to dunk. Dunking's an art. Don't let it soak too long. A dip and plop in your mouth. If you let it in there too long it'll get soft and fall off. It's all a matter of timing. I ought to write a book about it." Frank Capra was taught how to dunk by Will Rogers.

A CARROT for breakfast, which Ellie (Claudette Colbert) has refused, is eaten by Peter (Clark Gable) in road scene before the couple begin hitchhiking.

128

There is a rainstorm, and a washed-out bridge causes Peter and Ellie to leave the bus and spend the night in a nearby auto camp, where Peter registers them into a single cabin because they have to conserve their dwindling supply of money.

One of the best-remembered scenes begins with Peter testing a cord he has strung parallel with the two beds. He hangs a blanket over the cord. "That, I suppose, makes everything quite all right?" says Ellie.

"Oh, this," Peter answers ingenuously. "Well, I like privacy when I retire. I'm very delicate in that respect—prying eyes annoy me. Behold—the walls of Jericho! Maybe not as thick as the ones that Joshua blew down with his trumpet, but a lot safer. See, I have no trumpet!"

They go to their own sides of the "wall." The camera moves outside to capture Ellie looking out at the rain.

Ellie asks that the light be turned out, and then, while he smokes in bed, she undresses. "Sex was so much in their minds, it charged the atmosphere," Capra was later to write in his autobiography.

The rain plays its obbligato on the roof, and the scene ends with a long shot of the two beds, each with a window at its head, separated by the modern equivalent of the "challenge" that made Joshua famous.

Each day on the road teaches Ellie more of life's reality, and it ends with her falling in love with Peter's protective, self-reliant maleness. Her father agrees with her new choice, and her hasty, unconsummated marriage is annulled to make way for the real thing.

The final scene is of a tourist-cabin manager (Harry Holman) and his wife (Maidel Turner), who is holding a cat, standing outside, a distance from a recently rented cabin, discussing why the newly arrived couple needed to have a rope and a blanket ("on a night like this?") and a toy trumpet! Then in swift succession the trumpet sounds, we see the blanket fall to the floor, and the lights go out!

ALAN HALE, right, as Danker, gives a lift to Peter and Ellie (Clark Gable and Claudette Colbert). He greets them kindheartedly, but turns out to be a road thief, picking people up and then stealing their luggage.

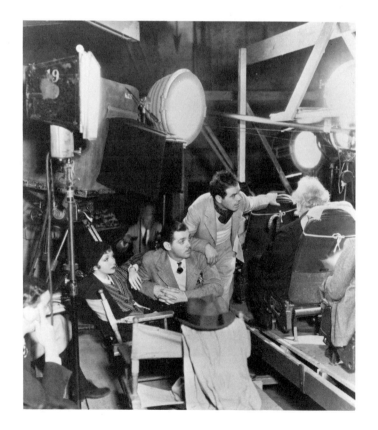

DIRECTOR AT WORK—Frank Capra (leaning over) lines up a shot of the bus interior while Claudette Colbert and Clark Gable wait for their next scene.

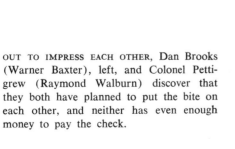

STARS of *Broadway Bill* in a photo on a theatre lobby display card—Left to right: Warner Baxter, Helen Vinson, Myrna Loy and Walter Connolly.

OUT TO IMPRESS EACH OTHER, Dan Brooks (Warner Baxter), left, and Colonel Pettigrew (Raymond Walburn) discover that they both have planned to put the bite on each other, and neither has even enough money to pay the check.

130

A Columbia Picture. A Frank Capra Production. Produced by Harry Cohn. Directed by Frank Capra. Screenplay by Robert Riskin, based on a story by Mark Hellinger. Photographed by Joseph Walker. Edited by Gene Havlick. Sound Engineer: Edward Bernds. Assistant Director: C. C. Coleman. Running time: 90 minutes.

CAST:

Dan Brooks, Warner Baxter; *Alice Higgins*, Myrna Loy; *J. L. Higgins*, Walter Connolly; *Margaret Brooks*, Helen Vinson; *Eddie Morgan*, Douglas Dumbrille; *Colonel Pettigrew*, Raymond Walburn; *Happy McGuire*, Lynne Overman; *Whitey*, Clarence Muse; *Edna*, Margaret Hamilton; *Ted Williams, Dan's Jockey*, Frankie Darro; *Joe*, George Cooper; *Henry Early*, George Meeker; *Arthur Winslow*, Jason Robards; *Jimmy Baker*, Ed Tucker; *Presiding Judge*, Edmund Breese; *Mrs. Peterson, Secretary*, Clara Blandick; *Switchboard Operator*, Lucille Ball; *Collins*, Charles C. Wilson; *Pop Jones*, Harry Todd; *Morgan's Henchmen*: Ward Bond, Charles Levison (Lane); *Mrs. Early*, Helen Flint; *Mrs. Winslow*, Helene Millard; *Whitehall's Jockey*, Bob Tansill; *Mae, Nurse*, Inez Courtney; *J. P. Chase*, Claude Gillingwater; *James Whitehall*, Paul Harvey; *Interne*, James Blakely; *Orchestra Leader*, Alan Hale; *Rube*, Harry Holman; *Horse Trainer*, Forrester Harvey; *Veterinarian*, Charles Middleton; *Hot-dog-stand Owner*, Irving Bacon; *Mayor*, John Ince; *Waiter*, Herman Bing; *Headwaiter*, Edward Keane; *Cab Driver*, Kit Guard; *Jailer*, Stanley Blystone; *Secretary*, Bess Flowers; *Patient*, Ernie Adams; *Reporter*, Robert Allen; *Johnson, the Butler*, Tom Ricketts; *Bookkeeper*, Harry C. Bradley; *Mike*, A. R. Haysel; *Onlooker*, Eddy Chandler; *Policeman*, Dick Summer; *Secretary*, Joan Standing; *Deputy Sheriffs*: Ky Robinson, Frank Holliday; *Pawnbroker*, William H. Strauss; *Head Nurse*, Gladys Gale; *Conductor*, Harry Semels. Arthur Rankin, Dennis O'Keefe, Pat O'Malley.

CLARENCE MUSE:

The scene is the race track at Tanforan. Overhead, scurrying white clouds obscure the sun. A chill wind, which blows through one's clothing, whistles through the paddocks and over the deserted course. A fine drizzle adds to the general desolation of this lonely panorama.

They are making a motion picture at Tanforan— the odyssey of an immortal horse, Broadway Bill. Clarence Muse, who plays his trainer in the picture, is sitting dejectedly on the rail of the fence parallel with the course. Peeking out from under his coat is

WEALTHY SISTERS, Alice Higgins (Myrna Loy), left, and Margaret Brooks (Helen Vinson) discuss Dan Brooks, Margaret's husband, from opposite viewpoints.

Broadway Bill

1934

BROADWAY BILL'S MASCOT, a rooster by the name of Skeeter, is delivered by Alice Higgins (Myrna Loy) to Dan Brooks (Warner Baxter), left, and a smiling Whitey (Clarence Muse).

CRITICALLY ILL BROADWAY BILL is cared for by veterinarian (Charles Middleton), second from left, while Whitey (Clarence Muse), far left, and Dan Brooks and Alice Higgins (Warner Baxter and Myrna Loy) and the horse's mascot, the rooster Skeeter, look on.

the mournful head of Skeeter, the rooster "luck piece" of Broadway Bill's owner, Mr. Brooks, played by Warner Baxter.

Frank Capra, ace Columbia director of the picture, steps out of the trainer's quarters and stops alongside the dejected figure at the rail. Capra squints at the skies to see what chance there is that the sun will come out.

"I've never seen such rotten luck, Mr. Capra," Muse remarks, shaking his head sadly. "Here it is one o'clock, and we haven't shot a scene. You can't shoot your picture if this keeps up."

Capra squints at the sun. "Clarence," he smiles, "it'll be clear by two o'clock, and we can shoot all afternoon. Meanwhile, the boys are taking some necessary shots of Broadway Bill in the paddock. In this business you've got to be an optimist. Remember, the general can't afford to look at the dark side or fret about how superior are the forces of the enemy. If he did, nine cases out of ten he'd fold up his tent and sneak away like a coward in the night."

"I guess that's right," Muse responds, brightening visibly. "By the way, will you tell me what spell you cast on your actors to make them do the things they do?"

"Why, I don't know what you mean, Clarence."

"Well, take yesterday. They were burying Broadway Bill. Now, a dead horse doesn't mean a thing to me. But you walked around saying those sad, quiet little things about this great old race horse and his fighting heart—so that when they finally lowered the body into that grave, tears were streaming from my eyes and I was sick with sorrow over his death."

"That's not magic, Clarence. I just gave you the spirit of the scene. The rest is the fine actor in yourself which responds to the stimulus."

"But that's only a part of it, Mr. Capra. Remember when we sat in the kitchen of your house and swapped stories? Here you are, the great director with more than half a dozen smash hits, talking with me so naturally and pleasant. No airs, no frills, no putting on. You haven't lost the common touch. That's why you are a great director."

"You're very kind, Clarence. I think I'd rather hear you say that than get a five-hundred-dollar raise. I really mean it. And if by losing the common touch, you mean going high-hat before my old friends who've come up the road to success with me and helped me to make mine, then it'll never happen. I just couldn't do it."

"Well, Lord bless me! Look, Mr. Capra, the sun *is* coming out—and it's just two o'clock. What are you—a wizard?"

"Just a lucky guy, Clarence. Come on, let's go to work! Lights, camera! Bring Broadway Bill out here! Come on, boys, step on it!"

—Letter to the authors from Muse-A-While Ranch, Perris, California, September 3, 1974.

EDWARD BERNDS:

Capra wanted Clark Gable for the leading role in *Broadway Bill*. It was just right for him. In fact, the part had been written for him. But Capra couldn't get him.

I recall that originally, in the movie, after the stormy night when the race horse Broadway Bill is rained on in the barn and clothing and blankets are put on him to keep him warm and dry, there was a fade-out and then, after the tremendous tension of the storm, a fade-in on a nice, sunny, peaceful day. However, the mood was still to be serious, because we would soon learn that Broadway Bill was critically ill. It was a long shot of the barn and Capra (thinking of what would have happened realistically) had put all the wet clothes and blankets on a clothesline, presumably to dry.

Well, when we previewed this version, the first and only time, there was a tremendous laugh when the audience saw the clothesline. Naturally, the scene came out. That's one of the things you preview for. Capra told me kind of ruefully, "I thought I knew some things about comedy, but I never dreamed they'd laugh at that. It just goes to show that you can't outfigure audiences."

—Told to the authors on tape from Van Nuys, California, September 23, 1974.

RAYMOND WALBURN:

I really have three favorite parts in my Hollywood career, and the part of the race-track tout in *Broadway Bill* is one of them. . . . I loved that old boy!

—Quoted in John McCabe's biographical study of Raymond Walburn, reprinted in THE REAL STARS *Number 2, edited by Leonard Maltin (Curtis Books, 1973).*

Married into the wealthy family of J. L. Higgins (Walter Connolly), Dan Brooks (Warner Baxter) revolts at the imperious confinement to rigid business and social values. His love for horses leads him to bolt the family circle with Whitey (Clarence Muse), his groom, and sleek, fast race horse Broadway Bill.

Unmarried Alice Higgins (Myrna Loy), his independent sister-in-law, joins him at the track as they work to train Bill, win the big race, and so prove that Dan has the capacity as well as the right to lead his own life. Alice and Dan are drawn into a comradeship that leads to love.

Bigtime gamblers are thwarted, and the race is won by Broadway Bill, but his heart bursts on the finish line. Capra stages a poignant burial for the horse alongside the famous track.

Dan's marriage to Margaret (Helen Vinson) having failed, he is free to return to the world of horse training with a perfectly sympathetic and loving mate, Alice. Even J. L. Higgins himself sees the joy of their way of life—and decides to follow their example!

THE FRANK CAPRA CREW for *Broadway Bill*—Top row: George Hager, gaffer; Jimmy Lloyd, head grip; Al Later, best boy (assistant to the gaffer); Bob Charlesworth, electrician. Middle row: Irving (Buster) Libbot, mike man; George Kelley, operative cameraman; Joseph Walker, cameraman; Gene (?), dialogue coach; Edward Bernds, sound engineer. Bottom row: Irving Lippman, still cameraman; George Rhein, prop man; Frank Capra; C. C. (Buddy) Coleman, assistant director.

133

A NEW LAUGH-AND-LOVE
TEAM TAKES AMERICA
BY STORM!

Gary COOPER

Mr. DEEDS
Goes to Town

Jean ARTHUR

GEORGE BANCROFT
LIONEL STANDER
DOUGLASS DUMBRILLE
H. B. WARNER

Screen play by Robert Riskin · Story by Clarence Budington Kelland

Another GREAT FRANK CAPRA PRODUCTION

A COLUMBIA PICTURE

A Columbia Picture. A Frank Capra Production. Produced and directed by Frank Capra. Screenplay by Robert Riskin, based on the story "Opera Hat" by Clarence Budington Kelland. Photographed by Joseph Walker. Special camera effects by E. Roy Davidson. Art direction by Stephen Goosson. Edited by Gene Havlick. Musical direction by Howard Jackson. Sound Engineer: Edward Bernds. Costumes by Samuel Lange. Assistant Director: C. C. Coleman. Running time: 115 minutes.

CAST:

Longfellow Deeds, Gary Cooper; *Babe Bennett*, Jean Arthur; *MacWade*, George Bancroft; *Cornelius Cobb*, Lionel Stander; *John Cedar*, Douglass Dumbrille; *Judge Walker*, H. B. Warner; *Walter*, Raymond Walburn; *Madame Pomponi*, Margaret Matzenauer; *Bodyguard*, Warren Hymer; *Theresa*, Muriel Evans; *Mabel Dawson*, Ruth Donnelly; *Mal*, Spencer Charters; *Mrs. Meredith*, Emma Dunn; *Psychiatrist*, Wryley Birch; *Budington*, Arthur Hoyt; *Farmer*, John Wray; *Mr. Semple*, Jameson Thomas; *Mrs. Semple*, Mayo Methot; *Waiter*, Gene Morgan; *Morrow*, Walter Catlett; *Jane Faulkner*, Margaret Seddon; *Amy Faulkner*, Margaret McWade; *Butler*, Barnett Parker; *James Cedar*, Stanley Andrews; *Arthur Cedar*, Pierre Watkin; *Swenson*, Christian Rub; *Dr. Malcolm*, Russell Hicks; *Dr. Frazier*, Gustav von Seyffertitz; *Dr. Fosdick*, Edward Le Saint; *Hallor*, Charles Levison (Charles Lane); *Frank*, Irving Bacon; *Bob*, George Cooper; *Anderson*, Harry C. Bradley; *Second Bodyguard*, Edward Gargan; *Douglas*, Edwin Maxwell; *First Deputy*, Paul Hurst; *Italian*, Paul Porcasi; *Tailor*, Franklin Pangborn; *Farmers' Spokesman*, George F. ("Gabby") Hayes; *Cabby*, Billy Bevan; *Reporter*, Bud Flannigan (Dennis O'Keefe); *Brookfield*, George Meeker; *Court Clerk*, Charles Wilson; *Lawyer*, Dale Van Sickel; *Henneberry*, Eddie Kane; *Writer*, Jay Eaton; *Bailiff*, Lee Shumway; *Board Members*: John Picorri, Edward Keane; *Reporter*, Jack Mower; *Interne*, James Millican; *Guard*, Harry Holden; *Shop Girl*, Mary Lou Dix; *Hat-check Girls*: Patricia Monroe, Lillian Ross; *Cigarette Girl*, Peggy Page; *Shop Girl*, Janet Eastman. Cecil Cunningham, Bess Flowers, Ann Doran, Beatrice Curtis, Beatrice Blinn, Pauline Wagner, Frank Hammond, Charles Sullivan, Flo Wix, Hal Budlong, Ethel Palmer, Juanita Crosland, Vacey O'Davoren, Bessie Wade.

JEAN ARTHUR:

Working with Mr. Capra has given me some of the happiest moments of my life. There was a feeling of great warmth and protection and a feeling that everyone, cast and crew, was working together to-

Mr. Deeds Goes to Town

1936

NEWS OF INHERITANCE is told to Longfellow Deeds (Gary Cooper), center, by Cornelius Cobb (Lionel Stander), left, and attorney John Cedar (Douglass Dumbrille), right, while Mr. Deeds' housekeeper, Mrs. Meredith (Emma Dunn), serves coffee.

FAREWELL
LONGFELLOW DE
THE PRIDE OF MANDRAKE

136   MR. DEEDS' FRIENDS in Mandrake Falls, Vermont, celebrate his good fortune as Longfellow
(Gary Cooper), with tuba, prepares to board a train for New York City.

ward the goal. Mr. Capra brought out the best in people. I think he should be drafted as "director" of the United Nations.

—Letter to the authors from Carmel, California,
April 8, 1974.

LIONEL STANDER:

I remember the filming of *Mr. Deeds Goes to Town* and Frank Capra quite vividly.

Mr. Capra told me that he had wanted Ned Sparks to play the role but that Harry Cohn had insisted on me—I was under contract to the studio, and Ned Sparks was a freelance player. Capra had reluctantly submitted to Cohn's dictate.

After he saw the rushes, even though my concept of the role differed from his, he liked what I did and kept me in the film without any further conflict with Cohn.

I felt that Sparks would have been excellent in the role but naturally with a different quality than mine. It was a good part, and any competent actor would have given it gloss.

—Letter to the authors from Rome, Italy,
February 28, 1974.

EDWARD BERNDS:

The enormous empathy created for Longfellow Deeds, especially in the courtroom scene, the "rooting interest" as it's called by the movie industry, accounts for the tremendous success of this picture, and it was a pure product of its time.

I remember well the opening scenes of *Deeds.* We shot them first, which of course, isn't always done. The scenes were of the lawyer Douglass Dumbrille and his henchman going to Mandrake Falls, Vermont, to inform Longfellow Deeds of his inheritance. We shot them on Fox Studios' New England street, not at our own Columbia Ranch.

The next day Capra reshot almost all of what we'd done the first day. He told me, "We were trying for too many laughs. We've got to make the audience like this guy and believe him and not think he's a jerk. Once they get to liking him, we can do anything we want." So we reshot a somewhat toned-down version in which laughs were sacrificed and a more believable Longfellow Deeds emerged.

I think the success of the picture is the proof that Capra was right. Apparently he had thought deeply that night about what he had done and in his way

DOUBLE-DECKER BUS is enjoyed by Babe Bennett (Jean Arthur) and Longfellow Deeds (Gary Cooper). Longfellow says of his sightseeing: "The aquarium was swell. If I lived in New York I'd go there every day!"

SUFFERING WITH HANGOVER, Longfellow Deeds (Gary Cooper) is helped into his slippers by his valet, Walter (Raymond Walburn), prior to being served a prairie oyster.

communicated with the as-yet-unborn audience. Certainly his decision was right.

—*Told to the authors on tape from Van Nuys, California*, September 23, 1974.

GARY COOPER:

[*Mr. Deeds Goes to Town*] was the most enjoyable [film] I ever made. I liked Mr. Deeds. Heck of a good fellow. Wish I could meet him somewhere.

—*From* THE GARY COOPER STORY *Copyright* 1970 *by George Carpozi, Jr. Published by Arlington House, New Rochelle, New York. All rights reserved. Used with permission.*

RAYMOND WALBURN:

I played Gary Cooper's valet in *Mr. Deeds Goes to Town*, and at one point in the script when I had to bring Mr. Deeds a Bromo to cure his hangover, Frank Capra stopped the scene because it was too trite, too conventional. He asked if anyone had any idea of how to give the scene a little zip. I thought of an old play I'd been in years before in which the maid had brought in a hangover remedy called a "prairie oyster." I told this to Frank, and he loved the sound of it. Now, Frank was a realist so he had the property man make up a real prairie oyster. I believe it was made up of Angostura bitters, an egg and sherry. Coop and I faithfully went through the scene and he drank it bottoms up, naturally.

—*Quoted in John McCabe's biographical study of Raymond Walburn, reprinted in* THE REAL STARS *Number 2, edited by Leonard Maltin (Curtis Books, 1973).*

PETER DE VRIES:

There is a reference to *Mr. Deeds Goes to Town* in my new novel, *The Glory of the Hummingbird* (a title taken from a line in T. S. Eliot's *Marina*), in connection with a tuba-playing paterfamilias going through a period of melancholia worse than Gary Cooper's, in which he says he will never play another note, the bird is silenced, and is about to give legal instructions that his instrument be buried with him, necessitating a second grave.

—*Letter to the authors from Westport, Connecticut,* September 29, 1974.

IN CENTRAL PARK, Babe Bennett (Jean Arthur) sings "Swanee River" and beats out the rhythm on a trash can while Longfellow Deeds (Gary Cooper) accompanies her with his vocal imitation of tuba sounds.

GRAHAM GREENE:

Mr. Deeds is Capra's finest film (it is on quite a different intellectual level from the spirited and delightful *It Happened One Night*), and that means it is a comedy quite unmatched on the screen. For Capra has what Lubitsch, the witty playboy, has not: a sense of responsibility, and what Clair, whimsical, poetic, a little precious and *à la mode*, has not, a kinship with his audience, a sense of common life, a morality: he has what even Chaplin has not, complete mastery of his medium, and that medium the sound-film, not the film with sound attached to it. Like Lang, he hears all the time just as clearly as he sees and just as selectively. I do not think anyone can watch *Mr. Deeds* for long without being aware of a technician as great as Lang employed on a theme which profoundly moves him: the theme of

goodness and simplicity manhandled in a deeply selfish and brutal world.

—From THE SPECTATOR, August 28, 1936. *Reprinted in* GRAHAM GREENE ON FILM, COLLECTED FILM CRITICISM 1935–1940. *Copyright* 1972 *by Graham Greene and reprinted by permission of Simon and Schuster.*

(Graham Greene wrote to the authors from London, England, October 17, 1974, concerning his memories of Capra films, but suggested the use of his contemporary reviews.)

MARK VAN DOREN:

Mr. Deeds is something different and better. As Robert Riskin conceived him, as Frank Capra directed him, and as Gary Cooper very admirably acted him, he becomes indeed one of the most interesting figures ever thrown on the screen. Truly an innocent,

COMIC RUTH DONNELLY, left, playing the part of Mabel Dawson, roommate of Babe Bennett (Jean Arthur), who is being escorted out of her apartment by Longfellow Deeds (Gary Cooper), hides photographers, left to right, Frank and Bob (Irving Bacon and George Cooper).

truly a virtuous and rational young man, he is so empty of spiritual pride as in the end, when it has been made clear to him that the world is corrupt and crazy, to desire nothing save silence even in the court where his sanity is being tried. The weakness of the film is not that he rises at last in defense of himself, but that his defense succeeds; the implication being that New York henceforth will honor such men, whereas we know of course that it will do nothing of the sort as long as it consists of people like ourselves. The perfect irony would have been for Mr. Deeds' completely brilliant and convincing argument to fail of its practical purpose. Yet perfect irony happens in literature only about once in a thousand years, so with a bow to it we can go on to say that *Mr. Deeds* is really a very intelligent affair, a film no less charming than Mr. Capra's *It Happened One Night* at the same time that it is more profound.

The idea which fills it almost to the limit is an idea of eternal importance, and it has been translated

IN COURTROOM, Babe Bennet (Jean Arthur) stands up to defend Longfellow Deeds. McWade (George Bancroft) is seated to her left.

with great skill into the concrete language of art: nowhere more so, as I have suggested, than at those moments when Gary Cooper as Mr. Deeds grows modest about his virtue and all but ashamed of it. He is never quite ashamed. It is rather that he cannot understand why other people do not have the virtue too. To him his wisdom is not wisdom; it is a minimum of horse sense, it is merely the starting-point for an inquiry. That is what throws the wisdom of the world into its proper relief; and what makes the film on the whole both so interesting and so plausible.

—THE NATION; *reprinted in* THE PRIVATE READER, *by Mark Van Doren* (Henry Holt and Company, 1942).

Mr. Deeds Goes to Town was voted the Best Picture of 1936 by the New York Film Critics and the National Board of Review. In Hollywood, Capra won an Oscar for Best Director, and the film was nominated for four other Oscars for Best Picture, Best Actor (Gary Cooper), Best Screenplay, and Best Sound Recording.

Tuba-playing, twenty-eight-year-old happy Vermont owner of a tallow works and writer of rhymes for greeting cards, Longfellow Deeds (Gary Cooper) inherits twenty million dollars. "I wonder," he asks his dead uncle's incredulous lawyer John Cedar (Douglass Dumbrille) and press agent Cornelius Cobb (Lionel Stander), "why he left me all that money? I don't need it."

The inheritance brings Deeds to New York, where he is put upon by all varieties of parasites and phonies. When he determines to give the money away, by giving acreage and livestock to impoverished farmers who will work, venal relatives and lawyers move to have him committed to an insane asylum.

Babe Bennett (Jean Arthur) is a newspaperwoman out to get Deeds's "inside" story. But finding him so genuine, she falls in love with him and fights for him. First, however, he has to suffer the ultimate disillusionment in the big city—her deceiving him about her identity while she covered him in the press.

To test this unbelievable fact, Deeds telephones her using her real name. We see him walk in tortured circles as he only half-talks with her while absorbing the unbearable truth. Gary Cooper's face reflects a quickly changing range of expressions, all despairing, before he pauses in the shadow behind a huge pillar to cry. It may well be the most poignant representation of male sensitivity in a Capra film.

TIMID SISTERS TESTIFY—Amy and Jane Faulkner (Margaret McWade and Margaret Seddon), left to right, claim in court that Longfellow Deeds is "pixilated."

At the sanity hearing, Deeds is at first too dispirited to speak on his own behalf, but when he does, he carries the day.

A high note of humor is injected into the hearing by the two elderly, old-maid Faulkner sisters from Deeds's hometown, Mandrake Falls. Being timid, they wish to testify together, and they whisper back and forth before replying to a question. Their verdict is that Deeds is "pixilated" (defined as an early-American expression for the pixies having got him). But as we learn at a climactic moment when Deeds cross-examines them, they believe everyone (including the judge) is pixilated—everyone, of course, except themselves!

Deeds is carried out in triumph on the shoulders of the unemployed beneficiaries of his largesse. Babe is left quietly crying. And the Faulkner sisters remain in place. Before long the hero returns, picks up his girl, and carries her out triumphantly.

"Still pixilated," says one of the sisters.

"He sure is!" returns the other.

DIRECTOR AND STAR—Frank Capra and Gary Cooper wait for a scene to be set up.

(*Opposite page*) TIBETAN TRIBESMEN converge on plane, being hijacked to Shangri-La, for the purpose of refueling it. The Tibetans were played by Pala Indians from the San Diego Mountains.

A Columbia Picture. A Frank Capra Production. Produced and directed by Frank Capra. Screenplay by Robert Riskin, based on the novel *Lost Horizon*, by James Hilton. Photographed by Joseph Walker. Aerial photography by Elmer Dyer. Special camera effects by E. Roy Davidson and Ganahl Carson. Art direction by Stephen Goosson. Interior decoration by Babs Johnstone. Edited by Gene Havlick and Gene Milford. Musical score by Dimitri Tiomkin. Musical Director: Max Steiner. Costumes by Ernst Dryden. Technical Advisor: Harrison Forman. Assistant Director: C. C. Coleman. Running time: 118 minutes.

CAST:

Robert Conway, Ronald Colman; *Sondra*, Jane Wyatt; *George Conway*, John Howard; *Maria*, Margo; *Henry Barnard*, Thomas Mitchell; *Alexander P. Lovett*, Edward Everett Horton; *Gloria Stone*, Isabel Jewell; *Chang*, H. B. Warner; *High Lama*, Sam Jaffe; *Lord Gainsford*, Hugh Buckler; *Prime Minister*, David Torrance; *Carstairs*, John Miltern; *First Man*, Lawrence Grant; *Wynant*, John Burton; *Meeker*, John T. Murray; *Seiveking*, Max Rabinowitz; *Bandit Leaders*: Willie Fung, Victor Wong; *Montaigne*, John Tettener; *Assistant Foreign Secretary*, Boyd Irwin, Sr.; *Foreign Secretary*, Leonard Mudie; *Steward*, David Clyde; *Radio Operators*: Neil Fitzgerald, Darby Clark; *Talu*, Val Durand; *Aviator*, Dennis D'Auburn; *Fenner*, Milton Owen; *Chinese Priest*, George Chan; *Shanghai Airport*

Lost Horizon

1937

Official, Richard Loo; *Missionaries*: Wryley Birch, Carl Stockdale, Ruth Robinson, Margaret McWade; *Passengers*: Beatrice Curtis, Mary Lou Dix, Beatrice Blinn, Arthur Rankin; *Leader of Porters*, Noble Johnson; *Porters*: Chief Big Tree, Eli Casey, Richard Robles, James Smith; *Englishmen*: Eric Wilton, Barry Winton, Robert Corey, Henry Mowbray, Wedgwood Nowell; *Servants*: Ernesto Zambrano, Richard Master, Alex Shoulder, Manuel Kalili; *Voices*, Hall Johnson Choir.

JANE WYATT:

Lost Horizon was, of course, a very important time in my life. I had expected to be completely overawed by those two giants Capra and Colman. Except for the first couple of days, I wasn't, although I think some of my acting in that picture looks as though I was!

Frank was wonderfully kind and always tried to put everyone at his ease. He didn't want any artifice at all—only truth. He stands out in my mind as one of the very few directors who almost insisted that the actors go to the rushes. A great many directors guard their rushes zealously. Sometimes this comes from lack of security, but usually it is because they have a mistaken notion that actors will be put off by seeing themselves. Actually, I think that once an actor sees himself doing something wrong—or not achieving what the director wanted—he is able to rectify it the next time. One of the great joys of *Lost Horizon* was going to the dailies with Frank and hearing his comments.

I think one of Frank's great qualities as a director was in creating a climate in which the actor could be himself and could expand. You never felt tied up in knots or frustrated.

To sum up, Capra was gentle, witty, and most understanding. But when I read his brilliant book I was entertained to find what a really tough, gutsy character he was! I guess to achieve what he did you have to be. I have never met anyone who didn't like Mr. Frank Capra!

—*Letter to the authors from Los Angeles, California,*
May 3, 1974.

JOHN HOWARD:

Frank Capra will always be one of my most favorite people; and when I hear his name, I immediately see that infectious grin which had the power to still all storms. I have always been sorry I had only one

144

CRASH LANDING IN HIMALAYAS—An emissary from Shangri-La, Chang (H. B. Warner), greets emerging plane crash survivors, left to right: Robert Conway (Ronald Colman), George Conway (John Howard), Alexander P. Lovett (Edward Everett Horton) and Henry Barnard (Thomas Mitchell).

145

opportunity to work with Frank, but that picture was, of course, something rather special.

—*Letter to the authors from Los Angeles, California,*
May 8, 1974.

SAM JAFFE:

Long before the film world proclaimed his genius, I knew Frank Capra was the unsung hero of Hollywood. *It Happened One Night, Mr. Deeds Goes to Town,* and *Lost Horizon* are but a few of his many wonderful films, most of which are not only a hall of fame of their own but would enhance any film hall of fame.

As a director, his was a happy marriage of science and art. In addition to those gifts, there was always his great warmth, which made the actor reach down to bring out his very best. What actor can ask for more!

—*Letter to the authors from Beverly Hills, California,*
April 18, 1974.

SAM JAFFE:

Concerning my makeup as the High Lama: to get the crinkly, wrinkly appearance of old age, first cigarette paper was chosen, then oatmeal—without cream, of course!—and then fish skin. Finally, the makeup man at M.G.M., Mr. Hawkes, took a cast of my face and used two built-in pieces, one for each side of my face. These pieces had furrows in lieu of lines so the camera could be brought up as close as necessary. These two set pieces could be cast as often as needed.

My hands were made up by the Columbia makeup man. Concerning my voice, Mr. Capra and I felt that since Shangri-La possessed such health-preserving miracles—the speedy healing of the Lama's leg and the youthful appearance of Margo—rather than the halting, hesitating, feeble quality associated with age, the Lama's voice should reflect a sort of benign simplicity.

—*Letter to the authors from Beverly Hills, California,*
May 7, 1974.

FRANK CAPRA:

. . . about the tests that were supposed to have been made of some twenty-three actors for the part of the High Lama in *Lost Horizon.*

I looked up the clippings from *Lost Horizon* just to refresh my own memory about what actors were tested—if any. You must remember that I hated tests, thought they were wholly unfair to actors and of very little use to directors.

I will quote you some of the clippings verbatim, but first, bear in mind that shooting on the film started *March 23, 1936.* That date is important.

Almost one year earlier, June 23, 1935, Beckley wrote in the *Raleigh* (West Virginia) *Reporter:*

. . . since then Walter Connolly has been in every film directed by Capra. He is set again for a role in *Lost Horizon,* Capra's next. Connolly has been in all Capra pictures from *The Bitter Tea of General Yen* to *Broadway Bill.*

That was pure speculation, since only Ronald Colman had been cast that far ahead of the starting date. Sure I wanted Connolly in all my films. The part I had in mind for him was not the High Lama (the High Lama was a frail two-hundred-year-old hermit; Connolly had a paunch that would have fitted him for the part of Cannon).

The news item that really set the stage for the canard that Connolly had been cast, or tested, for the High Lama was this squib in the *Los Angeles Examiner,* dated 12 March 1936, just eleven days before the first day of shooting:

. . . Jane Wyatt, billed as a society girl, plays opposite Ronnie with that excellent little actress, Isabel Jewell, in the second lead, and Walter Connolly as the Grand Lama. . . .

It was pure nonsense. I wanted Connolly to play the fugitive industrialist who had fleeced his stockholders, not the High Lama. But Connolly was committed to another assignment.

About six weeks after the film began shooting, this item came out in the *New York Telegraph,* 27 April 1936, about *Thomas Mitchell* being hired for the industrialist's role:

. . . others in the cast include Edward Everett Horton, Isabel Jewell, Thomas Mitchell.

Three days later, 30 April 1936, the *Detroit News* published this item:

. . . others cast so far are Jane Wyatt, Edward Everett Horton, and the studio is reportedly dickering for the services of Charles Laughton. . . .

Pure speculation about Laughton. He would have been far too fat to play the part of a two-hundred-year-old ascetic.

146

(*Opposite page*) SHANGRI-LA SET with Ronald Colman, as Robert Conway, posed in foreground.

CHANG CONFRONTED—Robert Conway (Ronald Colman), pointing finger, demands of Chang (H. B. Warner), seated left: "For some reason we are being held prisoners here and we want to know why." Other kidnapped travelers are, left to right: Gloria Stone (Isabel Jewell), Alexander P. Lovett (Edward Everett Horton) and Henry Barnard (Thomas Mitchell).

A couple of months after the film had been in production, Louella Parsons printed this item in her column (30 June 1936):

News that Sam Jaffe had been selected to play the Grand Lama in *Lost Horizon* brings to mind a dramatic and touching story told in connection with this very part. Ronald Colman, C. Aubrey Smith and other members of the English colony had A. E. Anson brought in from the desert to take a test with director Frank Capra. Anson, terribly ill, made the trip to Columbia Studios in an ambulance.

A few days later, Ronnie, who plays the lead in *Lost Horizon*, carried his friend the cheerful tidings that he had been engaged at a larger salary than he had ever received. Two days later Anson passed away in his sleep, happy over his good fortune. Jaffe, who now falls heir to the role, is one of Hollywood's better actors. . . .

As usual with Louella, she got the facts screwed up a bit. My recollection of this incident, as published in my book, is much closer to the truth. But the item does show that the film had been in production about two and a half months before we cast the High Lama's part.

The test business was as follows: A test of A. E. Anson. He died *after* the test. A decision to test Henry Walthall. He died *before* we could test him. A test of Sam Jaffe. He survived and got the part. No other tests were made.

Almost one year later, 14 February 1937, the *Boston Herald* summed up the High Lama highjinks with this *almost* factual item:

. . . from the very beginning, the role of the High Lama was dogged by disaster and difficulty. . . . Capra finally selected A. E. Anson, who came up from Arizona where he was recuperating from an illness, to take a test for the part. But before he was called for actual production, that fine old actor died.

148

STARS OF "LOST HORIZON"—Ronald Colman and Jane Wyatt as Robert Conway and Sondra in a posed publicity still.

DISARMED—George Conway (John Howard) has been knocked unconscious by his brother, Robert (Ronald Colman), left, when in a frenzy he pursued Chang (H. B. Warner) with a gun. Onlookers are, left to right: Henry Barnard (Thomas Mitchell), Alexander P. Lovett (Edward Everett Horton) and Gloria Stone (Isabel Jewell).

The next choice [right] from among the many who had taken screen tests [wrong] was Henry B. Walthall, the famous "Little Colonel" of Griffith's "Birth of a Nation." He, too, died before the cameras started grinding.

After these two tragedies had left the High Lama role still unfilled, someone remembered Sam Jaffe, the fine character actor who created the role of Kringelein in the stage production of "Grand Hotel." Jaffe was summoned to Hollywood, tested, and given the part.

—*Letter to the authors from La Quinta, California,*
July 26, 1974.

EDWARD EVERETT HORTON:

I liked doing *Lost Horizon* with Frank Capra. I had read the Hilton book. Suddenly I got a call from Mr. Capra. He wanted me to come down and be in the picture. "Oh," I said, "Mr. Capra, what could I play in it? I don't see anything." He said, "What I want you to do is not in the book. I am going to write it in just for you." Well, you couldn't say anything to that. I was a paleontologist. Did you ever see *Lost Horizon*? Well, I'm the fellow who carries the vertebrae of a prehistoric animal around in a little box. We are all in the airplane, and I discover that we are going in the wrong direction. I say, "Something must be done about this." Then we get to Shangri-La, and I like it there.

Capra was entirely different from Lubitsch. Everybody who worked for Capra had had stage experience. We were all stage actors. He hand picked them. He said to me one day, in a fabricated room up there

150

ANXIOUS TO LEAVE SHANGRI-LA, George Conway (John Howard), standing, is told by Henry Barnard (Thomas Mitchell) and Gloria Stone (Isabel Jewell) that they have decided to stay.

in the Himalaya Mountains, a great big place with wonderful Chinese embroideries, all built on that set, "Edward, in this scene I want to get over a feeling, not of fear, but sort of an eerie feeling. What goes on here? A mysterious something. What do you think?"

"Well, Mr. Capra, I don't know."

"What do you mean you don't know? You've been on the stage for fifteen, twenty, thirty-five years. What do you mean you don't know?"

I knew I had made a mistake and covered up quickly. "Well, I don't know quite what you mean by eerie. If I were in a room like this and I happened to see that long curtain moving back and forth, I'd be a little . . ."

"That's it. That's it. You're behind the curtain."

"I am?"

"Yes, you're behind the curtain."

So I went over and stood behind the curtain.

"Now sell me the fact that you're behind the curtain. I can't feel it unless I see some sort of a form of your body. Get up closer to it."

"What am I doing?"

"Give him a sword, one of those samurai swords. Now let's see the sword come out back and forth in front of the curtain."

"What am I doing?"

"You're sharpening a pencil or something like that."

"Ed, I'm stuck." He then said, "How do I know it's you?"

"I have no idea, Mr. Capra, unless I thought I heard something and I looked around the curtain to see what . . ."

151

HIGH LAMA (Sam Jaffe), right, reveals to Robert Conway (Ronald Colman) that he had him brought to Shangri-La to take his place when he dies.

PLANNING TO ESCAPE from Shangri-La are Maria (Margo) and George Conway (John Howard) in this posed still.

"That's it, that's just right. Now it's nobody, so you go over to the desk." I went over and just as I sat down I jumped up.

"What's the matter?"

"I forgot the sword."

"Oh, well, go and get it." Now at the desk he said, "Go ahead, what do you want to do?"

What do I want to do? I mean, what can you do behind a desk? I'm trying to see if there's any dust on it. Then I saw a Chinese lacquer box. I opened the thing and looked in it. And as I looked up, I saw that it had a mirror in it, and there's my face! I screamed and shut the thing.

"Perfect, that's just right," he said.

Well, it was fun working with Capra because you were thinking all the time and you tried to please him. He knew what he was after, but he wanted to see how you'd get around to it. Both Capra and Lubitsch were extraordinary directors.

—From THE REAL TINSEL, *by Bernard Rosenberg and Harry Silverstein, Copyright 1970 by Bernard Rosenberg and Harry Silverstein; reprinted by permission of Macmillan Publishing Co., Inc.*

EDWARD BERNDS:

I could talk to Capra, go to him with ideas. Sometimes he accepted them, sometimes he didn't, but he always received them with patience and never rejected them summarily. Of course, I never shouted

152

MINIATURE SET—"We re-created the mountain-locked Valley of the Blue Moon—its peaceful village by a peaceful stream, under the tranquil primacy of the lamasery on a cliff—in miniature."—Frank Capra in *The Name Above the Title.*

my ideas from the housetops. I got his ear quietly and discreetly, and I felt well rewarded if he used any part of my idea. I recall once I was fairly bursting with impatience waiting to get his ear about something that bothered me about a scene. He seemed to be unaware of my presence, but when he finished with the actor he was talking to he turned to me with a smile and said, "All right, let's have it. What's bothering you?"

I recall one idea of mine he used. In *Lost Horizon* I felt that the scene refueling the plane when we were shooting in the desert with the wild Tibetan horsemen—pouring gasoline into the plane from five-gallon cans through spouts—was slow and undramatic. My suggestion was to achieve a faster, barbaric tempo by having the wild tribesmen hack

off the tops of the gas cans with their bayonets and slosh the gasoline out. I thought that would give the impression of wildness and speed and be a hell of a lot more exciting.

Capra's face radiated magnificently at the idea. He accepted it. He would listen to anybody in the crew. He would listen, period.

—Told to the authors on tape from Van Nuys, California, September 23, 1974.

COLLEEN MOORE:

My favorite Capra film is *Lost Horizon*. When it was first released, I saw it several times. Since then I have seen it many more times on television. The message of love in this film has to make those who

153

DIRECTOR AND CAST relax during the making of *Lost Horizon*—left to right: Thomas Mitchell, Ronald Colman, Frank Capra, John Howard and Edward Everett Horton.

see it better people. *Lost Horizon* has a great spiritual quality that envelops the viewer, and I remember no other film up to that time with such a personal message.

> —*Letter to the authors from Templeton, California,*
> September 14, 1974.

ALAN ARKIN:

The only work of Mr. Capra's that I am really familiar with is *Lost Horizon,* but it had an enormous effect on me.

Every once in a while there is a film that gets into levels so profound that if one is working on it the best one can do is hint, suggest, and hopefully just keep out of the way. I think to be able to do this effectively is the most courageous thing a director

can do, and I think Mr. Capra did it brilliantly—not because of camera moves or trick lighting, but because of the spirit that dominated the work.

This spirit pointed me in a direction that I had had intimations of before, but *Lost Horizon* gave me the sure knowledge that it was tangible, there to be found. For this Mr. Capra has my eternal gratitude.

> —*Letter to the authors from New York, New York,*
> April 17, 1974.

The *New York Times* selected *Lost Horizon* as one of the ten best films of 1937. The film won two Academy Awards—for Best Art Direction and Best Film Editing—and it was nominated in five other categories—Best Picture, Best Supporting Actor (H. B. Warner), Best Musical Score (Dimitri Tiomkin),

Best Sound Recording, and Best Assistant Director.

The film begins, in brilliantly directed documentary style, with Robert Conway (Ronald Colman), "man of the East"—soldier, diplomat, public hero—evacuating white people who are in danger of being butchered in a local revolution in China.

Conway and four others are aboard the last plane out, in which they are kidnapped and transported to Shangri-La, located in a temperate valley sheltered on all sides by the Himalayas.

As Conway and the other characters come to learn, the mysterious place is a repository of the culture of Western civilization, presided over by the High Lama (Sam Jaffe), a Belgian priest, Father Perrault, who was the first European to reach the valley. He has been there for some two hundred years, mysteriously sustained by the beneficent quality of life. However, wisely looking to the future, he has had Conway kidnapped so that he may offer him the role of his successor.

As Shangri-La acts upon the visitors, all but Conway's brother, George (John Howard), influenced in part by Maria (Margo), fall under its benign influence. Maria, the Eve in this Garden of Eden (once brilliantly photographed through the bars of an enclosing gate), has always sought an escape from the intolerable boredom she experiences. Chang (H. B. Warner) has warned Conway that she was twenty when she arrived at Shangri-La in 1888 and that were she to leave the valley she would assume the characteristics of her actual age in all respects.

Conway, in loyalty to his headstrong brother, leaves with him and Maria, turning his back on his love for Sondra (Jane Wyatt), who has truly rendered Shangri-La paradise for him, and on the expectations of the High Lama, who has just died.

En route through the fury of blowing snow, Maria ages and dies, a frenzied George plunges to his death, and Conway stumbles on—to be finally rescued.

Determined to return to the mountain treasure-house he was chosen to preside over, Conway outwits his countryman Lord Gainsford (Hugh Buckler), who was sent to bring him safely back to London.

For ten months Conway pursues every possible and all-but-impossible means of returning to Shangri-La. At the film's end, we see amid the massive mountains a tiny, struggling Conway reach the gate into the valley. The bells ring. We again see Shangri-La.

ONE OF THE ANIMALS used in *Lost Horizon* is admired on the set by Frank Capra, center, Jane Wyatt and Ronald Colman.

155

Frank Capra's
YOU CAN'T TAKE IT WITH YOU

with

JEAN **ARTHUR** · LIONEL **BARRYMORE** JAMES **STEWART** EDWARD **ARNOLD**

MISCHA AUER · ANN MILLER SPRING BYINGTON

SAMUEL S. HINDS · DONALD MEEK H. B. WARNER

Based on the Pulitzer Prize Play by GEORGE S. KAUFMAN and MOSS HART
Screen Play by ROBERT RISKIN

156

(*Opposite page*) DIRECTOR AND CAST—Left to right: Halliwell Hobbes, Donald Meek, Mary Forbes, Edward Arnold, James Stewart, Jean Arthur, Frank Capra, Lionel Barrymore, Ann Miller, Mischa Auer, Spring Byington, Samuel S. Hinds, Dub Taylor, Lillian Yarbo, Eddie Anderson.

A Columbia Picture. Produced and directed by Frank Capra. Screenplay by Robert Riskin, based on the Pulitzer Prize play *You Can't Take It with You*, by George S. Kaufman and Moss Hart. Photographed by Joseph Walker. Art direction by Stephen Goosson. Associate: Lionel Banks. Edited by Gene Havlick. Musical score by Dimitri Tiomkin. Musical Director: Morris Stoloff. Miss Arthur's gowns by Bernard Newman and Irene. Sound Engineer: Ed Bernds. Assistant Director: Arthur Black. Running time: 127 minutes.

CAST:

Alice Sycamore, Jean Arthur; *Martin Vanderhof*, Lionel Barrymore; *Tony Kirby*, James Stewart; *Anthony P. Kirby*, Edward Arnold; *Kolenkhov*, Mischa Auer; *Essie Carmichael*, Ann Miller; *Penny Sycamore*, Spring Byington; *Paul Sycamore*, Samuel S. Hinds; *Poppins*, Donald Meek; *Ramsey*, H. B. Warner; *De Pinna*, Halliwell Hobbes; *Ed Carmichael*, Dub Taylor; *Mrs. Anthony P. Kirby*, Mary Forbes; *Rheba*, Lillian Yarbo; *Donald*, Eddie Anderson; *John Blakely*, Clarence Wilson; *Professor*, Josef Swickard; *Maggie O'Neill*, Ann Doran; *Schmidt*, Christian Rub; *Mrs. Schmidt*, Bodil Rosing; *Henderson*, Charles Lane; *Judge*, Harry Davenport; *Attorneys*: Pierre Watkin, Edwin Maxwell, Russell Hicks; *Kirby's Assistant*, Byron Foulger; *Kirby's Secretary*, Ian Wolfe; *Henry*, Irving Bacon; *Hammond*, Chester Clute; *Jailer*: James Flavin; *Inmates*: Pert Kelton, Kit Guard; *Strong-arm Man*, Dick Curtis; *Detectives*: James Burke, Ward Bond; *Board Member*, Edward Keane; *Court Attendant*, Edward Hearn; *Diners*: Robert Greig, John Hamilton, Major Sam Harris; *Plainclothes Policemen*: Eddy Chandler, Edgar Dearing.

You Can't Take It With You

1938

INTERNAL REVENUE MAN, Henderson (Charles Lane), right, tries to convince unconventional Grandpa Vanderhof (Lionel Barrymore) that he must pay his income tax.

UNEXPECTED WORK—Tony (James Stewart) and Alice (Jean Arthur) prepare an unplanned dinner in kitchen of Vanderhof home when the Kirby family arrives on the wrong night.

"CONFIDENTIALLY, IT STINKS!" is the judgment of Kolenkhov (Mischa Auer), holding his nose, as expressed to Grandpa Vanderhof (Lionel Barrymore), right, about the painting being held by its subject, De Pinna (Halliwell Hobbes).

ANN MILLER:

Frank Capra had a great sense of humor and was the greatest director of them all in my book.

—Letter to the authors from Paper Mill Playhouse, New Jersey, May 2, 1974.

DUB TAYLOR:

On a rainy afternoon, I sat contemplating the fact that we hadn't any money and my wife was pregnant. Reading the trade papers, I learned that a xylophone player was needed for Frank Capra's *You Can't Take It with You.*

Walking over to Columbia Pictures in the rain with great hopes, I was to meet the casting director, Bobby Mayo. He told me they needed a xylophone player, but they wanted someone who could also act. I told Mr. Mayo I had been and still was in vaude-

ville—whenever I could get a job. Mr. Mayo said, "Well, Dub, don't call us, we'll call you."

The very next day, Bobby Mayo *did* call me and told me to come over right away to meet Frank Capra. I had never met him, but this happy, smiling man came into the office (I was soaking wet, since it was still raining and of course I didn't have a car and couldn't afford a cab) and said in a Southern drawl, "What do you-all say, boy!" To this day I'm still kidded about my Southern accent.

Mr. Capra took me into his private office and asked me if I had ever made a movie. I told him no, but I had to do something pretty quick, since my wife was going to have a baby.

Mr. Capra then told Bobby Mayo to have me make a screen test in the morning with ZaSu Pitts. I also made a test with Ann Miller. A few months went by, and I hadn't heard a word from the studio, but I

G-MEN ARRIVE at Vanderhof home—Actors, left to right: James Stewart, Jean Arthur, Lionel Barrymore, Edgar Dearing, Donald Meek, Ann Miller, Mischa Auer, Dub Taylor, James Burke, Mary Forbes, Spring Byington, Eddy Chandler, Edward Arnold, Ward Bond, Halliwell Hobbes.

159

IRATE INDUSTRIALIST Anthony P. Kirby (Edward Arnold) is thrown in jail with his son, Tony (James Stewart), by mistake. The cop to the right of Arnold is James Flavin.

kept reading in the paper about different actors making tests for the part of Ed Carmichael in *You Can't Take It with You.*

I decided to call Columbia Studios and ask to speak with Frank Capra. I told his secretary I was Dub Taylor, that I had made two tests for *You Can't Take It with You*, and that I was going to Australia. I could hear Mr. Capra in the background say for me to come over right away.

When I arrived Mr. Capra said, "Dub, the picture doesn't start for two months, but I want you for the part of Ed Carmichael." He then told me I shouldn't worry, 'cause the part called for a zany guy and I should just relax and be myself. He told me they would have a xylophone player teach me to play the xylophone. I told Mr. Capra I did play the xylophone, but he said, "I know, but we still have to have someone teach you—you will be put on half salary (three hundred fifty dollars a week) until the picture starts, and then seven hundred dollars a week." As a matter of fact, I learned four numbers. This took three months, and it also took care of the cost of our expected baby.

At the close of the picture, Mr. Capra told me to get all the experience I could in any type picture. He also gave me a large photograph of the two of us

PROSTITUTE, played by Pert Kelton, evaluates fur coat worn by Mrs. Kirby (Mary Forbes), who is accidentally in jail with, left to right: Alice Sycamore (Jean Arthur), Essie Carmichael (Ann Miller), Penny Sycamore (Spring Byington), holding birdcage, and Rheba (Lillian Yarbo).

160

FINANCIALLY RUINED, Ramsey (H. B. Warner), is restrained from appealing to unbending Anthony P. Kirby (Edward Arnold) by attorney (Pierre Watkin), left, and Kirby's secretary (Ian Wolfe).

taken on the set, which he autographed, "To Dub. I dare anyone to be around you three seconds without smiling. Frank Capra."

Since that time I've worked for Mr. Capra many times, and whenever I start a new movie, I mentally thank Mr. Capra for giving me my start with *You Can't Take It with You*. I've made approximately 480 pictures, and I did get the experience!

Mr. Capra is one of the nicest, most gentle, humble, and beautiful persons I have ever had the pleasure of knowing.

—*Letter to the authors from Woodland Hills,*
California, September 14, 1974.

JAMES FLAVIN:

The thing I remember so well about Frank Capra is that he was always such a gentleman. That was a rare thing in those days, a gentleman and a great director.

—*Letter to the authors from Los Angeles, California,*
August 19, 1974.

With *You Can't Take It with You*, Frank Capra won his third Oscar for Best Director and his second for Best Picture. The film was also nominated for Academy Awards in five other categories—Best Sup-porting Actress (Spring Byington), Best Screenplay, Best Cinematography, Best Film Editing, and Best Sound Recording.

This was the first film in which Lionel Barrymore showed the effects of his crippling arthritis. Soon the affliction would cause him to play all his roles sitting down, usually in a wheelchair, but in *You Can't Take It with You*, Barrymore appears on crutches—and *not* in a wheelchair, as has been erroneously reported in print. Capra wanted him for the part of Grandpa Vanderhof, so to accommodate the actor he put a cast on Barrymore's foot and had him use crutches and speak one explanatory line early in the film about having sprained his foot when, on a dare from his granddaughter, he slid down the banister! It was a perfectly believable explanation, considering the daring quality of Grandpa Vanderhof's lifestyle.

Capra imposed a parallel plot or subplot on the original play: He made Anthony P. Kirby important, not only as a banker, but as a grasping tycoon, head of the largest individual munitions monopoly in the world, out to gobble up the Vanderhof house and those of his neighbors to construct still more factories.

Capra added a marvelously entertaining character

MOVING DAY—Grandpa Vanderhof (Lionel Barrymore) tells inquiring Tony (James Stewart) that he can't give him any information about the whereabouts of Alice, after the couple have come to a parting of the ways. Ed Carmichael (Dub Taylor) wears football helmet. Visiting neighbor Maggie O'Neill (Ann Doran) tells Vanderhof, "Things are certainly going to be dead around here without you, Grandpa."

not in the original play—Mr. Poppins, played by delightful Donald Meek—who makes ingenious toys and masks for fun. He fits very nicely into the Vanderhof household. Scott Meredith reports in his biography *George S. Kaufman and His Friends* (Doubleday, 1974) that when Capra and Kaufman met, the playwright asked, "Who's this guy Poppins?" Capra gestured vaguely and easily dismissed the matter with a casual: "Oh, you know."

Frank Capra's *You Can't Take It with You* is otherwise largely true to the play. It's a fast-moving farce about the carefree antics of the Vanderhof family, whose members are all uninhibited, happy, and free to do their own thing, in sharp contrast to the Kirbys, who are burdened down with money and social responsibilities. The motto of Grandpa Vanderhof is: "You can't take it with you! The only thing you can take with you is the love of your friends." The film is an indictment of valuing money and position over kindness toward, and love for, one's fellowman.

The final scene is of Grandpa at home presiding over the dinner table, which now includes the Kirbys. At grace, he tells the Lord, "We've all got our health, and as far as anything else is concerned —we'll leave it up to you."

HAPPY ENDING—Actors, clockwise around table: Donald Meek, Halliwell Hobbes, Samuel S. Hinds, Mischa Auer, Mary Forbes, Eddie Anderson, Lionel Barrymore, Spring Byington, Lillian Yarbo, Edward Arnold, Jean Arthur, James Stewart, Ann Miller, Dub Taylor.

FRENETIC ACTIVITY of Vanderhof household, soon to be interrupted by the arrival of the Kirbys, is photographed under the direction of Frank Capra, seated on the right.

LIONEL BARRYMORE'S 60TH BIRTHDAY, on April 28, 1938, is celebrated at a surprise party by the cast and crew on the set of *You Can't Take It With You*.

NEWLY APPOINTED SENATOR, Jefferson Smith (James Stewart), timidly stands to announce at a banquet in his home state before he leaves for Washington, "I'll do nothing to disgrace the office of the United States Senator." His mother (Beulah Bondi) is on the left and on the right are Governor Hubert Hopper (Guy Kibbee) and his wife, Emma Hopper (Ruth Donnelly).

A Columbia Picture. Produced and directed by Frank Capra. Screenplay by Sidney Buchman, based on a story, "The Gentleman from Montana," by Lewis R. Foster. Photographed by Joseph Walker. Montage effects by Slavko Vorkapich. Art direction by Lionel Banks. Edited by Gene Havlick and Al Clark. Musical score by Dimitri Tiomkin. Musical Director: M. W. Stoloff. Gowns by Kalloch. Sound Engineer: Ed Bernds. Second-unit Director: Charles Vidor. Assistant Director: Arthur S. Black. Technical Adviser: Jim Preston. Running time: 125 minutes.

CAST:

Clarissa Saunders, Jean Arthur; *Jefferson Smith*, James Stewart; *Senator Joseph Paine*, Claude Rains; *Jim Taylor*, Edward Arnold; *Governor Hubert Hopper,* Guy Kibbee; *Diz Moore*, Thomas Mitchell; *Chick McGann*, Eugene Pallette; *Ma Smith*, Beulah Bondi; *Senator Agnew (Senate Majority Leader)*, H. B. Warner; *President of the Senate*, Harry Carey; *Susan Paine,* Astrid Allwyn; *Emma Hopper*, Ruth Donnelly; *Senator MacPherson*, Grant Mitchell; *Senator Monroe*, Porter Hall; *Senator Barnes (Senate Minority Leader)*, Pierre Watkin; *Nosey*, Charles Lane; *Bill Griffith*, William Demarest; *Carl Cook*, Dick Elliott; *The Hopper Boys*: Billy Watson, Delmar Watson, John Russell, Harry Watson, Gary Watson, Baby Dumpling (Larry Simms); *Broadcaster*, H. V. Kaltenborn; *Announcer*, Kenneth Carpenter; *Sweeney*, Jack Carson; *Summers*, Joe King; *Flood*, Paul Stanton; *Allen*, Russell Simpson; *Senator Hodges*, Stanley Andrews; *Senator Pickett*, Walter Soderling; *Senator Byron*, Frank Jaquet; *Senator Carlisle*, Ferris Taylor; *Senator Burdette*, Carl Stockdale; *Senator Dwight*, Alan Bridge; *Senator Gower*, Edmund Cobb; *Senator Dearhorn*, Frederick Burton; *Senator Hammett*, Harry Bailey; *Senator Ashman,* Wyndham Standing; *Senator Holland*, Robert Walker; *Senator Carlton*, Wright Kramer; *Senator Grainger,* Victor Travers; *Senator Fernwick*, John Ince; *Senator Lancaster*, Sam Ash; *Senator Albert*, Philo McCullough; *Senator Alfred*, Frank O'Connor; *Senator Atwater*, Harry Stafford; *Senator Manchester*, Jack Richardon; *Mrs. Edwards*, Vera Lewis; *Mrs. McGann*, Dora Clemant; *Mrs. Taylor*, Laura Treadwell; *Paine's Secretaries*: Ann Doran, Helen Jerome Eddy, Beatrice Curtis; *Francis Scott Key*, Douglas Evans; *Ragner*, Allan Cavan; *Diggs*, Maurice Costello; *Schultz*, Lloyd Whitlock; *Jane Hopper*, Myonne Walsh; *Chief Clerk*, Arthur Loft; *Senate Reporters*: Eddie Fetherston, Ed

ENTHUSIASTIC ABOUT WASHINGTON, Jefferson Smith (James Stewart), center, tells his newly acquired secretary, Clarissa Saunders (Jean Arthur), and her friend, reporter Diz Moore (Thomas Mitchell), of his sightseeing tour, the reason for being late in getting to his office. Speaking of the Lincoln Memorial, he says, "And Mr. Lincoln just sitting there as though he was waiting for me." To which, Saunders quips, "He's got nothing on me."

Mr. Smith Goes to Washington

1939

CAPRA TOUCH—In this scene in Senator Paine's home, awkward Jefferson Smith (James Stewart), left, nervously plays with his hat and repeatedly drops it on the floor in the intimidating presence of enticing Susan Paine (Astrid Allwyn), daughter of Senator Paine (Claude Rains).

DISGUSTED WITH CORRUPTION she sees around her, Saunders (Jean Arthur), intoxicated, has quit her job, and with possessions from her desk, is waiting for an elevator in the company of cohort Diz Moore (Thomas Mitchell).

Randolph, Milton Kibbee, Vernon Dent, Michael Gale, Ed Brewer, Anne Cornwall, James Millican, Mabel Forrest, Nick Copeland, Dulce Daye; *Hopper's Secretary*, Byron Foulger; *Handwriting Experts*: Frank Puglia, Erville Alderson, Maurice Cass; *Senate Chaplain*, Rev. Neal Dodd; *Soapbox Speaker*, Louis Jean Heydt; *Reporters*: Dub Taylor, William Arnold, George Chandler, Donald Kerr, Clyde Dilson, William Newell, Gene Morgan, George McKay, Matt McHugh, Evelyn Knapp, Jack Gardner, Eddie Kane, Hal Cooke, James McNamara, Jack Egan, Ed Chandler; *Inventor*, Frank Austin; *Foreign Diplomats*: Count Stefenelli, Alex Novinsky; *Editor*, Robert Emmett Kean; *Butler*, Olaf Hytten; *Page Boy*, Dickie Jones; *Porter*, Snowflake; *Doorman*, Arthur Thalasso; *Senate Guard*, Dave Willock; *Speakers*: Robert Middlemass, Alec Craig, Harry Hayden; *Family Man*, Wade Boteler; *Committeeman*, Lloyd Ingraham; *Committeewoman*, Flo Wix; *Photographers*: Hank Mann, Jack Cooper; *Waiter*, George Cooper; *Barber*, Gino Corrado; *Civil War Veteran*, Lafe McKee. Frances Gifford, Lorna Gray, Adrian Booth, Linda Winters (Dorothy Comingore), Mary Gordon, Bessie Wade, Emma Tansey, Harry Depp, Wilfred Lucas, Tommy Bupp, Layne Tom, Jr., Walter Sande, Harlan Briggs, Dick Fiske, John Dilson, Edward Earle.

CORRUPT BIGWIGS, left to right, Senator Paine (Claude Rains), Jim Taylor (Edward Arnold) and Governor Hopper (Guy Kibbee) discuss how to handle their latest stooge, Senator Jefferson Smith (James Stewart), who appears to be getting out of hand.

FACTS OF POLITICAL LIFE, as seen by bosses, are explained to disillusioned Senator Jefferson Smith (James Stewart), seated, by Jim Taylor (Edward Arnold). Chick McGann (Eugene Pallette) is on the left, and the three men on the right are, from left to right: Ragner (Allan Cavan), Diggs (Maurice Costello) and Schultz (Lloyd Whitlock).

RUTH DONNELLY:

Regarding my recollections of the memorable days I spent making both *Mr. Deeds Goes to Town* and *Mr. Smith Goes to Washington* at Columbia Studios with Frank Capra, they will ever remain two of the happiest films I made during my long career in Hollywood.

Mr. Capra was a dream director to work for, as I found George M. Cohan to be in my earlier days in the theater on Broadway. They both had that wonderful quality of permitting an actor to have complete control of the portrayal of his role, to have the intelligence to believe in himself.

Because the actor knew that Frank Capra was tops in Hollywood during those days, he felt not only flattered but honored to be cast in a Capra film.

He, like John Ford, had great respect for the talented actor—especially those who had proved themselves in the theater. And he had a tendency to use them as often as possible in his casts. They were days to remember when films brought joy and beauty and entertainment to the sparkling cultural world that once we knew. It all seems like a dream, compared to the sordid, carnal-minded, unbelievable nothingness the filmmakers indulge in today.

I thank God for every moment of my career on the stage and screen and for the great opportunity of having worked with one of the greatest of them all—*Frank Capra.* "Long will he *live!*"

—Letter to the authors from New York, New York,
February 4, 1974.

SENATOR GEORGE MCGOVERN:

The Capra film *Mr. Smith Goes to Washington* definitely helped to awaken my early interest in our national government.

—Letter to the authors from Washington, D.C.,
February 6, 1974.

THE HONORABLE MARGARET CHASE SMITH:

I thoroughly enjoyed the films of Frank Capra. I particularly liked *Mr. Smith Goes to Washington,* since many of my friends and supporters thought the story had some striking similarity to my own career, and there was some talk of *Mrs. Smith Goes to Washington.*

—Letter to the authors from Washington, D.C.,
March 19, 1974.

168

"LET HIM SPEAK!" shouts Saunders (Jean Arthur) from the gallery of the Senate Chamber. Harry Carey, portraying the Vice President, is in the chair of the President of the Senate.

TELEGRAMS OF DISAPPROVAL, deviously instigated by corrupt influential powers, anguish Jefferson Smith (James Stewart) during his filibuster.

HELEN GAHAGAN DOUGLAS:

As in politics, so in filmmaking—nothing of moment can be accomplished without cooperation. Frank Capra's fine films are the product, in large measure, of his wonderful "stock company" of supporting actors and actresses, whom he not only appreciated and respected, but directed superbly. "One man—one film," yes; but films creatively employing many and wonderfully varied individual talents.

—*Told to the authors in Fairlee, Vermont,*
July 19, 1974.

MELVYN DOUGLAS:

I am a great admirer of Mr. Capra's work and remember *Mr. Smith Goes to Washington* as a particularly courageous film for the time in which it was made.

—*Letter to the authors from Fairlee, Vermont,*
May 13, 1974.

LEONARD BERNSTEIN:

Mr. Smith Goes to Washington was a turning point in my life. In a way that had not happened at school, I experienced a revelatory insight into the nature of democracy—one that has never faded.

—*Letter to the authors from New York, New York,*
March 18, 1974.

GRAHAM GREENE:

[*Mr. Smith Goes to Washington*] is a great film, even though it is not a great story, acted by a magnificent cast, so that Capra can afford to fling away on tiny parts men like Eugene Pallette, Guy Kibbee, Thomas Mitchell and Harry Carey. A week later one remembers vividly the big body of Pallette stuck in a telephone-box, the family dinner of the weak crooked Governor (Kibbee) whom even his children pester over the nomination, the whole authentic atmosphere of big bland crookery between boss and politician—the "Joes" and the "Jims," the Christian names and comradeship, the wide unspoken references, and one remembers too the faces chosen and shot with Capra care—worried political faces, Grub Street faces, acquisitive social faces and faces that won't give themselves away.

—*From* THE SPECTATOR, *January 5, 1940. Reprinted in*
GRAHAM GREENE ON FILM, COLLECTED FILM CRITICISM
1935–1940. *Copyright 1972 by Graham Greene;*
reprinted by permission of Simon and Schuster.

Mr. Smith Goes to Washington was selected by the *New York Times* as one of the ten best pictures of 1939, and James Stewart won The New York Film Critics Circle Award for Best Actor. In Hollywood, the film won an Oscar for Best Original Story (Lewis R. Foster) and received ten other nominations for Best Picture, Best Director, Best Actor (James Stewart), Best Supporting Actor (Claude Rains), Best Supporting Actor (Harry Carey), Best Screenplay, Best Art Direction, Best Film Editing, Best Musical Score, and Best Sound Recording.

Mr. Smith Goes to Washington is the story of young, idealistic Jefferson Smith (James Stewart), newly appointed junior senator. He is sent to Washington, where unbeknown to him, he is expected by the senior senator, Joseph Paine (Claude Rains), and the state's political boss, Jim Taylor (Edward Arnold), to go naïvely along with a money-making scheme that will raise real estate values for a few political insiders.

Smith inherits a fine office, a savvy, attractive secretary, Clarissa Saunders (Jean Arthur), and her good friend, Washington reporter Diz Moore (Thomas Mitchell). However, quickly disillusioned by his minor status in the Washington establishment and by unfriendly newspaper coverage, Smith decides to resign. He is hoodwinked into staying by Senator Paine, who advises him to sponsor a bill for a national Boy Rangers camp, a group Smith has always supported.

When the corrupt bill nears a vote, Saunders tells Smith the facts and pilots him into the fight of his lifetime, which ends up being a one-man filibuster in the United States Senate against a massive state machine. Capra daringly exposes the almost limitless, tentacular hold of corruption upon modern society.

Smith, struggling on through physical exhaustion and almost voiceless hoarseness, fears that he is fighting "just another lost cause." But he believes that such causes, regardless of the odds, are "the only ones worth fighting for."

Smith faints. Paine, dashing from the Senate Chamber, attempts to shoot himself but fails. He returns, dramatically, to shout that it is all true. "I'm not fit for office!" he shouts wildly.

Pandemonium breaks loose (perfectly choreographed by Capra) as Smith revives to the applause of the Senate and the gallery and to Clarissa's "Yippee!"

In real Washington, Capra's film received strong Senate disapproval. Majority Leader Alben W.

Barkley was among those who spoke publicly; he pointed out, among other things, that the idea that the entire Senate membership would walk out on Smith when he is attacked by a corrupt senator, as happens in the film, "was so grotesque it was funny. It showed the Senate made up of crooks, led by crooks, listening to a crook. . . . It was so vicious an idea it was a source of disgust and hilarity to every member of Congress who saw it."

Movie reviewer Frank S. Nugent, in the *New York Times*, had a different perspective: "[Capra] is operating, of course, under the protection of that unwritten clause in the Bill of Rights entitling every voting citizen to at least one free swing at the Senate. Mr. Capra's swing is from the floor and in the best of humor; if it fails to rock that august body to its heels—from laughter as much as injured dignity—it won't be his fault but the Senate's, and we should really begin to worry about the upper house."

BETWEEN SCENES—Left to right: James Stewart, Jean Arthur and Frank Capra.

DISTINGUISHED VISITOR on the set of *Mr. Smith Goes to Washington* with Frank Capra was Clare Boothe Luce, who wrote to the authors of this book from Honolulu, Hawaii, on January 8, 1975: "I hardly recognize myself in this photo. There never was anyone called Clare Luce *that* young and slim! I do remember visiting the set of *Mr. Smith Goes to Washington*. There's no doubt that Capra was one of the all-time director greats, and a very attractive man."

CAUGHT BETWEEN TAKES in a moment of thought are, left to right: Claude Rains, Frank Capra and Edward Arnold.

H. V. KALTENBORN, left, famed newsbroadcaster of the 1930s and 1940s, played himself in *Mr. Smith Goes to Washington*. Director Frank Capra goes over his script with him.

173

"JOHN DOE" CANDIDATE—Long John Willoughby (Gary Cooper), center, is scrutinized in newspaper office by Ann Mitchell (Barbara Stanwyck) and editor Henry Connell (James Gleason).

174

A Warner Bros. Picture. A Frank Capra Production. Produced and directed by Frank Capra. Screenplay by Robert Riskin, based on a story by Richard Connell and Robert Presnell. Photographed by George Barnes. Montage effects by Slavko Vorkapich. Special effects by Jack Cosgrove. Art direction by Stephen Goosson. Edited by Daniel Mandell. Musical score by Dimitri Tiomkin. Musical Director: Leo F. Forbstein. Choral arrangements by Hall Johnson. Gowns by Natalie Visart. Sound by C. A. Riggs. Assistant Director: Arthur S. Black. Running time: 135 minutes.

CAST:

Long John Willoughby (John Doe), Gary Cooper; *Ann Mitchell*, Barbara Stanwyck; *D. B. Norton*, Edward Arnold; *The "Colonel,"* Walter Brennan; *Mrs. Mitchell,* Spring Byington; *Henry Connell*, James Gleason; *Mayor Lovett*, Gene Lockhart; *Ted Sheldon*, Rod La Rocque; *Beany*, Irving Bacon; *Bert Hansen*, Regis Toomey; *Mrs. Hansen*, Ann Doran; *"Sourpuss" Smithers*, J. Farrell MacDonald; *Angelface*, Warren Hymer; *Mayor Hawkins*, Harry Holman; *Mrs. Hawkins*, Sarah Edwards; *Spencer*, Andrew Tombes; *Hammett*, Pierre Watkin; *Weston*, Stanley Andrews; *Bennett*, Mitchell Lewis; *Barrington*, Walter Soderling; *Charlie Dawson*, Charles C. Wilson; *Governor*, Vaughan Glaser; *Dan*, Sterling Holloway; *Radio Announcers*: Mike Frankovich, Knox Manning, Selmer Jackson, John B. Hughes; *Pop Dwyer*, Aldrich Bowker; *Mrs. Brewster*, Mrs. Gardner Crane; *Mike*, Pat Flaherty; *Ann's Sisters*: Carlotta Jelm, Tina Thayer; *Red, Office Boy*, Bennie Bartlett; *Radio MC*, Edward Earle; *Sheriff*, James McNamara; *Mr. Delaney*, Lafe McKee; *Mrs. Delaney*, Emma Tansey; *Grubbel*, Frank Austin; *Relief Administrator*, Edward Keane; *Joe, Newsman*, Edward McWade; *Bixler*, Guy Usher; *Policeman*, Edmund Cobb; *Midget*, Billy Curtis; *Lady Midget*, Johnny Fern; *Jim, Governor's Associate*, John Hamilton; *Governor's Associate*, William Forrest; *Fired Reporter*, Charles K. French; *Mayor's Secretary*, Edward Hearn; *Mattie, Newspaper Secretary*, Bess Flowers; *Ed, Photographer*, Hank Mann; *Photographer*, James Millican; *Mug*, Gene Morgan; *Political Manager*, Ed Stanley; *Sign Painter*, Garry Owen; *Butler*, Cyril Thornton; *Man*, Vernon Dent; Hall Johnson Choir; *Autograph Hounds*: Suzanne Carnahan (Susan Peters), Maris Wrixon; *Telephone Operator*, Gail Newbray; *Ex-owner of* Bulletin, Harry Davenport; *GOP Man*, Paul Everton; *Bum*, Forrester Harvey.

ROBERT RISKIN:

To be associated with a director who possesses a keen understanding and a profound sympathy for your "outpouring" and who, at the same time, is the master of his own craft, is the acme of every screen

Meet John Doe

1941

HARMONICA PLAYERS—The "Colonel" (Walter Brennan), left, and Long John Willoughby (Gary Cooper), who bum around together, show off their musical expertise to interested Ann Mitchell (Barbara Stanwyck) after the two men have been served a much needed meal in the newspaper office.

175

NEW MAN—With new clothes and the new name of John Doe, Long John Willoughby (Gary Cooper) accepts a cigar from newspaperman, Beany (Irving Bacon), while the "Colonel" (Walter Brennan), still in his hobo's clothes, looks on with disdain at the effeteness of it all. Other newspaper man, Angelface (Warren Hymer), wonders if the John Doe scheme will work.

NEWSPAPER TYCOON, D. B. Norton (Edward Arnold), at his palatial estate, discusses the profitable use of the John Doe creation with Ann Mitchell (Barbara Stanwyck).

writer's ambition. A singular experience for a writer is to see his characters come to life on the screen in their true and unmarred form. This, Frank Capra accomplishes for you in his masterful and individual way—and generally, just for good measure, throws in some little tidbit of his own, to heighten and clarify your original conception.

—*From "Meet the Creators of John Doe, Meet John Doe Himself," by Robert Riskin in* CLICK *magazine,*
March 1941.

EDWARD ARNOLD:

Frank Capra is one of the few directors who can, without apparent effort, always reach the human side of an actor or player. This, I think, accounts largely for his outstanding successes. And I say this with all due respect to other directors.

—*From* LORENZO GOES TO HOLLYWOOD, *the autobiography of Edward Arnold, in collaboration with Frances Fisher Dubuc* (Liveright Publishing Corporation, New York, 1940).

REGIS TOOMEY:

I first met Frank Capra in 1929 in the basement of the B. H. Dyas store, now the Hollywood-Broadway. He was buying a fishing rod. I did not know who he was but he knew me because my first picture had just been released and I had received the usual newcomer press reviews.

I remember we talked for several minutes before I knew whom I was talking to. The one thing I distinctly remember from that conversation was a remark he made about his attitude toward the actor of long experience when directing. He said, "I always try to give an actor a chance to show me how he thinks the part should be played. If an actor has worked at his craft for a number of years, and I am paying him a thousand dollars a week, I want to find out what he thinks before I start to tell him what I think."

When we were taking leave of each other he said,

"Regis, someday I will have a part that I particularly want you to play. I hope you will be available."

In 1939 I got word that Frank Capra wanted to see me. It had been ten years since I had first met Frank, and I had never seen enough of him to really get to know him, so it wasn't exactly like going in to be interviewed by a pal. He turned out to be exactly that. When I arrived at his office, he gave me the warm and friendly greeting characteristic of his Italian background.

He came right to the point—there was a part in his new picture that he wanted me to play. "Remember," he said, "I told you I would send for you someday, but I never thought it would take this long."

He gave me fourteen pages of script and told me

REGIS TOOMEY AND ANN DORAN, playing the roles of Bert Hansen, shaking hands with John Doe (Gary Cooper), and Mrs. Hansen, on extreme right, epitomize the John Doe movement when they tell of their own John Doe Club, the influence of which has caused them to become friendly with "Sourpuss" Smithers (J. Farrell MacDonald), to the right of Toomey. The "Colonel" (Walter Brennan), with bag in hand, unimpressed, is ready to leave. Between Cooper and Toomey are Ann Mitchell (Barbara Stanwyck) and D. B. Norton (Edward Arnold).

to take it home and read it and let him know the next morning if I would care to do it. I went home and immediately sat down and started to read what he had given me. The fourteen pages—*one speech!* I memorized it that night.

When I arrived at Frank's office at ten the next morning, he asked me if I wanted to do it. You're damned right I wanted to do it! He was very pleased. He asked me if I would mind reading the speech for the author of the script, Robert Riskin, since it was a key speech in the play, explaining the John Doe movement. He told me that Bob would like to hear what it sounded like. He assured me that this reading had nothing to do with my getting the part—it was mine.

Bob came into the office and sat down. They both looked at me, and I said, "Okay?" And away we went. Neither of them had any idea that I had memorized the speech, and I can remember Frank turning the pages of his script as I went on.

When I finished he looked up with that wonderful toothy grin and said, "We will get to this in about six weeks. I want you do it just the way you did it now."

In due time I reported to Warner Bros. to begin work on *Meet John Doe*. My first scene was the long speech. This was the first time I had seen Frank since reading the speech for him and Riskin. He greeted me warmly and started lining up the shot. We were all set to go. Everyone was in place, and we were ready for rehearsal.

Frank called me over. "How do you feel about this, Regis?" he asked. "You don't want to rehearse it, do you?"

I said, "If it is all right with you, I'd just as soon take a crack at it." So we rolled for our first take. It took about four minutes.

Frank said, "Print it," and that was that. Six times we did the scene from different angles, and each time it was a print on one take. And that was Frank Capra directing. I'll never forget him.

—Letter to the authors from Los Angeles, California,
September 17, 1974.

ANN DORAN:

The mere mention of Mr. Capra's name brings back a flood of warm memories. We who were fortunate enough to be a part of his pictures cherish every minute spent under his kind, deft, unassuming, and miraculous direction. We often said that we weren't sure how he directed, but we did agree that he could make a post give a good performance.

178

TOTALITARIAN-MINDED AMERICANS are told off by John Doe (Gary Cooper), in raincoat, observed by Ann Mitchell (Barbara Stanwyck). D. B. Norton (Edward Arnold) is at head of table, at the foot is Ted Sheldon (Rod La Rocque), with back to camera, and reading clockwise are: Barrington (Walter Soderling); unidentified; Bennett (Mitchell Lewis); Hammett (Pierre Watkin); and Weston (Stanley Andrews).

I never heard him shout in anger or frustration. His chair was right under the camera lens, and he was readily available for a quiet talk any time an actor or actress needed guidance. He had a way of making every performer feel that his part, no matter how small, was vital to the success of the scene and the picture.

During his preparation for production, each performer, from star to special-business extra, was called in for a conference. Those individual talks covered your character, who and what you were, how you contributed to the story, why you were included, your relationship to every other person. With that kind of care in dealing with his actors, is it any wonder that we all felt a part of every picture? We all did the very best we could never to let him down.

Before starting rehearsal on any scene that involved a number of characters, we sat in a circle off the set to discuss the scene. Mr. Capra explained it fully, its importance to the picture as a whole, its purpose and place in the story. Then we started reading from the script. Since we all were fully aware of our characters, we were privileged to make suggestions concerning changes in dialogue or sequence of speaking. He listened, weighed, and accepted or rejected. Most important, he listened. If he rejected, he explained why, and you understood that the scene was more important than any individual.

Every picture he did was a reflection of his soul. He had an enormous capacity for humor, concern for the dignity of the human animal, and understanding of the little man's struggle for peace of mind. He never belittled anyone, but he could poke fun at human frailty and the pompous ass. The little man always won, not because he was the little man, but because he had an all-consuming passion for goodwill to all men.

—Letter to the authors from Hollywood, California,
February 10, 1974.

Mr. Smith Goes to Washington ended Capra's contract with Columbia Pictures and Harry Cohn. Now, wishing to be on his own, he formed an independent company in partnership with his old friend the writer Robert Riskin. Jack Warner of Warner Bros. agreed to meet the new team's financial and artistic demands, so Capra and Riskin made their first independent production, *Meet John Doe*, at Warner Bros. The film received generally favorable notices and was a box-office success, and writers

BROKEN MAN—John Doe (Gary Cooper) is disheartened and disillusioned when he learns that Ann Mitchell (Barbara Stanwyck) has fallen under the corrupting influence of D. B. Norton.

180

(*Opposite page*) TO PREVENT HIS SUICIDE, Ann Mitchell (Barbara Stanwyck) clings to John Doe (Gary Cooper) on Christmas Eve atop the building from which he intends to jump. They are looking at their foes, the men who are plotting to rule America dictatorially, and who have gathered at the scene to tell Doe that his suicide will be in vain.

THREE CLOSE FRIENDS enjoy each other's company on the set of *Meet John Doe*—left to right: Frank Capra, Barbara Stanwyck and Gary Cooper.

Richard Connell and Robert Presnell were nominated for Oscars for Best Original Story.

Although the film was a financial success, the high corporate taxes, payable in advance, brought about the dissolution of the new Capra-Riskin corporation.

The theme of *Meet John Doe* was topical. Hitler's war, now raging in Europe, was based on theories of Aryan superiority culminating in Hitler's apotheosis as a Germanic demigod. Even in America Bund leaders were appearing, and pseudo-intellectual talk about "the wave of the future" had its fashionable exponents. *Meet John Doe* was a grim warning against any native brand of fascism.

Newspaper writer Ann Mitchell (Barbara Stanwyck) invents a character named "John Doe" and has him write a letter to the newspaper to protest all the injustices suffered by the "little man." Reader

MAKERS OF "MEET JOHN DOE"—Left to right: Irving Bacon, James Gleason, Barbara Stanwyck, Robert Riskin, Frank Capra, Gary Cooper, Walter Brennan and Spring Byington.

response is so great that she and editor Henry Connell (James Gleason) search for a real John Doe, who will be the author of a new column to be called "I Protest" (actually to be written by Ann). Long John Willoughby (Gary Cooper), an ex-baseball player now with a bad pitching arm and out of work, fits the bill exactly. The column is a success, and circulation goes up.

We see the new owner of the newspaper, D. B. Norton (Edward Arnold), watching his personal army of uniformed motorcyclists drill. His absolute leadership of the men whose uniforms and souls he buys is underscored because only he is not in uniform.

The column is succeeded by a radio broadcast, which leads to the formation of John Doe clubs nationwide. The clubs boom, and as the first na-

tional convention looms, the real leader, D. B. Norton, prepares with serpentine efficiency to use it to raise himself into the American presidency. Men who acquire power (Long John is about to learn) must use it themselves or yield it.

Ann is dazzled by the success of her creation, but Connell tells Long John, in an impassioned scene in a bar (where he has taken refuge from himself and a foreboding Capra rainstorm) what Norton is up to.

Awakened, Long John tells Norton he will expose his false position at the convention, but powerful Norton discredits him before he can and then has his men cut the microphone wires to snatch Long John's voice away from his followers.

On Christmas Eve, Long John goes to City Hall to keep the original John Doe pledge, contained in

Ann's first letter, to commit suicide by jumping from the top of the building. It is snowing, and the monolithic structure, all cold stone and steel, is a dramatic presence in its own right. Ann, now contrite and in love with Long John, is there to plead with him to *live* for what he believes in. Norton and his associates are present also, and the camera records their granitic faces, devoid of human feeling.

Ann faints, and Long John, with Ann in his arms, silently walks toward another group on that rooftop, the faithful John Does determined to rebuild the movement without Norton's evil influence.

As Connell strides to join them in that task, he turns back for a moment to deliver the closing line: "There you are, Norton—the people. Try and lick that!"

LOOKING THROUGH EYEPIECE of camera, director Frank Capra studies a shot of Barbara Stanwyck, typing away as newspaperwoman Ann Mitchell.

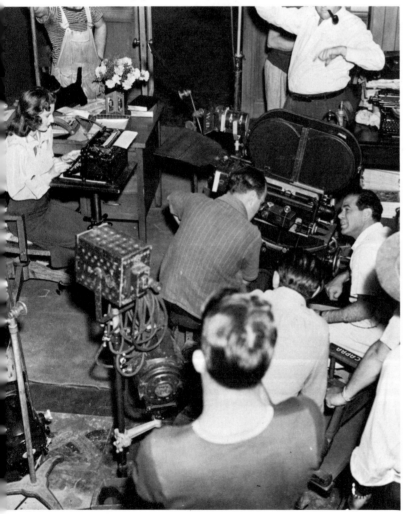

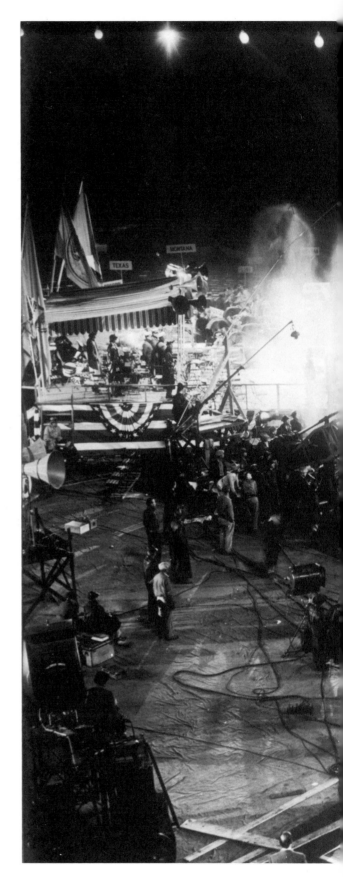

RAIN SPECTACLE—Frank Capra, on camera boom, directs the climactic John Doe Convention scene.

IN THE MIDST OF MURDER—The romance of Mortimer Brewster (Cary Grant) and Elaine Harper (Priscilla Lane) is interrupted by "murder" in the Brewster family.

186

A Warner Bros. Picture. A Frank Capra Production. Produced and directed by Frank Capra. Screenplay by Julius J. Epstein and Philip G. Epstein, based on the play *Arsenic and Old Lace*, by Joseph Kesselring, originally produced on stage by Howard Lindsay and Russel Crouse. Photographed by Sol Polito. Art direction by Max Parker. Edited by Daniel Mandell. Musical score by Max Steiner. Musical Director: Leo F. Forbstein. Orchestral arrangements by Hugo Friedhofer. Sound by C. A. Riggs. Gowns by Orry-Kelly. Makeup by Perc Westmore. Special effects by Byron Haskin and Robert Burks. Dialogue Director: Harold Winston. Assistant Director: Russ Saunders. Running time: 118 minutes.

CAST:

Mortimer Brewster, Cary Grant; *Elaine Harper*, Priscilla Lane; *Jonathan Brewster*, Raymond Massey; *Officer O'Hara*, Jack Carson; *Mr. Witherspoon*, Edward Everett Horton; *Doctor Einstein*, Peter Lorre; *Lieutenant Rooney*, James Gleason; *Abby Brewster*, Josephine Hull; *Martha Brewster*, Jean Adair; *"Teddy Roosevelt" Brewster*, John Alexander; *The Reverend Dr. Harper*, Grant Mitchell; *Officer Brophy*, Edward McNamara; *Taxicab Driver*, Garry Owen; *Saunders*, John Ridgely; *Judge Cullman*, Vaughan Glaser; *Doctor Gilchrist*, Chester Clute; *Reporter*, Charles Lane; *Mr. Gibbs*, Edward McWade; *Man in Phone Booth*, Leo White; *Marriage License Clerk*, Spencer Charters; *Photographer*, Hank Mann; *Umpire*, Lee Phelps.

PRISCILLA LANE:

It was a great pleasure working with Frank. He's a grand person as well as a great director. I was quite flattered when he asked that I play the fem lead in *Arsenic and Old Lace*. I remember everyone was quite impressed with the set of Brooklyn and with the streetcar running in the background. It was complete with the big bridge. I loved making the picture and working with the whole cast.

—*Letter to the authors from Derry, New Hampshire,*
March 11, 1974.

CHARLES LANE:

Over the many years and hundreds of pictures, I have worked for practically all the directors that have made their appearance in this town. I haven't the slightest hesitation in saying Frank Capra was by far the most talented.

Capra's technical knowledge was never approached by any other director. He knew more

Arsenic and Old Lace

1944 (Filmed in 1941)

SUPPORTING PLAYERS Charles Lane, right, as a reporter and Hank Mann as a photographer—on the lookout for news at the Marriage License Bureau—spot Mortimer Brewster, famous self-designated symbol of bachelorhood, waiting in line with Elaine Harper and trying to hide behind dark glasses!

"WHAT'S THIS, THE OREGON?" exclaims "Teddy" Brewster (John Alexander), holding ship model which he has just discovered in a box of old toys being donated by his aunts to Officers Brophy and O'Hara (Edward McNamara and Jack Carson), left to right, for needy children. A visitor in the house is next door neighbor, The Reverend Dr. Harper (Grant Mitchell). The Brewster sisters are Martha (Jean Adair), left, and Abby (Josephine Hull).

TRYING TO REASON WITH HIS AUNTS, Mortimer Brewster (Cary Grant) explains that serving arsenic in wine to unhappy old men whom they feel sorry for is "not a nice thing to do—people wouldn't understand." Abby Brewster (Josephine Hull), left, and Martha Brewster (Jean Adair) sit on the window seat in which resposes their latest victim.

about the sound department than the head sound man and more about the camera than the head cameraman. He also had uncanny intuition in regard to the script and was able with an added line here and a cut there to make a clumsy scene wonderfully playable.

But in my opinion, all these talents were secondary to his ability to establish a relationship with the performer. I realize this attribute is necessary in any enterprise, but in our insane, irrational business I have always felt it to be the most important. Of course, Capra was *the boss.* He was the one and only authority on the set, the embodiment of the "one man, one picture," method. (I may be an old-fashioned goat, but God, I wish we had that method back, instead of production by committee, as we now have.)

As far as the actors were concerned, he knew who we were, our abilities and shortcomings. There were never any interminable interviews and auditions. If he thought you were right for the role, he hired you, period. No one else told him anything about you. It was his decision. The result: When you walked onto that set the first morning, you had a wonderful feeling of security that you were there because Capra wanted you and no one else. If you don't think that helped a poor, terrified little punk, I can assure you it did!

The atmosphere on a Capra set was always uncomplicated and creative, with a professional discipline that left no room for half measures. Thinking back on my association with him, I can't recall a single incident that could be described as difficult or embarrassing. That says an awful lot!

—Letter to the authors from Los Angeles, California
March 3, 1974.

"COME TO PANAMA WITH ME," says "Teddy" Brewster (John Alexander), referring to the basement, and offering a pith helmet to Dr. Einstein (Peter Lorre), left, while exasperated Jonathan Brewster (Raymond Massey) fumes.

Joseph Kesselring's enormously funny and successful play *Arsenic and Old Lace*, with one set and a small cast, is the script that Frank Capra turned to when he decided to make a quick film to support his family while he would be serving voluntarily as a major in the United States army signal corps.

On December 8, 1941, the cast and crew halted work long enough to listen to President Roosevelt's declaration-of-war address to Congress. On the same day, two signal-corps officers came to the studio to swear Capra into the army. He was granted six weeks' leave of absence to finish, edit, and preview the picture.

Arsenic and Old Lace was filmed during a four-week vacation of Josephine Hull, Jean Adair, and John Alexander from the Broadway play in 1941; Capra and Jack Warner had agreed with the stipulation, however, not to release the movie until after the play had closed on Broadway, which turned out to be three and a half years later, in 1944.

Raymond Massey was made up to look like Boris Karloff, who was playing the part on Broadway. Capra wanted to use Karloff in the film, as he told the authors, but the producers of the play felt that for box-office reasons, they had to have at least *one* of the original stars appearing on Broadway during the month Hull, Adair, and Alexander would be away. If possible, the mimicry of Massey made up as Karloff made the jokes about the character's resemblance to Karloff even funnier.

Capra left the play essentially unchanged and did not embellish it with any special social significance.

The pixielike Brewster sisters, Abby (Josephine Hull) and Martha (Jean Adair), have living with them their nephew "Teddy" Brewster (John Alexander), who believes he is President Theodore Roosevelt.

The ladies' eccentricity is to painlessly kill off lonely old men with a glass of elderberry wine to which has been added arsenic, strychnine, and cyanide ("One of our gentlemen found time to say, 'How delicious.'") and have "Teddy" bury them in the cellar as yellow-fever victims of the Panama Canal digging!

COMMITMENT PAPERS for "Teddy" Brewster (John Alexander) are brought by befuddled Mr. Witherspoon (Edward Everett Horton), center, Superintendent of Happy Dale Sanitarium, who assumes police Lieutenant Rooney (James Gleason), right, is his patient. Startled Mortimer Brewster (Cary Grant) looks on.

"NOT THE MELBOURNE METHOD!" Dr. Einstein (Peter Lorre), right, begs of Jonathan Brewster (Raymond Massey), left, who is about to torture to death his brother, Mortimer Brewster (Cary Grant), by the Australian madman's slow technique.

When nephew Mortimer Brewster (Cary Grant) discovers a body in the window seat, he points out to his darling aunts that "People just don't go into window seats and die."

They agree: "No, dear. He died first." They then reluctantly tell him of their "activity" and advise him to forget he ever saw the gentleman, adding, "We never dreamed you'd peek."

We learn there are twelve bodies buried in the cellar. When Mortimer opens the cellar door he is frightened by a silent four-footed arrival up the cellar stairs. "The cat's in on it, too!" is his comment. Capra added that touch. He told the authors, "Whenever you want to liven up a situation, add a cat!"

Mortimer's criminally insane brother, Jonathan (Raymond Massey), and his sidekick, plastic surgeon Doctor Einstein (Peter Lorre), arrive to use the Brewster house as a hideout. They bring the truly macabre, sinister note to the plot. Mortimer and his bride Elaine (Priscilla Lane) finally get free of the unbelievable household. The police and the asylum take over, and Mortimer discovers to his immense relief that he is not a blood-related Brewster at all!

As in the play, Capra filmed the final scene in which Happy Dale Sanitarium superintendent Mr. Witherspoon (Edward Everett Horton) falls victim

191

to the innocent poisoners, but audience reaction in the first preview, Capra told the authors, was swift and sure: "They threw rocks at the screen. They didn't want their beloved Edward Everett Horton killed off! So I tacked on a different ending, with Cary Grant chasing Priscilla Lane through the cemetery. No, the audience would not have Horton die. It's one of those cases in which the strong personality of an actor overrides the dictates of the script. On the stage, there was distance between the audience and the players, but the closer film medium has a way of making everything seem realistic. I'm sure the movie audience was right about Horton. Audiences are always right!"

SCENE CUT OUT OF FILM by Frank Capra because preview audience made it known that it didn't want lovable Edward Everett Horton to die. Here he is as Mr. Witherspoon drinking the poisoned wine, watched over by well-intentioned Abby Brewster (Josephine Hull), left, and Martha Brewster (Jean Adair).

THERE WAS FUN on the set as well as before the cameras during the making of *Arsenic and Old Lace* among, left to right, Frank Capra, Cary Grant and Priscilla Lane.

INGENIOUS SET—Cary Grant, left, and Frank Capra look over the script of *Arsenic and Old Lace* on the film's fascinating set, which featured, using an actual distance of only forty feet, a believable three-dimensional effect of distance behind cemetery—of houses, the Brooklyn Bridge and the Manhattan skyline.

194

INTRODUCTION

Morale plays a decisive part in any war: The greatest generals in history have known how to marshal it to their cause's advantage. In modern times, with rapid mass dissemination of information, ideas have become more potent than ever, and during the period of the Second World War propaganda battles were waged for possession of people's minds and the destruction of their will to resist.

Americans were particularly vulnerable because of the emotional loyalties and normal rivalries resulting from their differing social, economic, racial, national, and religious origins. Further, the failure of the League of Nations, which had attempted to embody the idealism of the First World War, led to a skepticism of "crusades." Despite President Franklin Delano Roosevelt's all but clairvoyant grasp of the real issues and the threat to this nation, the majority of the American people remained apathetic. Only the body blow of Pearl Harbor united an isolationist-minded people.

Men in the armed forces were typical Americans and shared the doubts of their fellow countrymen. In the seven *Why We Fight* information films shown to every member of the fighting forces, the War Department gave the American GI a factual sense of identification with his country's past, more zest for the best possible future, and a comradely appreciation for the men of many nations by whose side he was to fight. Above all, the series showed, vividly and memorably, the deeds of those he was called upon to fight. Each individual felt a new pride in his mission—he knew that if he didn't win, the perpetrators of unspeakable cruelties and hideous crimes would. He was fighting for America against inhuman foes devoid not only of morality, but of common decency.

The conception to tell each soldier why he must fight and why he might have to die was General George C. Marshall's. This masterly chief of staff turned over the concept's implementation and execution to Frank Capra.

Capra was shown the most potent filmic weapon ever forged, Leni Riefenstahl's *Triumph of the Will,* a visual battering ram designed to break down all resistance to German supremacy. To counter this kind of mind-numbing onslaught, Capra summoned his belief in the tenet "Ye shall know the truth, and the truth shall make you free." He decided that the way to make ourselves strong enough to resist this new barbarism was to see it for what it truly was—

Why We Fight Series and Other World War II films

through the *enemy's* acts, books, speeches, films and newsreels. It was an idea of stunning simplicity.

Although Capra was the director and/or supervisor of these films, the project required the creative help of a brilliant and dedicated staff, of which the five key men were director Anatole Litvak, writers Anthony Veiller and Eric Knight, documentary-film man Edgar Peterson, and head film editor William Hornbeck. Other writers who worked on the series included Robert Heller, James Hilton, Alan Rivkin, Leonard Spiegelgass, William L. Shirer, and Bill Henry. Never before or since has film been used so elaborately or on such a scale to educate so vast an audience. Capra's 834th Photo Signal Detachment succeeded totally, whereas comparable attempts by navy and air-force units and by directors as able as Hitchcock and Lubitsch failed.

In addition to the famous *Why We Fight* series, Capra made other vital informational or morale-building films required by the changing wartime situation at home and abroad.

Colonel Capra was awarded the Distinguished Service Medal (the highest American military decoration for noncombat service), upon his release from active duty in June 1945, after almost three and a half years in uniform. In a farewell letter to General Marshall, of whom he had grown very fond, Capra wrote: "You have been an inspiration to me and will remain so the rest of my life."

GENERAL OF THE ARMY GEORGE C. MARSHALL, CHIEF OF STAFF, UNITED STATES ARMY:

Your *Why We Fight* series had a tremendous influence on morale and understanding, and I think *Prelude to War* and *The Nazis Strike* will stand as motion-picture classics of that character....

Altogether you have done a grand job and I want you to know that I am very grateful.

—Letter to Colonel Frank Capra from Washington, D.C., June 5, 1945.

GENERAL OF THE ARMY OMAR N. BRADLEY:

[General Bradley believes that *freedom* is what Frank Capra's work was created to defend.]

Freedom—no word was ever spoken that has held out greater hope, demanded greater sacrifice, needed more to be nurtured, blessed more the giver, damned more its destroyer, or come closer to being God's will on Earth. May Americans ever be its protector.

—Letter to the authors from Los Angeles, California, March 9, 1974.

GENERAL MARK W. CLARK, U.S.A., RET.:

After the Korean War, I entered education as president of The Citadel with full knowledge that I was leaving the largest educational complex in the world—the U.S. Army. A large portion of the efficiency of the army's educational system must be accorded modern audio-visual aids.

We found early in the game that soldiers could be quickly taught almost any subject through the medium of motion pictures. At the same time, we developed new respect for the value of such films in building morale, teaching Americanism, and instilling the spirit to fight.

Frank Capra, an unsurpassed artist of the movies, was of inestimable value in this regard. The army was fortunate to be able to draw on his special talents for some of our most effective films, and the public was fortunate to be entertained by the genius of Mr. Capra, which gave us genuine glimpses of ourselves and our surroundings through the medium of film.

—Letter to the authors from Charleston, South Carolina, August 5, 1974.

GENERAL JAMES H. DOOLITTLE, U.S.A., RET.:

I am a lifetime admirer of Frank Capra.

—Letter to the authors from Los Angeles, California, July 8, 1974.

THE HONORABLE W. AVERELL HARRIMAN:

I have a very high regard for Frank Capra and his work. I knew him during the war when he did the documentaries *The Battle of Britain* and *The Battle of Russia*. I know that Churchill was personally deeply moved and enthusiastic about the one on Britain, and the film was well received in Britain.

I was Ambassador to Moscow when Capra came there, and the Russian leaders, including Stalin, appreciated greatly the war documentary. Stalin personally expressed himself favorably on the film. This whole thing was rather rare for Stalin.

—Letter to the authors from Washington, D.C. April 24, 1974.

GENERAL WILLIAM C. WESTMORELAND, U.S.A., RET.

I believe that the *Why We Fight* series made a very substantial contribution to the proper orientation of our men during World War II. It placed into sharp focus the threat of the aggressors and the implications if we did not take up arms and contribute sweat, blood, and lives to stop the Nazis and the Japanese in their efforts toward world conquest. *Why We Fight* was masterfully done and is a tribute to the ingenuity and the talent of its creator, Frank Capra.

—*Letter to the authors from Charleston, South Carolina*, March 8, 1974.

MICHAEL R. MCADAM, A.C.E.

Colonel Capra's sense of humor? Terrific! It had to be—look at the cast of characters he had to contend with. The greatest picture-making talent ever assembled—names such as Darryl F. Zanuck (had colonel eagles so huge he couldn't pin them on, he had to *bolt* them on!), William Wyler, George Stevens, Sam Briskin, Ted Geisel (Doctor Seuss), John Gunther, Eric Knight, Leonard Spiegelgass, Carl Foreman, and Irving Wallace, some of them privates then, but certainly a few ranks higher now.

I could go on and on citing other outstanding names, but I won't, because I might leave out my own—Sergeant Michael R. McAdam, film editor, once cited by none other than Colonel Anatole Litvak for a Good Humor Medal! I'm sure the good colonel meant the Good Conduct Medal, but who am I to argue? It was just that kind of a unit, the greatest for making army films, the poorest for establishing beachheads except at choice Hollywood niteries.

Which reminds me—Capra got a call one *noon* to come and get two of the world's greatest gag writers (three-thousand-dollar-a-week class). They had been picked up by the MPs at a choice nitery out of uniform—dressed in their field jackets, strictly a *top* army no-no!

That little escapade, augmented by others equally bizarre, did it. For some time Capra had been getting chin music from the Washington brass to make soldiers out of us, something he knew *God* couldn't even do. But now something must be done to get the brass off his back so his beloved little unit could get back to the job they knew best, making pictures. But what, what device would immediately show the brass that making soldiers out of us was just an impossible dream!

Finally an idea occurred to him. He called for our first sergeant and proceeded to tell him about it. The sarge was an army man with almost twenty years' service behind him and a top drill sergeant at that. He almost deserted right there when the colonel told him his plan.

The plan? It was a *pip!* Our ingenuous colonel was going to expose his darlings to the unsuspecting public by marching them, guns and all, down Western Avenue! *What a fiasco it was!* We started out two abreast, but in spite of the frantic cries of the sarge, two blocks later we were single file—one file on each side of the street!

Needless to say, we never finished the march, nor did we ever march again! Colonel Capra had made his point. The noble experiment had failed. Soldiers we were not. Now the brass knew it. They called Colonel Capra and suggested he keep us as much out of public view as humanly possible. Gleefully, he agreed. His plan had succeeded, thanks in part to the many irate citizens on Western Avenue. They had telegraphed the brass demanding that the Capra unit be kept behind walls. "They are nothing but a menace to Western Avenue traffic and a deterrent to bond buying!"

Yes, Capra's quite a colonel. Was then—is now.

—*Letter to the authors from Sherman Oaks, California*, November 4, 1974.

JAMES AGEE:

I can only urge you to write your Congressman, if he can read. For these films are responsible, irreplaceable pieces of teaching. [*The Battle of Britain*], one hour's calculated hammering of the eye and ear, can tell you more about that battle than you are ever likely otherwise to suspect, short of having been there. [*The Battle of Russia*], though it is a lucid piece of exposition, is cut neither for fact nor for political needlepoint but purely, resourcefully, and with immensely powerful effect, for emotion. It is by no means an ultimate handling of its material, but it is better than the Russian records from which it was drawn, and next to the tearful magnificence of *The Birth of a Nation* is, I believe, the best and most important war film ever assembled in this country.

—*From* THE NATION, October 30, 1943.
Reprinted in AGEE ON FILM, REVIEWS AND COMMENTS, *by James Agee* (McDowell Obolensky, 1958).

197

DISDAIN FOR RELIGION by the Nazis is dramatically presented when a rock is thrown through a church's stained glass window and Hitler's face is revealed.

WHY WE FIGHT: PRELUDE TO WAR 1942

JAMES AGEE:

Prelude to War is the first of the army orientation films put out by Lieutenant Colonel Frank Capra's special-services unit. It is the sort of thing one can expect when capable film makers work for a great and many-leveled audience—the best, I suspect, which this country has ever had—under no obligation to baby or cajole, and for a serious purpose.

. . . More shrewdness has been used here to make screen images point, edge, impregnate, or explode the spoken text than I have ever seen used before; at times the border line is crossed into full cinematic possibility, and words serve the screen instead or even do it the greatest service, of withdrawal. For a film made up chiefly of old newsreels and confiscated enemy footage, a surprising amount is new, and a surprising amount of the new is excellent. There is

an eye for the unprecedented powers which can reside in simple record photographs—the ferocious inadvertent caricature, the moment when a street becomes tragic rather than a mere street, the intricate human and political evidence in unknown faces —which is here equaled only by the quiet, dry-touched forcefulness with which such images are cut in. A newsreel poll of American war sentiment in 1939 is brilliantly used. There is a long, pouring, speechless sequence, intelligently sustained by rudimentary drumbeats, of marching children, youths, and men which is a virtuoso job of selection and cutting, and the grimmest image of fascism I have seen on a screen.

—*From* THE NATION, June 12, 1943.
Reprinted in AGEE ON FILM, REVIEWS AND COMMENTS,
by James Agee (McDowell Obolensky, 1958).

The march of history toward increased human freedom is seen to reverse itself in Germany (a state of eighty million, which proclaims its citizens the master race and is intent upon enslaving all others to work for it), in Italy (where Il Duce promises to forty-five million Italians to restore the glory that was Rome), in Japan (a small country geographically, which possesses a fanatical devotion to its god-emperor and whose military leaders tell their seventy million people "the Pacific is ours").

Capra's technique in conveying quantitative information such as population figures, or in illustrating complex battle strategy, was to use animation, supplied by the masters of line in motion, Walt Disney and his best animators.

While the democracies disarmed and America wanted peace so much that its people decided not to fight again unless attacked, the Axis powers carried out their carefully hatched plans for world domination. For Japan it meant first conquering China as a source of raw materials. We see tragic film records of helpless victims of the bombings and shellings. Germany and Italy cry out, in propaganda moves, that they lack raw materials—at the same time that they build the greatest war machine the world has ever seen. Italy conquers Ethiopia, the possessor of one old plane, by dive bombing spear-carrying warriors on horseback.

To film compiled with extraordinary eloquence, dramatic impact is added by Dimitri Tiomkin's musical score and the selective use of John Huston's voice as narrator.

The conclusion is clear: "What we are fighting" is "freedom's oldest enemy: the passion of the few to rule the many." Two worlds, one slave and one free, confront each other. One must die, and one must live. And "170 years of American freedom decrees our answer!"

Prelude to War won an Academy Award as Best Documentary (1942), and in 1944 the *Why We Fight* series received the New York Film Critics Award in the same category.

As General Marshall said in a 1957 interview, "I required that every soldier see the film before he left the United States." In the same interview he records, "The president was thrilled by it." It was viewed by our English-speaking Allies in English and by our other Allies in their own languages. It was released to the American public in movie houses throughout the country.

The first of the most widely publicized and successful documentaries to be created during World War II was launched to both warm acceptance and critical acclaim.

Running time: 53 minutes.

FASCIST SALUTE is taught to a youth by an Italian soldier.

199

PRAGUE CITIZENS are forced to "Heil, Hitler" when the Nazis march into their beloved city after conquering Czechoslovakia.

WARSAW—A young girl, who has been made a refugee by the Nazis.

WHY WE FIGHT: THE NAZIS STRIKE
1943

This second film in the *Why We Fight* series summarizes the German militaristic thrust, bringing it up to date by showing the great rally at Nuremberg and the institute devoted to geopolitics at Munich. The Nazi blueprint was to dominate what geopoliticians called the "world island," representing seven-eighths of the population of the world. To accomplish this they established bunds or parties of agents all over the world (and the film shows the American "fuehrer," Fritz Kuhn, addressing a mass rally in New York's Madison Square Garden); at the same time, they forged arms at home and trained an army limited to 100,000 men by the Peace Treaty at Versailles (but they were 100,000 officers!).

In swift succession, the viewer witnesses the fall of the demilitarized Rhineland, Austria, Czechoslovakia, and Poland. The Munich Agreement (Chamberlain fatuously proclaiming: "Peace in our time")

FRENCH REFUGEES on the move.

included Germany's last territorial demand in Europe, Hitler told the cowed and assenting British and French. With the fall of Czechoslovakia, the Russians, disillusioned by the West and anxious to buy time, signed a Non-Aggression Pact with the Germans on August 21, 1939.

Hitler marched on Poland and conquered her in 27 days.

Thanks to the power of film, the battering of Warsaw is graphically preserved and portrayed. The Nazi bombing and bombardment were irresistible. Relatives wept over the bodies of their dead. France called up her reserves. Britain, unprepared, but in fulfillment of her treaty obligation, declared war on Germany. Winston Churchill spoke out: "Lift up your hearts. All will come right. Out of the depths of sorrow and of sacrifice will be born again the glory of mankind."

Narrators: Walter Huston, Anthony Veiller.
Running time: 42 minutes.

WHY WE FIGHT: DIVIDE AND CONQUER
1943

The history lesson of Nazi conquest continues in *Divide and Conquer*, which shows the fall of Denmark, Norway, Belgium, Holland and France. Hitler's master race timetable was on inexorable schedule.

NORWAY INVADED and Nazi orders are posted.

The British and the French, along with the British Commonwealth, had declared war. The British Navy, ready for action, swept German shipping from the sea and instituted a blockade. Britain must be defeated by Germany, but first on Hitler's list came Norway, whose submarine and air bases were needed to fight the British blockade.

Denmark, as a springboard for the Norwegian attack, fell in a matter of hours. Treacherously, Norway fell because of "Trojan Horse" German ships in Norwegian ports and the internal aid of Fifth Columnist Norwegian traitor, Quisling.

Next, Luxembourg, Belgium and Holland are attacked simultaneously. Flame throwers burn out defenses, and endless miles of refugees clogging the roads become yet another Nazi weapon of war as, bombed from their homes, they impede Allied movement to the east. Rotterdam we see bombed into rubble, as 30,000 men, women and children are killed in 90 minutes.

So Hitler divided and so he conquered.

Dive bombers and mass (45,000 armored vehicles) tank attacks speed the fall of France. At Dunkirk, by miracle, under foggy weather, 211,500 British troops and 112,500 French and Belgian troops are rescued by small craft out of British harbors and brought to England. At the moment France is being overwhelmed, Italy attacks. Although the American Department of State cut it from the President's speech, F.D.R. angrily proclaimed anyway: "The hand that held the dagger has struck it into the back of its neighbor."

France's terms of surrender: 400 million francs a day to support the Nazi occupation army, and 2 million French prisoners of war sent to Germany as slave workers and hostages (and to insure a decrease in the French birth rate for the future). Hitler proclaimed: "There will be a class of subject alien races; we need not hesitate to call them slaves."

Narrators: Walter Huston, Anthony Veiller.

Running time: 58 minutes.

KNOW YOUR ALLY—BRITAIN 1943

Because they share a common language, Americans and Britons can know just enough about each other to make for confusion. England is an old country; America is a new country. The British are reticent; Americans are not. This film shows both the differences and the similarities between the two countries, and clearly what they agree on is of far greater importance than differences in customs.

SEAFARING TRADITION of Englishmen, none of whom live more than 100 miles from the sea because of their small island country, is shown by an old man of the sea passing on information to a little boy.

SPIRIT OF THE BRITISH is revealed in this scene of laughing women helping to salvage furniture from a bombed out home.

DIFFERENCE between American and British traffic regulations is illustrated by a GI putting up a necessary sign for American soldiers stationed in England.

Americans, living in a large country, build porches on their houses to sit on and greet their neighbors, whereas the British box their houses in with hedges to have privacy in a country with a large population for a small land mass. A difference like this is dictated by the facts of life. What the two peoples share and what we inherited from the older country is free representative government and freedom of speech, press, and religion.

The role of the king as servant and symbol of the people is explained, and the evolving nature of the British Commonwealth of Nations is clearly outlined. The great sacrifices that war has brought to the fortress island are delineated in detail. We see a horse-drawn hearse: The war victims are buried, and the next day is faced grimly but defiantly. The factory work goes on to prepare for the day the country can strike back.

(It was the British, when they did take to the air, who showed the Germans that destruction could be brought to their own soil.)

Running time: 42 minutes.

WHY WE FIGHT: THE BATTLE OF BRITAIN
1943

In captured German film we see Hitler at Paris, ecstatic in victory, and then at Dunkirk and at Calais looking across twenty-one miles of the English Channel, eight minutes away by plane, at the single obstacle (smaller than Wyoming in size) that stands between him and world domination. He had 100 million slave laborers at his command; now there would be six weeks of final preparation for the invasion.

Britain did not have enough material to equip one modern division; her Air Force was outnumbered 10 to 1. But there was the spirit of the English people! Or, as the film says it—there was something Hitler could not understand: "In a democracy it is not the government that makes war—it's the people."

On August 8, 1940, the Battle of Britain began. In the first ten days the Germans launched 26 major air attacks: 697 German planes were downed, 153 British. From August 24 to September 5: 562 German planes were shot down either over the Channel or over Britain, and 219 British.

The Germans postpone the invasion. The spirit of the people must be crushed first. The decision is made to attack London, and on September 7 the first

PLANE SPOTTERS on one of Britain's coasts on the alert for German raiders.

205

LONDON GIRL feeds her cat in doorway of her blitzed home.

blow brings 375 German planes over the city. The Londoners went underground or into shelters, and for 28 days they took the concentrated rage of the frustrated enemy. On September 15, 500 planes were sent over and 200 individual dog fights took place in the first half-hour. The Luftwaffe lost 185 planes that day. In these highly concentrated attacks, 50 million pounds of explosives were dropped— 7,000 persons were killed, 10,000 more wounded, and hits had been scored on Saint Paul's Cathedral, Westminster Abbey, Buckingham Palace and the Houses of Parliament. The royal family and the people of London were bound together in courage, while rescue squads worked night and day and life went on, somehow, and the hideous delayed action bombs exploded at will.

Hitler, in yet another rage of frustration, ordered that London be firebombed. A million incendiary bombs set 1500 different sections of the city aflame —they merged to make the greatest fire in recorded history. Water mains were shattered, and the Nazis had picked the night when a low tide made the use of temporary hoses in the Thames impossible.

Fireweed would soon grow up in bombed-out rubble-cleared areas. London had survived. In one year, as the invasion threat faded, 2,375 German planes and their crews were shot down. A grave is photographed with the flowers bearing a ribbon saying simply, "Mother." Forty thousand Britons died; 50,000 more were seriously wounded or injured. But the legend of Nazi invincibility was destroyed. Defeated, Hitler had to turn to the East.

Standing alone, Britain had won a year of precious time for herself and for America. It was won by character, and by the Royal Air Force, on whom the Prime Minister bestowed that imperishable accolade: "Never in the field of human conflict was so much owed by so many to so few." Such, says this film, is the mettle of our Allies.

Narrator: Walter Huston.

Running time: 54 minutes.

WHY WE FIGHT: THE BATTLE OF RUSSIA
1943

This film, which was shown in two parts because of its length, begins by recalling that from 1242 to the present, every attempted foreign invasion of Russia failed. The Union of Soviet Socialist Republics, made up of nine million square miles, comprises a sixth of the earth's surface and is three times

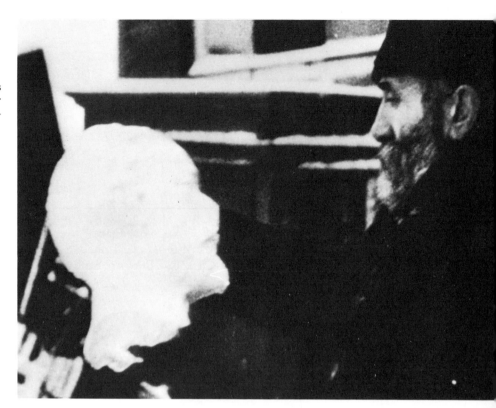

BROKEN TSCHAIKOVSKY BUST is examined by a musician after the Germans wrecked Tschaikovsky's home, a shrine.

RUSSIAN GUERILLA FIGHTER.

the size of the United States. It has a population of 193 million people who represent many races, colors and creeds, and speak 100 languages. The film shows a cross-section of this huge population to set aside in the viewer's mind any simple Russian stereotype.

Hitler hurled 200 divisions (two million men) against the Red Army with the aim of annihilating it on the frontier. The Russian strategy was to yield land (at one point 500,000 square miles were in German hands), suck the enemy in deeper, turn on them with "pincer movements," kill, and again retreat. This made a long war inevitable and called in Russia's historic ally, winter.

The Russians made their cities into fortresses, slowing down the vaunted German blitzkrieg. The screen shows one such city, Sevastopol, which halted the German advance for eight and a half months, as it defended itself street by street, house by house, room by room.

In Part II, Russian foot soldiers, dressed in white, rout Germans in the winter's snow. For the first time in the war, the Germans retreat and are themselves strafed and bombed. Towns and cities are retaken by their owners, who find the unburied bodies of the raped and murdered.

Hitler's order to take Stalingrad regardless of cost led to 162 days of the heaviest fighting in history. Winter and encircling reserves from Siberia not only free the heroic city, but lead to the capture of 24 German generals and 330,000 men, the equivalent of 22 divisions. At a cost in human life too staggering to be reckoned, Russia broke the back of the invincible Germans and recaptured 185,000 square miles of "Mother Russia."

The genius of this film is that we see fully the horror of total war, reflected in the faces of the living and the dead Russians—the price that they paid to remain themselves.

Narrators: Walter Huston, Anthony Veiller.
Running time: 80 minutes.

WHY WE FIGHT: THE BATTLE OF CHINA 1944

The Battle of China makes a remote people and their country relevant to the fighting man whose ally they are. A clip of Madame Chiang Kai-Shek addressing a Joint Session of the Congress of the United States is representative of what this informational film is saying: "The oldest and the youngest of the world's great nations, together with the British Commonwealth, fight side by side in the struggle

CHIANG KAI-SHEK assures his people that they will defeat the invading Japanese.

209

that is as old as China herself: the struggle of freedom against slavery, civilization against barbarism, good against evil. Upon their victory depends the future of mankind."

There follow immediately, composites of marching Chinese troops, seemingly endless in number, that appear to be coming from all directions and, by that technique, conveying invincibility in numbers.

China has a 4,000-year history: it was 168 years ago that Washington crossed the Delaware; 452 years ago that Columbus discovered America; 3,400 years ago that Moses led the Jews out of captivity; 3,700 years ago that the pyramids were built. And in all that history, China never waged a war of conquest. But in 1937 after six years of Japanese attack, the Chinese were aroused and united by the bloody massacre at the fall of Nanking, where berserk soldiers of the Japanese emperor raped, tortured and butchered 40,000 men, women and children. This attempt to tear the heart out of the people gave birth to the will to resist.

Territory was yielded slowly to buy time to build a war machine. Thirty million people rose and moved 2,000 miles, west, riding, walking, crawling —in the greatest mass migration ever recorded. They carried 300 million pounds of factory machinery, libraries, schools, hospitals, and when the last train carried the last load, its tracks and ties were also lifted and transported over the mountains. Every river was heavily laden with barges and sampans weighted down to the water, and men on shore harnessed together by ropes pulled boats in the shallow waters. When seen on film, this superhuman accomplishment creates an awesome respect for a determined people. Once behind the mountains, the Chinese literally dug in, building their factories and homes underground, having anticipated the destruction that enemy bombers would attempt to rain on them.

When the Japanese Navy blocked China to cut off supplies to these factories, the Chinese built the Burma Road on which thousands of trucks shuttled over hairpin curves, often at elevations close to 10,000 feet. Experts stated that with modern equipment such a route would take six to seven years to build; hundreds of thousands of Chinese carved the supply line out of the mountains in less than one year. American General Claire Chennault's voluntary "Flying Tigers" defended this hard-won lifeline against air attack.

The Tanaka Plan of Japan, calling for the conquest, in turn, of Manchuria, China, bases in the South Pacific, and the United States, bogged down

211

THE WALL OF CHINA, a symbol of defense, and Chinese soldiers on the march to fight for their country.

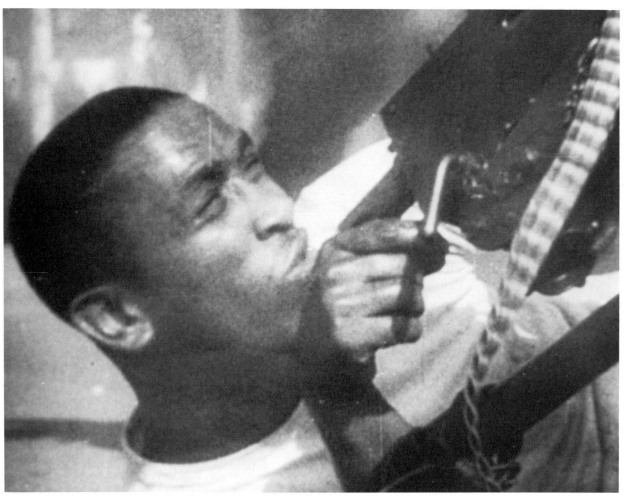

FIGHTING SAILOR mans an anti-aircraft gun aboard ship during the attack at Pearl Harbor.

after the first victory. China would not be conquered. The Japanese decided to proceed to phases 3 and 4 at once. The time seemed right. Russia and Britain were totally occupied, and an awakening United States was appropriating funds to build a two-ocean Navy. The attack on Pearl Harbor was carried out.

Narrator: Walter Huston.
Running time: 60 minutes.

THE NEGRO SOLDIER   1944

This film was ordered by the army to boost the morale of Negro troops and to give white troops, especially, the historic record of the Negroes' roots in America.

In the America of 1944 this was not an easy subject to handle. Because the pitfalls were so many and so obvious, skepticism, particularly among Negroes, ran high, making the film's success and real contribution all the more praiseworthy. Perhaps Langston Hughes best summed it up when he called it "the most remarkable Negro film ever flashed on the American screen," adding that it was "distinctly and thrillingly worthwhile."

The viewer learns that a Negro, Crispus Attucks, was the first man to die in the Boston Massacre, that two of his race were at Concord Bridge and one, Peter Salem, at Bunker Hill.

While Hitler calls it "criminal madness" to educate a Negro, America knows that throughout its history it has profited from the contributions of Negroes in war, in industry, in intellectual life, and in the arts.

The French raised a monument to our Negro troops in April 1918, and this film shows that it was summarily destroyed by the Nazis in 1941.

212

MOTHER reads a letter in church from her son who has been selected for Officer's Candidate School.

MAN OF GOD listens as woman member of his church reads a letter from her son in the service. He preaches of the need for America to win the war for humanity's sake.

The film is highly personalized when a Negro mother reads a letter aloud in church from her soldier son, who is now going to Officer's Candidate School. Although this represents only a beginning, three times as many Negro officers had already been commissioned as in World War I.

Running time: 41 minutes.

TUNISIAN VICTORY 1944

Following the popular success of the British army's *Desert Victory* in public theaters, the American army called on Capra to make a joint British-American film on the joint British-American victory in North Africa.

The opening shot is of the crow's-nest of a ship at sea—out for eighteen hours, its destination a military secret. Then it and the American ships with it meet up with the British flotilla for a combined operation.

By flashback we are present when the president of the United States welcomes the prime minister of Great Britain to Washington on June 18, 1942. By morning of the next day a bold and revolutionary decision has been reached—"bold because in this, our darkest hour, we dared to take the offensive; revolutionary because that offensive was conceived, planned, and executed by the peoples of two nations."

In 125 days the operation, code named "Acrobat," brought together in split-second efficiency hundreds of thousands of men and their millions of tons of equipment from bases three thousand miles apart. It resulted in the greatest mass surrender of fully equipped troops in modern history, as 266,000 Germans capitulated and so ended the ambitious Axis African adventure with its grave threat to the outcome of the war.

Tunisian Victory documents the preparation, shows the battle action, describes the strategy by animated maps, takes time off to show the troops celebrate Christmas 1942, and ends with justifiable pride in an Allied victory of unprecedented proportion.

Running time: 76 minutes.

WHY WE FIGHT: WAR COMES TO AMERICA 1945

War Comes to America begins with brief shots showing the early settlers, scenes of the Revolution,

214

AMERICAN TROOP SHIP—En route to Africa, GIs are entertained by piano-playing soldier.

TANKS played a vital role on the North African front.

MAKESHIFT BATHS on the desert front.

FRANKLIN D. ROOSEVELT visiting the troops in North Africa. Between him and the driver is General Mark W. Clark.

AMERICA ENLISTS to fight a war against dictatorial powers.

PEARL HARBOR, after the attack on America by the Japanese.

the varied landscape, the addition of states, the influx of immigrants, the building of cities, a veterans' cemetery. It is stated that courage, sweat, blood built the nation, and brought to the greatest number of people the highest standard of living in the world's history. And America is flexible: we make mistakes, we see the results, we correct the mistakes.

Powerful when seen in hindsight, are the events of our time to which we responded at first apathetically but of which, especially as we are educated by President Franklin D. Roosevelt, we increasingly become aware. Our isolationism was entrenched. The Spanish Civil War, additionally a battleground for German, Italian and Russian air forces, did not alert us. Japan's all-out war on China did not alter the neutral position we held tenaciously, nor did it keep us from profiting by the sale of scrap iron and gasoline to the dastardly Japanese. Austria, Czechoslovakia, Albania are taken over. War comes. France falls. The Compiègne Forest Armistice report by William L. Shirer is followed by film shots of Paris, while on the sound track "The Last Time I Saw Paris" is sung. The heartbreak is there for some Americans, but only for some. The threat of Fifth Columns is considered unreal (although the movies and theatre portray its reality): German and Japanese glider clubs thrive in Brazil; German pilots train in Ecuador, within bombing distance of the Panama Canal; Argentina is hospitable to German nationals engaged in all varieties of espionage and propaganda.

217

BURNING OF REICHSTAG in Berlin. The fire was set deliberately by Hitler to symbolize the end of the old Weimar Republic.

Slowly, America looks outward. Edward R. Murrow reports from a blitzed London. Charles Lindbergh speaks out at an America First rally to say that England is losing the war and we must not risk aiding her; Wendell Willkie takes the opposite stance. Americans are divided. But events inexorably force them out of the ostrich posture. And it is on December 7, 1941 that the Empire of Japan, miscalculating the character of Americans, attacks what they took to be a "divided" and unprepared nation, spills American blood at Pearl Harbor, and on that fateful Sunday united a people that would massively help to defeat all the triumphing enemies of human freedom. As it unfolds, this film is a history lesson of unparalleled power that was shown in a classroom of millions.

Narrator: Walter Huston.
Running time: 70 minutes.

HERE IS GERMANY   1945

Using the same technique of showing the Germans through their own films and newsreels, *Here*

Is Germany makes the point: "Just as our will for freedom is born of a heroic tradition, so the Germans' thirst for power springs from their historic past."

A typical German, "Karl Schmidt," is shown born into the goose-stepping heritage of his grandfather and father. The Prussian state created Germany, and its myth of superiority became the German myth; its militarism, Germany's militarism.

An armistice, not an unconditional surrender, ended the First World War for Germany. The Allies will not make that mistake again. With the rise of Hitler, "Karl Schmidt" heard only one voice from his earliest childhood, the voice of Der Führer, and he saw Hitler's face displayed everywhere.

Hitler's total control of the state is embodied in his words: "In my schools, a youth will grow up before which the world will shrink back," and "Today Germany—tomorrow the world!"

The Germans, isolated and indoctrinated, held a false view of both the world and themselves. Their mythic superiority as a race was to be broken by the clash with reality that followed when they attempted world conquest.

To ensure that this pattern of militarism is not passed to yet another generation, defeated Germany will this time be occupied and educated into world citizenship.

Running time: 52 minutes.

KNOW YOUR ENEMY—JAPAN 1945

The most fascinating portions of this highly informative film deal with the Japanese way of life, of which most Americans know so little. With a fierce sense of ethnic superiority, the Japanese believe themselves to be descended from gods and destined to rule the earth. The rising sun is a symbol of the emperor, who is a visible god, a direct descendant of the sun, whose person cannot be touched. He is the source of all that is; all acts are his.

The dead are present as ghosts, and the living are links in that chain of the living dead, who watch over the living to see that the god-emperor is obeyed. In 1870 the state added the doctrine that the emperor was supreme over all the races of the world; there were no longer the seven seas, but the one sea of Japan. Japanese soldiers who die in battle become warrior gods enshrined in a sacred temple.

Film shows the silent, victorious return of the ashes of soldiers—for which food and drink and lighted cigarettes are provided in all honor. To sur-

render in battle is to shame one's living family and all one's ancestors. It follows that for these people there is no moral right or wrong, no individual conscience, just blind, total obedience to one's superior.

When Christianity reached Japan in the sixteenth century, its influence in dignifying the lives of serfs troubled the warlords, who caused churches to be destroyed and Christians to be executed. The closed-door policy that prevailed then for two hundred years (during which the Western world advanced more than in the previous thousand years) was so complete that even shipwrecked foreign sailors were automatically tortured and beheaded.

Narrators: Walter Huston, Dana Andrews.

Running time: 60 minutes.

YOUR JOB IN GERMANY 1945

This film begins with the title: "The motion picture you are about to see is a training film prepared by the War Department for the U.S. Army of Occupation in Germany, so that they will be fully instructed and advised concerning their all-important mission."

The film goes on to tell each member of the occupying American army that he will see picturesque ruins, flowers, "mighty pretty scenery," but "Don't let it fool you. You are in enemy country.

JAPAN'S PLAN of world conquest is illustrated by this drawing. The sign reads, "Let us extend the capitol and cover the eight corners of the world under one roof," which is *Hakko Ichiu*, the Japanese word for this doctrine, and it is held by Jimmu, the first God-Emperor, whose descendants (including Hirohito) become Emperors of all the races of the world.

219

WAR LORDS—"Japan's system of regimentation is so perfect it made Hitler's mouth water. On top of the heap of this social structure are the leaders of the Army and Navy—the war lords who surround the Emperor."

GERMAN HAND is extended, but American occupation forces are warned not to take it.

Be alert. Be suspicious of everyone—you are up against German history."

Pictorially, we review chapters out of the German past: Bismarck, the Kaiser, Hitler. This time it "took everything we had to beat it—legs, fingers, arms. It took years never to return." It could happen again. "That is why you occupy Germany: to make that next war impossible."

Every German is a potential source of trouble, for although the Nazi party is gone, the thinking remains. Only yesterday these "civilians" were soldiers, officials, school children molded by Hitler. You are not to argue or try to educate people; others will be sent to do that. "You are soldiers only."

To say, "Sorry," and offer a hand is not enough for a German to do to reenter the civilized fold. "They're not sorry they caused the war, only sorry they lost it."

A hand dominates the screen, and the viewer hears that this is "the hand that heiled Hitler, the hand that dropped bombs, the hand that held the whip over slaves, the hand that withheld food, massacred, killed, cripped—don't clasp *that* hand!"

Some of the millions of Germans may be good, but which ones? We cannot afford to make mistakes. The cycle of war followed by a phony peace followed by war "shall once and for all time come to an end—that is your job in Germany."

Narrator: Dana Andrews.

Running time: 15 minutes.

TWO DOWN AND ONE TO GO 1945

The significance of the title is that the war is not over and there can be no letup in effort. Germany and Italy (in General Marshall's words) "lie in the ruins of their own evil ambitions." Now Japan, committed to world domination or death ("We are prepared to lose ten million lives in our war with America."—Lieutenant General Homma, imperial Japanese army), will feel the concerted wrath of the Allies and suffer a like fate.

The Technicolor film is presented by Secretary of War Henry L. Stimson, shown at his desk. General George C. Marshall begins his remarks: "I salute the armed forces." With the use of world maps, the decision to defeat the European enemies first is fully detailed, and the necessity for the enormous job ahead is made clear.

Triumphant film footage accompanied by the joyous tolling of bells shows the reception of VE Day: the people, the troops, the flags, the leaders, the pope blessing a multitude from the balcony of Saint Peter's, Eisenhower flashing his inimitable smile.

Three caricatures by Arthur Syzk show Hitler with an *X* across his face and Mussolini with an *X* across his face, but Hirohito's face still menaces the world with its criminal cruelty.

One to go!

Running time: 9 minutes.

EMPEROR HIROHITO is the one remaining member of the triumvirate, which included Mussolini and Hitler, for America to defeat.

A TRAGEDY IS AVERTED when young George Bailey (Bobbie Anderson) tells druggist, Mr. Gower (H. B. Warner), who is griefstricken and drunk over the death of his son, that he has accidentally put poison in a prescription.

THE CHARLESTON is performed by George Bailey (James Stewart) and Mary Hatch (Donna Reed) at a high school dance—before they fall into the swimming pool!

An RKO-Radio Picture. A Liberty Films Production. Produced and directed by Frank Capra. Screenplay by Frances Goodrich, Albert Hackett, and Frank Capra, based on a story by Philip Van Doren Stern. Additional scenes by Jo Swerling. Photographed by Joseph Walker and Joseph Biroc. Special photographic effects by Russell A. Cully. Art direction by Jack Okey. Set decorations by Emile Kuri. Edited by William Hornbeck. Musical score written and directed by Dimitri Tiomkin. Sound by Richard Van Hessen and Clem Portman. Costumes by Edward Stevenson. Makeup by Gordon Bau. Assistant Director: Arthur S. Black. Running time: 129 minutes.

CAST:

George Bailey, James Stewart; *Mary Hatch,* Donna Reed; *Mr. Potter,* Lionel Barrymore; *Uncle Billy,* Thomas Mitchell; *Clarence Oddbody,* Henry Travers; *Mrs. Bailey,* Beulah Bondi; *Ernie,* Frank Faylen; *Bert,* Ward Bond; *Violet Bick,* Gloria Grahame; *Mr. Gower,* H. B. Warner; *Harry Bailey,* Todd Karns; *Mr. Bailey,* Samuel S. Hinds; *Cousin Millie,* Mary Treen; *Sam Wainwright,* Frank Albertson; *Ruth Dakin,* Virginia Patton; *Cousin Eustace,* Charles Williams; *Mrs. Hatch,* Sarah Edwards; *Annie,* Lillian Randolph; *Mr. Martini,* William Edmunds; *Mrs. Martini,* Argentina Brunetti; *George Bailey as a boy,* Bobbie Anderson; *Sam Wainwright as a boy,* Ronnie Ralph; *Mary Hatch as a girl,* Jean Gale; *Violet Bick as a girl,* Jeanine Anne Roose; *Marty Hatch as a boy,* Danny Mummert; *Harry Bailey as a boy,* Georgie Nokes; *Nick,* Sheldon Leonard; *Potter's Bodyguard,* Frank Hagney; *Joe, in luggage shop,* Ray Walker; *Potter's Rent Collector,* Charles Lane; *Janie Bailey,* Carol Coomes; *Zuzu Bailey,* Karolyn Grimes; *Pete Bailey,* Larry Simms; *Tommy Bailey,* Jimmy Hawkins; *Carter, Bank Examiner,* Charles Halton; *Tollhouse Keeper,* Tom Fadden; *High School Principal,* Harry Holman; *Tom, at Building and Loan,* Edward Kean; *Mr. Welch,* Stanley Andrews; *Marty Hatch,* Hal Landon; *Freddie,* Carl "Alfalfa" Switzer; *Mickey,* Bobby Scott; *Doctor Campbell,* Harry Cheshire; *Bank Teller,* Ed Featherstone; *Owner of House,* J. Farrell MacDonald; *Bill Poster,* Garry Owen; *Mrs. Wainwright,* Marian Carr; *Miss Davis,* Ellen Corby; *Mr. Potter's Secretary,* Almira Sessions.

JAMES STEWART:

In my opinion, Capra is one of the giants of the picture business and always will be. It is amazing the contribution that he made to the industry when it was young and just getting on its feet.

I remember when he called me about the story *It's a Wonderful Life.* We had both been out of the

It's a Wonderful Life

1946

MAKESHIFT CLOTHES are worn by clowning George Bailey (James Stewart) and Mary Hatch (Donna Reed), after their unexpected dip in the high school swimming pool.

TOWN TYRANT, Mr. Potter (Lionel Barrymore), right, is challenged by George Bailey (James Stewart), left, at a board meeting to discuss the future of George's late father's building and loan company. Others are, Uncle Billy (Thomas Mitchell), seated, Dr. Campbell (Harry Cheshire), behind Uncle Billy, and Potter's Bodyguard (Frank Hagney).

BEULAH BONDI, as Mrs. Bailey, second from right, sees Mary and George Bailey (Donna Reed and James Stewart), huddling under a shower of rice, off on their honeymoon. Others are, left to right, Ernie (Frank Faylen), Mr. Gower (H. B. Warner), Mrs. Hatch (Sarah Edwards), Violet Bick (Gloria Grahame) and Annie (Lillian Randolph).

ELLEN CORBY, at teller's window, hatless, in her one-line bit part of a depositor, Miss Davis, about to receive a kiss from James Stewart, who, as George Bailey, with his hand on the shoulder of his bride of less than one hour, Mary (Donna Reed), is offering to use his honeymoon money to avert impending panic. Uncle Billy (Thomas Mitchell) is behind Mary.

224

service for several months, and I had had no offers to play in pictures of any kind, but Frank called me and said he had an idea for a picture, and I went over to his house. He started a rather rambling story about a guardian angel and a man about to commit suicide and wishing he had never been born, and it was all rather confusing. However, I frankly didn't ask many questions and simply said that I would like, with all my heart, to play the part of George Bailey in *It's a Wonderful Life.*

Frank has had a great deal to do with the progress of my career over the years, and I will always be grateful to him.

—*Letter to the authors from Beverly Hills, California,*
January 17, 1974.

DONNA REED:

It's a Wonderful Life began in the spring of 1946. The war was over, and two of Hollywood's war heroes had come home to work together: James Stewart and Frank Capra were reunited, and I had been invited out of MGM to join them.

It was the best of times—inspired, extemporaneous, fun, *hard* work, and especially memorable for me. The great Capra was working with his sure and pure instinct for the human qualities—goodness, badness, courage, despair (love and death, with no fear of looking hard at the latter), especially as they are borne by the common man, our everyday kind of neighbor.

IN NEED OF HELP, Violet Bick (Gloria Grahame), thanks George Bailey (James Stewart) for a loan which will enable her to leave town and start a new life

MARY TREEN, as Cousin Millie, shares the good news on the telephone with George Bailey (James Stewart) that his brother, Harry Bailey (Todd Karns), has been awarded the Congressional Medal of Honor. Cousin Eustace (Charles Williams) is interrupting them to say that Carter, the bank examiner (Charles Halton), is there to look over the books at the Bailey Bros. Building and Loan Assn.

SHELDON LEONARD, in white shirt and apron, as bartender Nick, along with Mr. Martini (William Edmunds), kneeling right, comes to the aid of George Bailey (James Stewart), who has been punched and knocked down by Mr. Welch (Stanley Andrews), left, husband of a schoolteacher George had berated.

Capra loved his "neighbor" passionately and presented that good man with dogged determination to make him "big." There were no tricky camera angles or setups to hamper, restrict, or manipulate the always larger picture—the character on Capra's film.

I remember working *harder* for Capra than any other director before or after, for a deceptively simple, uncomplicated smalltown "girl and woman" character. I did things I had never done before— danced the Charleston a little, sang a little, fell over backward into a swimming pool (ending by using a double because I swam *very* little), played light comedy as well as drama, aged from eighteen to forty years—and he made it all look so simple and easy on screen. That's the trick of film acting—it must always look simple and easy, even if you've nearly killed yourself doing it.

On the set, Capra was untiring, with a commanding personality, and his hand-picked crews and cast liked him enormously. He was quick to laugh, given to salty quips, but quick to return to the seriousness of film work. He was quick and generous in his appreciation of a scene that satisfied him. His face hid nothing, revealed everything. He had the rare courage to "make things up" as we went along, depart from the script, even close down the set for a day to think out scenes. (No one had ever done *that* at MGM!)

Anyone with an idea was welcomed, in fact encouraged, to present it. Capra had *great* courage in his creative convictions, but if he was uncertain about a scene or idea, he also had the courage to admit that he needed time to *think (rare!),* and then took it *(rarer!).*

We made *It's a Wonderful Life* in less than three

DRYING OUT in bridge tollhouse after their river plunge, Clarence Oddbody (Henry Travers), left, tells George Bailey (James Stewart), right, that he is his guardian angel. Wide-eyed tollhouse keeper (Tom Fadden) is about to flee the scene.

BRIDGE SNOW SCENE—After being shown what life in Bedford Falls would have been like if he had never been born, George Bailey (James Stewart), right, is overjoyed when he discovers he is back in the real world. He shows a rose petal to his friend Bert, the cop (Ward Bond), that was given to him by his little girl.

months. It was such a brief encounter that now, looking back thirty years, it seems amazing that in so short a time we created such a remarkably moving film—thanks mostly to the wonderfully gifted Frank Capra!

—*Letter to the authors from Beverly Hills, California,* March 8, 1975.

BEULAH BONDI:

My recollections are now impressions of my returning home (after days or nights of shooting at the studio or on location) with an exalted feeling of accomplishment because of Frank Capra's understanding and generous giving of himself to each and every actor and detail.

Twenty-five years passed, after *It's a Wonderful Life* was made, before he and I met again and Time dissolved in a warm embrace!

My admiration for his work came early; my admiration and deep appreciation for the man are still increasing, because I know of the continued giving of himself and his experience to young people interested in acting.

—*Letter to the authors from Hollywood, California,* February 10, 1974.

SHELDON LEONARD:

I have worked with Frank Capra on the West Coast Council and National Board of the Directors

228

FRIENDS DONATE MONEY at end of film to help George Bailey (James Stewart), far left. Other actors are, left to right, Ward Bond, Donna Reed, Sarah Edwards, Todd Karns, an extra, Mary Treen, H. B. Warner, Gloria Grahame, Beulah Bondi, Frank Faylen, Thomas Mitchell and Charles Williams.

Guild of America, before and after his term as president and have always admired his skill and poise in difficult situations.

As an actor, I worked for him on two occasions—in *It's a Wonderful Life* and *Pocketful of Miracles*. It's interesting to note that both of these pictures have become classics liberally replayed during the Christmas period and even more appreciated now than when they were new.

From the actor's point of view, I saw Frank as exceedingly patient, imperturbable, and meticulous. I know of no one who rehearsed and inspected a scene more carefully before committing it to film than he.

For a while it was fashionable to dismiss Frank's work as oversentimental. Now that we are emerging from a dark period characterized by a lack of sentiment, the permanent appeal of his pictures is again becoming apparent.

—Letter to the authors from Los Angeles, California,
February 13, 1974.

MARY TREEN:

The total experience of working with Mr. Capra was one of the nicest experiences in my life. He is a gentle, soft-spoken man with a delightful sense of humor and laughing eyes, and to have been privileged to work under his direction was a *joy!*

—Letter to the authors from Hollywood, California,
March 28, 1974.

ELLEN CORBY:

Frank Capra proved long ago that a picture can be made without violence and still be a hit.

I love Frank Capra, and I feel so privileged to have worked for him. I think he was the first person to prove to me that there was no such thing as a small part. In *It's a Wonderful Life* I had only one line, and for that I received not only some nice compliments, but a kiss from Jimmy Stewart. (A piece of business that wasn't in the script!) Matter of fact, I'm not sure the dialogue was in the script—but Mr.

Capra's mind seemed to be channeled into that great creative source. He didn't just shoot what was on paper; he continued to create on the set.

It's a Wonderful Life was one of the first pictures I did when I went into acting after eleven years as a script supervisor. Fifty percent of me was still working behind the camera, and I was keenly interested in everything Mr. Capra did. He was head and shoulders above most of the directors I had worked with. He was quiet and inspiring. I wanted to please him more than anything else in the world. He didn't need noise to be forceful, and I loved the way he delegated the work so that Assistant Director Art Black and others made the noise and Mr. Capra watched the results with a twinkle, as though Art and the others were being naughty!

This is my forty-first year in the business, and it has been a wonderful life, partly because I have known such people as Frank Capra, who has instilled in me a desire to do my best—regardless. God bless Frank Capra.

—Letter to the authors from Los Angeles, California,
May 3, 1974.

DECEMBER 30, 1946   15c

Newsweek

THE MAGAZINE OF NEWS SIGNIFICANCE

The Return of Jimmy Stewart
(See 'Movies')

MAGAZINE COVER heralds the return to the screen of James Stewart, and the article inside mentions the return to film making of Frank Capra, after both men's service in World War II. Actors, left to right, are: Thomas Mitchell, Carol Cooms, Donna Reed, James Stewart, Jimmy Hawkins and Karolyn Grimes.

In postwar Hollywood, Capra joined with directors William Wyler and George Stevens and producer Samuel Briskin to form Liberty Films, Inc., and Capra directed its first feature, *It's a Wonderful Life.* For both Frank Capra and James Stewart, this film remains their favorite of all those they made. Capra shows it every Christmas Eve at his home in La Quinta, California.

For *It's a Wonderful Life,* Capra was honored with the Foreign Correspondents' Golden Globe Award as Best Director. And the Academy of Motion Picture Arts and Sciences honored the film by nominating it in five categories, for Best Picture, Best Director, Best Actor (James Stewart), Best Editing, and Best Sound Recording.

The film has two parts. The first, told in flashback to review the life of George Bailey (James Stewart) for Clarence Oddbody (Henry Travers), an angel about to be assigned to George, ends with George's decision to leap to his death from the Bedford Falls bridge. The second begins when Clarence appears and grants George his wish—never to have been born—and shows him what his world would have been like without him.

Circumstances throughout George's life had combined to keep him at home, although he always longed to travel and grow beyond his hometown. He has had a useful, loving life, but the forces of evil, represented by Henry F. Potter (Lionel Barrymore), rich and dominating, always made it necessary for George to fight continuously to keep the Bailey Building and Loan Company alive as the only alternative people had to falling under Potter's financial control. It is not the life George would have chosen for himself, and ultimately fate victimizes him beyond his endurance.

At this point, the prayers of those who love him are answered. His guardian angel gives him a new zest for life, and all the good he has done returns to rescue him and confound Potter. The miracle of friendship makes his Christmas merry!

Early in this film is one of the most spontaneously joyful of Capra scenes. George and Mary Hatch (Donna Reed), doing the Charleston at a high school dance, are unaware that beneath the gym floor, which slides back, is a water-filled swimming pool. Mary's jealous date triggers the mechanism, and the floor slowly and inexorably opens. Preoccupied in their dance-contest competition, George and Mary soon dance right into the pool—and good spiritedly continue to dance! The rest of the students jump in, and so does the high school principal (Harry Holman).

Capra told the authors that he got the idea for the scene when he discovered, while location shooting at Beverly Hills High School, that there was a swimming pool under the gym floor. "I've got to use it!" he said to himself at once.

SMILING ASSISTANT DIRECTOR Arthur S. Black, holds part of Donna Reed's costume while director Frank Capra, left, ponders a scene about to be rehearsed with James Stewart, right.

LOVE IS SWEEPING THE NATION!

Metro-Goldwyn-Mayer and Liberty Films Present

SPENCER TRACY
KATHARINE HEPBURN
VAN JOHNSON
ANGELA LANSBURY
ADOLPHE MENJOU · LEWIS STONE

FRANK CAPRA'S

State of the Union

BASED ON THE PLAY BY HOWARD LINDSAY AND RUSSEL CROUSE · SCREEN PLAY BY ANTHONY VEILLER AND
MYLES CONNOLLY · ASSOCIATE PRODUCER ANTHONY VEILLER · A METRO-GOLDWYN-MAYER PICTURE
PRODUCED AND DIRECTED BY FRANK CAPRA

A Metro-Goldwyn-Mayer Picture. A Liberty Films Production. Produced and directed by Frank Capra. Associate Producer: Anthony Veiller. Screenplay by Anthony Veiller and Myles Connolly, based on the Pulitzer Prize play *State of the Union*, by Howard Lindsay and Russel Crouse. Photographed by George J. Folsey. Art direction by Cedric Gibbons. Associate Art Director: Urie McCleary. Set Decorator: Emile Kuri. Edited by William Hornbeck. Special effects by A. Arnold Gillespie. Musical score by Victor Young. Costumes by Irene. Sound Engineer: Douglas Shearer. Assistant Director: Arthur S. Black, Jr. Running time: 124 minutes.

CAST:

Grant Matthews, Spencer Tracy; *Mary Matthews*, Katharine Hepburn; *"Spike" McManus*, Van Johnson; *Kay Thorndyke*, Angela Lansbury; *Jim Conover*, Adolphe Menjou; *Sam Thorndyke*, Lewis Stone; *Sam Parrish*, Howard Smith; *Bill Hardy*, Charles Dingle; *Lulubelle Alexander*, Maidel Turner; *Judge Alexander*, Raymond Walburn; *Norah*, Margaret Hamilton; *Leith, Radio Announcer*, Art Baker; *Senator Lauterbach*, Pierre Watkin; *Grace Orval Draper*, Florence Auer; *Buck Swenson*, Irving Bacon; *Blink Moran*, Charles Lane; *Joyce Matthews*, Patti Brady; *Grant Matthews, Jr.*, George Nokes; *Bellboy*, Carl "Alfalfa" Switzer; *Waiter*, Tom Fadden; *Barber*, Tom Pedi; *Jenny*, Rhea Mitchell; *First Reporter*, Arthur O'Connell; *Blonde Girl*, Marion Martin; *Wrestler*, Tor Johnson; *Senator*, Stanley Andrews; *Pilot*, Dave Willock; *Politician*, Russell Meeker; *Joe Crandall*, Frank L. Clarke; *Rusty Miller*, David Clarke; *Broder*, Dell Henderson; *Bradbury*, Edwin Cooper; *Crump*, Davison Clark; *Josephs*, Francis Pierlot; *Editor*, Brandon Beach; *Doctors*: Howard Mitchell, Boyd Davis; *Little Man*, Maurice Cass; *Crackpot*, Frank Austin; *Editor*, Sam Ash; *Businessman*, Mahlon Hamilton; *Brooklynite*, Garry Owen; *Television Man*, Eddie Phillips; *Secretary*, Eve Whitney.

KATHARINE HEPBURN:

I don't know any anecdotes about Capra—we didn't go in for all that analysis then. You could either do it or you couldn't do it. Capra could do it —his own way—his own lovely way.

I slid in there when Claudette Colbert and Capra had an irreversible difference of opinion. Both were stubborn. I got the job.

A funny, totally concentrated, imaginative, warm creature who felt violently, loved to laugh, and

PRESIDENTIAL HOPEFUL WITH LOVING WIFE, Grant Matthews (Spencer Tracy) and Mary Matthews (Katharine Hepburn).

NEAR DEATH at the beginning of *State of the Union*, newspaper magnate Sam Thorndyke (Lewis Stone) bequeaths to his daughter, Kay Thorndyke (Angela Lansbury), his chain of newspapers, and urges her to work to help elect a Republican President.

could lead an audience to water and make them drink.

—*Letter to the authors from Los Angeles, California,* April 15, 1974.

ANGELA LANSBURY:

Frank Capra was the kindest and most sensitive of men, with a funny way of half-finishing a sentence and then laughing. I was struck by his tremendous sense of humor, which always put actors and crew at ease. On the set of *State of the Union* laughter could be heard almost continuously. However, when difficulties arose, he was a natural conciliator, because he understood each individual's problems. This made him an ideal director to work with.

I remember, too, that on the set, Frank Capra set the tone by showing his regard for Spence and Katharine. He is a man with a lot of grace and inner sweetness. And it was contagious.

I was very young and, frankly, surprised to get the part. I understood that Mr. Capra saw me in the film *If Winter Comes*, and it was he who cast me. He saw that despite my youth I possessed the requisite "authority" for the part. Which was more than I saw!

Despite his ease and total lack of self-importance, this remarkable director knew what he wanted to

get on film, and everything he did on the set was funneled to that all-important end.

—*Told to the authors backstage in her Winter Garden dressing room between performances of* GYPSY *on Broadway,* December 4, 1974.

TOM FADDEN:

There was a funny incident in *State of the Union* regarding Tracy and me. Capra asked me if I could ad-lib, and when I said yes, he told me Tracy was one of the best (I suspect that Capra told Tracy the same thing about me). So Capra directed me to forget the script and start to ad-lib with Tracy in the scene.

As the waiter, I was a fan of the character Tracy played. He was my hero. In the scene we did together, I greeted him at the door, and then the ad-libbing began. Tracy asked me if I had worked for the hotel for a long time. I told him yes, for many years, and that my father had worked for the hotel too. Tracy asked me if I had any children. I told him, yes and told him how many and that it was getting harder to bring them up nowadays because of the increasing cost of living.

We said things like that, back and forth, while walking toward the camera, and we got so engrossed in our make-believe conversation that we were still talking after Frank shouted, "Cut!" The crew said

234

PRESIDENTIAL ASPIRATIONS of Grant Matthews (Spencer Tracy), on phone, are encouraged by, left to right, Jim Conover (Adolphe Menjou), "Spike" McManus (Van Johnson) and Kay Thorndyke (Angela Lansbury).

MARITAL SPAT—Having learned of her husband's continuing affair with Kay Thorndyke, Mary Matthews (Katharine Hepburn) refuses to sleep in the same bed with her husband, Grant (Spencer Tracy), who angrily volunteers to sleep on the hotel room floor.

235

TOM FADDEN, as the hotel waiter in the room service scene with, left to right: Mary Matthews (Katharine Hepburn), "Spike" McManus (Van Johnson), Grant Matthews (Spencer Tracy) and Jim Conover (Adolphe Menjou).

if the camera had not been there we would have been off the lot and out on the street. The scene was kept in as we made it.

Another thing—as I started to serve the food and drinks at the table, Hepburn started to tell me what to do. Capra told her, "Let Tom do it his way. I'm directing!"

—Letter to the authors from Vero Beach, Florida,
March 18, 1974.

TOM FADDEN:

Frank Capra was the best comedy director I ever worked for—because he knew how to protect a laugh. For instance, in the serving scene, according to the script, Van Johnson started to say something to Tracy, and as the waiter I interrupted him, saying, "Let him eat!" Johnson started talking again immediately, but Capra stopped him, saying, "Wait for Tom's laugh." So Capra was able to observe the scene from the audience's viewpoint.

—Told to the authors on the telephone from Vero Beach, Florida, September 14, 1974.

TOM PEDI:

When I worked for Frank Capra, I found him to be a very tolerant and understanding man. He knows how to get the best out of an actor.

VYING WOMEN—Mary Matthews (Katharine Hepburn), left, and Kay Thorndyke (Angela Lansbury) both have designs on Grant Matthews, one (Mary) for love and the other (Kay) for political gain. Observing the scene at a party are, left to right, "Spike" McManus (Van Johnson), Buck Swenson (Irving Bacon) and Jim Conover (Adolphe Menjou).

SPECIAL INTERESTS are represented by group surrounding Grant Matthews (Spencer Tracy), center. Kay Thorndyke (Angela Lansbury), with paper in hand, decides to broadcast speech that Grant's wife has refused to deliver. Others are, left to right, Grace Orval Draper (Florence Auer), Sam Parrish (Howard Smith), Bill Hardy (Charles Dingle), "Spike" McManus (Van Johnson), Jim Conover (Adolphe Menjou) and Senator Lauterbach (Pierre Watkin).

236

DRAMATIC CLIMAX occurs when Grant Matthews (Spencer Tracy), right, realizing that he has been using his wife, Mary (Katharine Hepburn), selfishly and dishonestly for political purposes, forceably prevents her from delivering a fraudulent speech on his behalf. Radio announcer Keith is played by Art Baker.

I recall only one incident that may add some light to the man. We had shot three days of bits and drabs of my scene, and I recall that on the third day and final shot of the scene something made me suggest to him that we shoot my monologue all in one take instead of breaking it up into bits and drabs the way we had done. I then realized the stupidity and nerve I had to even suggest that he reshoot the whole scene as I suggested it. To my surprise and relief, the scene was shot as I suggested it. The scene was with Spencer Tracy, Katharine Hepburn, Adolphe Menjou, and Van Johnson. Is that a beautiful man or is that a beautiful man? I may add, that is the way the scene remained in the picture.

I guess that is about all I can say about the man Frank Capra. I love him.

—*Letter to the authors from Los Angeles, California,*
April 5, 1974.

RKO Pictures would not meet the budget required by Liberty Films for filming *State of the Union*, so MGM took over the picture, mainly because of Spencer Tracy, who wanted to play the leading role and wanted to work with Capra.

State of the Union had its world premiere in Washington D.C., with President Harry S Truman in attendance.

The film is the story of an idealistic, successful business man, Grant Matthews (Spencer Tracy), being pushed toward nomination as the Republican candidate for president of the United States by special interest groups. His estranged wife, Mary (Katharine Hepburn), is caught up in her husband's mission and is willing to join him in his campaigning —to add her strength to his and, at the same time, dispel any possible rumors of his romantic attachment to Kay Thorndyke (Angela Lansbury), newspaper publisher and number-one backer of Matthews, who has teamed up with master politico James Conover (Adolphe Menjou).

The dramatic center is in the love Grant and Mary have for each other. Mary alone can question her husband's crumbling integrity as ambition lures him on. And she wins his soul back for him, because Grant sees that her love for him is causing even her granite incorruptibility to start on the downhill road of compromise.

DIRECTOR FLOORED—Frank Capra takes it easy while dialogue director, Harold Winston, center, rehearses Van Johnson and Katharine Hepburn.

STAR AND TWO LEADING LADIES—Bing Crosby, Coleen Gray, left, and Frances Gifford.

COMPLAINING HORSE OWNER, Whitehall (Paul Harvey), shakes his finger at long-suffering Racing Secretary (James Gleason) and objects to the condition of the track. Whitey (Clarence Muse), far left, and Dan Brooks (Bing Crosby) are stunned by the man's arrogant behavior.

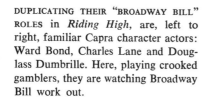

DUPLICATING THEIR "BROADWAY BILL" ROLES in *Riding High*, are, left to right, familiar Capra character actors: Ward Bond, Charles Lane and Douglass Dumbrille. Here, playing crooked gamblers, they are watching Broadway Bill work out.

238

A Paramount Picture. Produced and directed by Frank Capra. Screenplay by Robert Riskin. Additional dialogue by Melville Shavelson and Jack Rose. Based on a story by Mark Hellinger. A remake of Frank Capra's 1934 film *Broadway Bill*. Photographed by George Barnes and Ernest Laszlo. Process photography by Farciot Edouart. Art direction by Hans Dreier and Walter Tyler. Set decoration by Emile Kuri. Edited by William Hornbeck. Costumes by Edith Head. New songs ("Sunshine Cake," "Someplace on Anywhere Road," "The Horse Told Me," "We've Got a Sure Thing") by Johnny Burke and James Van Heusen. Vocal arrangements by Joseph J. Lilley. Musical direction by Victor Young. Music Associate: Troy Sanders. Sound recording by Hugo Grenzbach and John Cope. Western Electric Recording. Makeup supervision by Wally Westmore. Assistant Director: Arthur Black. Running time: 112 minutes.

CAST:

Dan Brooks, Bing Crosby; *Alice Higgins*, Coleen Gray; *J. L. Higgins*, Charles Bickford; *Margaret Higgins*, Frances Gifford; *Happy McGuire*, William Demarest; *Professor Pettigrew*, Raymond Walburn; *Racing Secretary*, James Gleason; *Lee*, Ward Bond; *Whitey*, Clarence Muse; *Pop Jones*, Percy Kilbride; *Johnson, Butler*, Harry Davenport; *Edna*, Margaret Hamilton; *Whitehall*, Paul Harvey; *Eddie Howard*, Douglass Dumbrille; *J. P. Chase*, Gene Lockhart; *Mathilda Early*, Marjorie Hoshelle; *Henry Early*, Rand Brooks; *Arthur Winslow*, Willard Waterman; *Mary Winslow*, Marjorie Lord; *Hamburger Man*, Irving Bacon; *Joe Frisco*, Himself; *Nurse*, Ann Doran; *Jockey Williams*, Frankie Darro; *Erickson*, Charles Lane; *Joe*, Dub Taylor; *Horse Player*, Oliver Hardy; *Bertie*, Max Baer; *Whitehall's Trainer*, Tom Fadden; *Maitre d'*, Byron Foulger; *Veterinarian*, Stanley Andrews; *Musicians*: Ish Kabibble, Candy Candido; *Pawnbroker*, Percy Helton; *Dan's Secretary*, Dorothy Newmann; *Butler*, Roger Davis; *Barber*, Victor Romito; *Maid*, Margaret Field; *Jailer*, Richard Kipling; *Deputies*: Edgar Dearing and Jim Nolan; *Harry*, Garry Owen.

BING CROSBY:

You know, when I learned that Paramount had secured Frank Capra to direct a picture I was going to be in, I was highly elated, because not only did I have great respect for Frank and for the great work he had done in the past, but I knew him personally from around the golf club and was very fond of him.

Making the picture was a joy. He's such a competent craftsman—knows his work so thoroughly and seems to create an air of amiability on the set that very few directors are able to achieve.

Riding High

1950

HILARIOUS SCENE in *Riding High* occurs when Professor Pettigrew (Raymond Walburn), left, bluffingly says about the demand of Pop Jones (Percy Kilbride), second from right, for payment of a $92.72 feed bill: "Let's pay this vulture off and be rid of him. How much is it, a thousand dollars?" Dan Brooks (Bing Crosby), between them—along with Happy McGuire (William Demarest), far right—adds to the fast talk.

239

"SUNSHINE CAKE," a musical number staged by Frank Capra in a spontaneous manner, is exuberantly sung and danced in the barn housing Broadway Bill by, left to right: Whitey (Clarence Muse), Alice Higgins (Coleen Gray) and Dan Brooks (Bing Crosby).

CAPRA TOUCH—While a rainstorm threatens the well-being of Broadway Bill, the mascot rooster, Skeeter, left, protects himself from the rain by sitting on the handle of a pail hanging upside down in the barn. Whitey (Clarence Muse) is bending over, left; Dan Brooks (Bing Crosby) looks up at the leaking roof; and Alice Higgins (Coleen Gray) is drying off Broadway Bill.

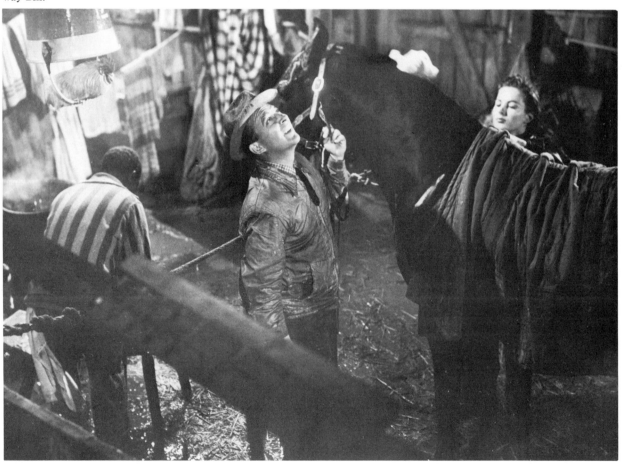

240

OLIVER HARDY, left, as a rube horse player, proves an easy mark for con artists Professor Pettigrew (Raymond Walburn), center, and Happy McGuire (William Demarest), right, who bilk him through chicanery.

He's the kind of director who instills confidence in an actor. You just put yourself in Frank's hands and do what he tells you, and it has got to come out all right.

Certainly the most gratifying factor in my career has been the fact that I've been associated with great men, and Frank Capra comes very high indeed on this list.

—Letter to the authors from Hillsborough, California,
September 17, 1974.

COLEEN GRAY:

God broke the mold after he made Frank Capra —truly one of his beloved sons, who must give him a great deal of pleasure.

In trying to describe Frank Capra without getting maudlin, lengthy, or overblown, I can say he is the most "full" human being I have ever known.

Working on *Riding High* was pure joy. Finishing it was pure pain. An amputation. All pictures are ultimately finished, and there is sadness as the close-knit cast and crew say goodbye and go their separate ways. But this had been a special picture for me. The Capra touch had made the difference.

—Letter to the authors from Los Angeles, California,
April 21, 1974.

ISH KABIBBLE, far right, accompanies the singing of "The Horse Told Me" on his cornet and joins in the singing, too, at a restaurant party with Professor Pettigrew (Raymond Walburn), in white hat, Dan Brooks (Bing Crosby), center, and Alice Higgins (Coleen Gray).

CROOKED JOCKEY, played by Frankie Darro, is mounted on Broadway Bill. Dan Brooks (Bing Crosby), left, gives a pep talk to his beloved horse before the big race, while Whitey (Clarence Muse) pats the animal affectionately.

ISH KABIBBLE:

It was one of the highlights of my movie days to have worked with Frank Capra, even though my portion took only a few days to shoot.

I remember the scene I did in *Riding High* very well. It was a party scene in which I sang and played the cornet. I felt very privileged to be asked to do the part. The little band that accompanied the song we sang, something about "The owner told the jockey and the jockey told the horse and the horse told me," was made up of some distinguished musicians of the day. Joe Venutti on the fiddle was one of them.

Regarding the scene, I had butterflies so bad and I never could learn and memorize lyrics, so during that scene if you could stop the film and look through a microscope, I am sure you would see that I had the words to the song typed and pasted all over the cornet I was holding. That way I could appear to be looking at Bing Crosby and the others, but actually was holding the horn so that out of the corner of my eye, I could see the words.

—Letter to the authors from Honolulu, Hawaii,
August 15, 1974.

CLARENCE MUSE:

Frank Capra was created for the make-believe (motion pictures). He started as a gag man bringing the entire Sicilian background into focus in every phase of his production.

He was always sitting in the front row as a spectator, laughing at his jokes, crying all through a tragedy, and reaching in his hip pocket, at the end, for a human burst of wholesome laughter.

This quality is the spiritual thing hidden in a formal script. Surrounded by great artists, he was always the ringmaster in life's great arena. The rules of circus life were never violated—no one must overlap his department. He is a man sent here with an objective: "Let's make life a smooth game, full of fun, understanding, dignity, and love." That's Brother Frank Capra's accomplishment.

—Letter to the authors from Muse-A-While Ranch, Perris, California, September 3, 1974.

DRUNKEN BUTLER, played by Harry Davenport, announces to J. L. Higgins (Charles Bickford), at the end of *Riding High*, "It's Mr. Brooks, sir. He says to release the Princess from the Dark Tower." The Princess referred to is Alice Higgins (Coleen Gray). Max Baer, as Bertie, is on the left.

LAUGHS ON THE SET of *Riding High* were common. It was a happy picture for all concerned. Taking a cigarette break between scenes are, from left to right: Frank Capra, William Demarest and Oliver Hardy.

Liberty Films was sold to Paramount Pictures, and at that studio, Frank Capra, having acquired the rights from Harry Cohn, chose to remake *Broadway Bill* as a musical with many of his stock company of supporting actors repeating their original roles.

Although the story is the same as *Broadway Bill* in all essentials and in many details (including actual racing and crowd scenes from the original), in this version Dan Brooks (Bing Crosby) is not married to Margaret Higgins (Frances Gifford), but is engaged to be married to her in three weeks.

The first scene with Broadway Bill concludes with a wonderful gambol between Dan and his horse. The horse doesn't want him to leave—as he must, to have dinner at J. L. Higgins's mansion—and follows him across the field, attempting, in playful rushes, to lure him back. Dan is drawn into sportive romping with Bill in a sequence so tenderly portraying their relationship as to seem almost choreographed, so graceful is its statement.

Higgins's butler, Johnson (Harry Davenport), adds a whimsical comic contrast to the tycoon's sterile household. Dan refers to the Higgins home as a mausoleum. In this frigid setting, where all drink their soup in unison (an imaginative long shot), Capra uses the strains of "Home, Sweet Home" as background music.

"Somewhere on Anywhere Road" is the song ingratiatingly sung by Dan and Whitey (Clarence Muse), the former with a horn, the latter with a drum accompaniment while driving away from the Higgins house on their way to the track. Broadway Bill, in his trailer, joins in, neighing.

William Demarest, as Happy McGuire, can perfectly deliver the response to the Crosby line, "How's your wallet?" with a sardonic, "I don't know. I ate it yesterday." Percy Kilbride, as Pop Jones, renting his ramshackle barn as a stable for Bill, can sound convincing when he says, after the door falls off, that it's "nice and comfortable inside!"

And the lighthearted "Sunshine Cake" musical number grows out of the scene in the barn when Alice (Coleen Gray) is making dinner, a chicken dinner (so Dan and Whitey can have an extra dollop of tomfoolery in a mock search for Skeeter, the mascot rooster). As for dessert, Alice says she has no flour, no baking powder, no eggs. Dan replies, "Who needs those things? We bake a cake every night here without them—don't we, Whitey?" Whitey concurs, "Out of sunshine!" The musical number has great spontaneity and no accompaniment other than kitchen utensils and Whitey's guitar. Capra employed direct recording of musical numbers throughout this film.

VISITOR TO SET of *Riding High* was Gary Cooper, center, seen here enjoying a conversation with Frank Capra while Bing Crosby feigns jealousy.

ODETTE MYRTIL, as a Gray Lady, far left, with, left to right, Bobby (Jacques Gencel), Suzi (Beverly Washburn), French Matron (Michele Lange) and Pete Garvey (Bing Crosby). Scene is in Pete's Paris office-apartment, where he's been working with UNESCO at start of film. Pete is packing his bag for reassignment, as a reporter, in the Far East, but he returns to America instead, taking Bobby and Suzi with him.

POSTER for *Here Comes the Groom*, with a photo of Pete Garvey (Bing Crosby) on the phone surrounded by orphans in his Paris office.

244

A Paramount Picture. A Frank Capra Production. Produced and directed by Frank Capra. Associate Producer: Irving Asher. Screenplay by Virginia Van Upp, Liam O'Brien, and Myles Connolly, based on a story by Robert Riskin and Liam O'Brien. Photographed by George Barnes. Special effects by Gordon Jennings and Paul Lerpae. Process photography by Farciot Edouart. Art direction by Hal Pereira and Earl Hedrick. Set decoration by Emile Kuri. Edited by Ellsworth Hoagland. Costumes by Edith Head. Musical direction by Joseph J. Lilley. Special orchestral arrangements by Van Cleave. Songs: "In the Cool, Cool, Cool of the Evening," by Johnny Mercer and Hoagy Carmichael; "Misto Cristofo Columbo," "Bonne Nuit," and "Your Own Little House," by Jay Livingston and Ray Evans. Dance direction by Charles O'Curran. Sound recording by Harry Mills and John Cope. Western Electric Recording. Makeup supervision by Wally Westmore. Assistant Director: Arthur S. Black. Running time: 113 minutes.

CAST:

Pete Garvey, Bing Crosby; *Emmadel Jones*, Jane Wyman; *Winifred Stanley*, Alexis Smith; *Wilbur Stanley*, Franchot Tone; *Pa Jones*, James Barton; *George Degnan*, Robert Keith; *Theresa*, Anna Maria Alberghetti; *Bobby*, Jacques Gencel; *Suzi*, Beverly Washburn; *Ma Jones*, Connie Gilchrist; *Mr. McGonigle*, Walter Catlett; *Mr. Godfrey*, Alan Reed; *Mrs. Godfrey*, Minna Gombell; *Governor*, Howard Freeman; *Aunt Abby*, Maidel Turner; *Uncle Elihu*, H. B. Warner; *Uncle Prentiss*, Nicholas Joy; *Uncle Adam*, Ian Wolfe; *Mrs. McGonigle*, Ellen Corby; *Policeman*, James Burke; *Baines*, Irving Bacon; *Paul Pippitt*, Ted Thorpe; *Radio Announcer*, Art Baker; *Aunt Amy*, Adeline de Walt Reynolds; *Herself*, Dorothy Lamour; *Himself*, Phil Harris; *Himself*, Louis Armstrong; *Herself*, Cass Daley; *Himself*, Frank Fontaine; *Burchard, FBI Agent*, Charles Lane; *Gray Lady*, Odette Myrtil; *Marcel*, Chris Appel; *Cusick*, Charles Halton; *Priest*, The Reverend Neal Dodd; *Mayor*, Charles Evans; *Man*, J. Farrell MacDonald; *Messenger*, Carl "Alfalfa" Switzer; *Newsreel Director*, Walter McGrail; *Newsreel Cameraman*, Howard Joslin; *Maid*, Laura Elliot; *French Matron*, Michele Lange; *Neighbor*, Donald Kerr; *Photographers*: Charles Sullivan, Ed Randolph; *Others*: Chester Conklin, James Finlayson, Bess Flowers; *Passengers on Airplane*: Almira Sessions, Frank Hagney, Julia Faye, Franklyn Farnum, Don Dunning.

CONNIE GILCHRIST:

What first comes to mind in connection with *Here Comes the Groom* is an episode with Jane Wyman.

Here Comes the Groom

1951

WAITING AT AIRPORT for Pete Garvey are his newspaper editor, George Degnan (Robert Keith), and his fiancee, Emmadel Jones (Jane Wyman). They are unintentionally stood up.

She was going through an odd tune, which I considered rather quaint, when she should have been having lunch.

"Why are you knockin' yourself out with that? Wait'll they hand you the music they're going to use."

"This *is* the music they're going to use!" says she. It was "In the Cool, Cool, Cool of the Evening," which won an Academy Award and dragged on for years. I have a feeling for this sort of thing!

Another recollection was the group of Mack Sennett veterans in the wedding scene at the church, from Jimmy Finlayson to Chester Conklin, who were posing as my husband's old, good buddies while the rest of the family were trying to elevate him to a proper sphere. James Barton had worked with most of them in the early days.

"How much d'ya think Jim is getting for this one?"

"Seven-fifty, at least."

"Naw, it's gotta be a thousand!"

"Twelve hundred, maybe?"

They ran it up the scale and down again. I cut in. "For your information, he's getting twenty-five hundred." Finlayson fell out of his pew. Actually, Jim was getting five thousand, but there was no sense in straining credulity too far.

—*Letter to the authors from Santa Monica, California,*
August 19, 1974.

CASS DALEY:

I had only a small part in *Here Comes the Groom*, you might say a cameo, but it was the thrill of my

PLANE JAMBOREE—Pete Garvey (Bing Crosby), center, sings "Misto Cristofo Columbo" with guest stars, playing U.S.O. entertainers: Frank Fontaine, left of him, and, to the right of him, Cass Daley, Dorothy Lamour and Louis Armstrong. Phil Harris is behind Lamour. The song humorously elucidates American history to Bobby and Suzi (Jacques Gencel and Beverly Washburn), seated, who are on their way to America.

career just to be next to, or on the same set with, Frank Capra—a gentleman if there ever was one and of course, one of the greatest!

—Letter to the authors from Las Vegas, Nevada,
March 22, 1974.

PHIL HARRIS:

Frank Capra has always been the epitome, as far as I am concerned, not only in the film industry, but in any of his undertakings.

—Letter to the authors from Palm Desert, California,
January 28, 1974.

ALAN REED:

Frank Capra has always impressed me as being one of the most forthright, practical, and level-headed creators the industry has ever produced. My working adventure with him lasted only two days, but it was a pleasure to watch him improvise from minute to minute during the shooting day. As I recall, he was surrounded, not by a group of sycophants but by equals with whom he would discuss, argue, listen, and finally make his decision—often against his original approach.

One personal anecdote, which left me quite unhappy at the time—but with more understanding as the years have gone by—requires a bit of background. There are vital differences between the way stars are handled and the way character people and bit players are handled. I don't mean to infer any unfairness or lack of courtesy to Frank Capra, but it is the accepted tradition of the industry that as soon as the master shot (the long shot) is finished, the closeups of the stars are done (while their makeup is fresh and spirits are buoyant), and the closeups of the lesser character people are put off to the end of a long day.

In *Here Comes the Groom* I played a world-renowned musical impresario, lured against his will to an orphanage to hear a young girl (Anna Maria Alberghetti) sing. She had a lovely voice, and the maestro's expression went from boredom to interest to enthusiasm and, at a crucial moment when he realized the child was blind, to tears. Well, during the long shot the scene played to perfection, the tears streamed forth naturally, and I felt great in my performance. This was at 9:00 A.M. Now came the long, long wait for my closeup. The moment finally arrived at 5:30 P.M., and hard as I tried, I could not reach inside for that magic moment. I was absolutely

DISAPPROVING OF MARRIAGE of his daughter to Wilbur Stanley, Pa Jones (James Barton), right, drunk in the midst of the decorations for his daughter's bridal shower, unburdens his unhappiness to Pete Garvey (Bing Crosby), who has been reading about the upcoming marriage in the newspaper. Pa Jones wants Pete to marry Emmadel and tells him, "You'll have to work fast, son. They're hauling her in this Saturday—in a forty million dollar net!"

SONG, "In the Cool, Cool, Cool of the Evening," which Capra took off Paramount's shelf and turned into a hit and Academy Award winner, is sung by clowning Emmadel Jones (Jane Wyman) and Pete Garvey (Bing Crosby).

247

dry-eyed. We finally had to use glycerine for the tears, and I was sick to realize that at the moment when it really counted it had to be done synthetically.

Frank Capra, who had been very patient through four or five takes and had then ordered the glycerine, was the epitome of kindness. When the final take was concluded, he put his arm around me and said, "Don't worry. They won't be able to tell the difference."

—*Letter to the authors from Los Angeles, California,* March 4, 1974.

ODETTE MYRTIL:

Frank Capra is one of the nicest men in Hollywood. My recollection of my stay with him is most pleasant—in fact, I would say *the* most pleasant of my career in Hollywood. Of course, the cast helped a lot, because it was difficult to argue with Bing Crosby and Jane Wyman and the darling little French kid who had been sent over from France and could not have been cuter.

I really haven't got any funny recollections, except my knocking off Bing Crosby's hat in my passionate embraces and finding out how bald he really was, and Mr. Capra making fun of it!

—*Letter to the authors from New Hope, Pennsylvania,* June 19, 1974.

IAN WOLFE:

I know how pleasantly and warmly Frank Capra handled and directed smaller players. He treated older actors with special kindness and care, which endeared him to me forever. For these reasons, I remember him with appreciation as a fine human being, in addition to being a master director.

—*Letter to the authors from Sherman Oaks, California,* March 10, 1974.

Fulfilling his contractual obligation, Frank Capra directed one more film for Paramount Pictures— *Here Comes the Groom.*

American newspaperman Pete Garvey (Bing Crosby), about to end a Paris assignment covering UNESCO and not able to bear leaving behind orphans Bobby (Jacques Gencel) and Suzi (Beverly Washburn), cables girlfriend Emmadel Jones (Jane Wyman): "Oil your lamp—the bridegroom cometh —meet me and expect surprise."

Their departure from France is delayed, however, and Emmadel, irate at having been stood up again

SPORTIVE WRESTLING MATCH between Winifred Stanley (Alexis Smith) and Pete Garvey (Bing Crosby). She is wearing Pete's pajamas because she got her clothes wet on the lawn when the sprinkler system accidentally went off.

248

after an almost endless repetition of such incidents, goes ahead with plans to marry her boss, millionaire Wilbur Stanley (Franchot Tone).

Pete arrives with Bobby and Suzi, who are in the United States on a permit. If Pete isn't married by the end of five days, the children have to go back to France. Emmadel's father (James Barton) says his beloved daughter is throwing herself away on Wilbur Stanley, who's not a man, but "a tradition—out of Lexington by the minutemen." Already the headlines tell of a fisherman's daughter set to wed forty million dollars.

The major musical number, "In the Cool, Cool, Cool of the Evening," is sung and danced in the Stanley real estate office, where Emmadel has agreed to take Pete, although the office is closed, and find him a house to lease. By a ruse, Pete manages to create a situation (by switching leases) that brings Wilbur Stanley to the scene of his attempt to move into a house already occupied by Mr. and Mrs. McGonigle (Walter Catlett and Ellen Corby).

Alone with his rival, Pete convinces him to let him and the children stay in the Stanley gate house and try to win Emmadel back. Wilbur agrees to the contest: Emmadel will both decide the winner and be the prize.

Pete turns Wilbur's beautiful but cold cousin Winifred (Alexis Smith) into a hip-swinging glamour girl not afraid to go after and win Wilbur, whom she has always loved. Emmadel marries Pete, insuring that the French orphans will have a home in America.

Not only did the song "In the Cool, Cool, Cool of the Evening" win an Academy Award, but Robert Riskin and Liam O'Brien were nominated for Oscars as writers in the Best Story category.

CONNIE GILCHRIST laughs with Bing Crosby on the set of *Here Comes the Groom.*

WEDDING REHEARSAL—In the foreground, from left to right: Wilbur Stanley (Franchot Tone)—and Emmadel Jones (Jane Wyman) and Winifred Stanley (Alexis Smith), who are about to come to blows. The Stanley family, seated in the background in the first row of chairs, are, from left to right: Uncle Adam (Ian Wolfe), Aunt Abby (Maidel Turner), Uncle Alihu (H. B. Warner), Aunt Amy (Adeline de Walt Reynolds) and Uncle Prentiss (Nicholas Joy).

VISITOR to the set of *Here Comes the Groom* was Harold Lloyd, right, who was greeted by Frank Capra and Jane Wyman.

249

MR. SUN AND FATHER TIME, speaking with the voices of Marvin Miller and Lionel Barrymore, respectively.

250

INTRODUCTION

For a five-year period, beginning in 1952, Frank Capra devoted his scientific flair and his cinematic knowhow to producing and writing four hour-long science films (three of which he also directed) for national television, to be sponsored by the Bell Telephone system.

American Telephone and Telegraph wanted the best man they could find to do a series on science that would entertain audiences as they learned. Capra was intrigued by this unique opportunity to bridge the gap between scientist and layman, to simplify the complex without distorting it, and to add a spiritual dimension that would point up the wholeness of man's knowledge.

As quoted in the April 2, 1957, issue of *Look* magazine, Frank Capra stated about science, believing it could be entertaining, "It is full of adventure stories. It appeals to the imagination. These things have to be brought out of the dry facts of science," and about his science films, "We do it with a little story or plot, documentary film and lots of animated cartoons. It's a unique concoction."

OUR MR. SUN   1956

FRANK P. KELLER, A.C.E.:

One morning in December of 1952, Frank Capra and I arrived together at the offices that were to become the headquarters of the Bell Telephone Science Series films. He was carrying an armload of reference books, and I was carrying an armload of film-editing equipment.

The next five years were an enriching experience in compilation, filmmaking, higher education, and human relations. During this period, Frank Capra was a perfect study of concentration as he wrote or reedited many versions of treatments and scripts. In the midst of the usual distractions of an office with phones ringing and numerous interruptions, Frank Capra could be seen sitting quietly at a typewriter oblivious of his surroundings and deep in his thoughts.

Early in our association, I learned that Mr. Capra's credo in picture making is, "Never be dull." In making these science films, he was determined that they would be entertaining as well as educational, so that the audience would be "held," and the scientific information would be almost unconsciously assimilated.

Television Science Films

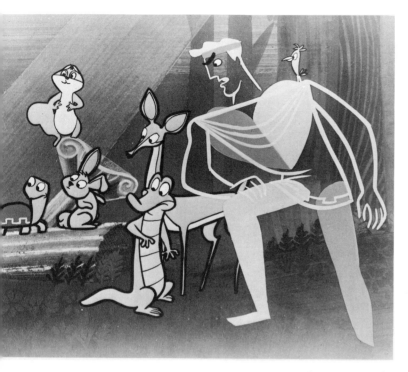

HEMO THE MAGNIFICENT, a cartoon man who represents the blood, speaks to his animal friends whose circulatory systems are compared with those of man.

THE HEART AS A PUMP and the circulatory system are explained in cartoon animation.

Working on these films caused us to have many experiences different than we would have had on normal theatrical productions. One of them was the people in the academic world with whom we were in contact. They, of course, had no film experience and were unfamiliar with the terms we used, and vice versa, so that at times we seemed to be speaking two different languages. Fortunately, Frank Capra had had a scientific education at Cal Tech so that he could interpret much of the detailed information into motion-picture terms and could create a film approach to illustrate scientific data.

—*Letter to the authors from Hollywood, California,*
November 8, 1974.

"The Bell Telephone System brings you the first in a new series of programs on science: man's effort to understand nature's laws." Thus *Our Mr. Sun* is introduced, and a frame showing the sun in all its magnificence also reminds viewers that "The heavens declare the glory of God."

Two principal live characters are used—Eddie Albert as a fiction writer and Doctor Frank Baxter as Doctor Research, in addition to an assistant played by Sterling Holloway—along with animated cartoon characters to entertainingly relate the fascinating scientific facts.

More important than the aesthetics of the sun, it is stated, is its great, untapped power. The sun is the source of 99 percent of all food and fuel, and solar power is the answer to tomorrow's energy needs, to heat houses and cook food. Solar batteries will fly planes, sail ships, and operate telephone lines.

"Man's greatest power source is his mind," so he will research himself into his next great adventure—the sun age, a time in which man will be "rich beyond all dreams," and even in desert wastes great cities will thrive, running on sunlight alone. In the words of Saint Francis, "Be praised, my Lord, in what you have created. Above all else, be praised in our brother, Master Sun."

An audience of twenty-four million saw *Our Mr. Sun.*

HEMO THE MAGNIFICENT 1957

The second of the science films, featuring Richard Carlson this time as a fiction writer, along with Doctor Frank Baxter as Doctor Research, and Sterling

Holloway as the assistant, deals with the blood, and the opening quotes the Book of Leviticus: "For the life of the flesh is in the blood."

Through animation, the viewer learns about the turtle's heart, the rabbit's heart, the bird's, the cat's, the elephant's—and the human heart, ¾ of a pound of the "strongest, toughest muscle" that "never tires." It paces itself on the scale of our activity, and it gives first priority to nourishing the brain cells which are always working, are non-replaceable and are non-repairable.

Extraordinary film shows the blood-flow highly magnified; animation clarifies the body's priorities for survival and the nature of shock, which is protective of life. Thus do we learn much about "that entirely wonderful sap," to use Goethe's definition of blood.

It was estimated that the audience for this picture on television was thirty-five million!

THE STRANGE CASE OF THE COSMIC RAYS   1957

BIL BAIRD:

Working with Frank Capra was one of the most exciting and exacting periods of our lives. He stretched the hell out of our capabilities, and we loved it—and him. Working in a new medium, it didn't occur to him that there might be limitations. So we stretched voices, gestures, and eyes, and I must say, we're still riding on what we learned.

Here we were, crew and puppeteers, a tiny concentration about forty feet square in the middle of one of the huge Sam Goldwyn studios—but everything focused on Capra. Nobody spoke till Capra asked for something, and I reckon it was because everybody knew that what he wanted was gonna be right.

—Letter to the authors from New York, New York,
April 13, 1975.

FRANK P. KELLER, A.C.E.:

Although producing authoritative science films was very difficult and at times frustrating, there were lighter moments too. One that I recall occurred while we were photographing a sequence for *The Strange Case of the Cosmic Rays.*

Three oversize puppets had been constructed to portray famous mystery writers seated at a table. This was to be the framing for the live-action part of the picture. Puppeteers on a platform above operated the figures and spoke the lines as they moved the lips of the puppets.

In directing the action and lines, Frank Capra began by looking up at the puppeteers as he gave his instructions. However, because the puppets were so skillfully handled, they became very believable as individual personages. After a short time, Mr. Capra found himself unconsciously giving directions to the puppets, rather than to the puppeteers. He enjoyed the humor of the situation as much as the rest of the crew.

—Letter to the authors from Hollywood, California,
November 8, 1974.

The tale of this strange case is told at "Ye Academy of Detection Arts and Sciences," presided over by Bil and Cora Baird's personable marionettes, representing Edgar Allan Poe, Charles Dickens, and Feodor Dostoevski, introduced by the regulars in the science series, Richard Carlson as a fiction writer and Doctor Frank Baxter as Doctor Research.

Speaking for the vast television audience, Dostoevski exclaims, "Science is for me a big bore!" But he and the audience soon change their minds as the mysterious phantom bandit (radiation), seen in animation, is traced beyond the earth to the outer universe and found to be embodied in cosmic rays.

BAIRD MARIONETTES on miniature set—from left to right: Charles Dickens, Edgar Allan Poe and Feodor Dostoevski with Frank Capra, left, and Bill Baird.

THE MAKING OF WEATHER, as shown in cartoon fashion by an apothecary putting the right natural ingredients together.

These rays are "pieces of matter from outer space, the same matter as on earth: proof of the oneness of matter." A lay public is drawn step by logically deductive and scientifically provable step into the thinking of scientists. A new awareness of the possibilities the future holds explains to us the reasons for research and the search for new facts leading to new discoveries.

THE UNCHAINED GODDESS   1958

RICHARD CARLSON:

Of course, Frank Capra is one of everyone's favorite people, as artist, as technician, as human being.

Anyone who has spent much time working on motion-picture sets is aware of the inevitable increasing hum of peripheral conversations between forty or fifty crew people, especially during any lull in the shooting. The constant pleas of assistant directors, "Let's hold the conversation, folks! Please, quiet, folks!"

On Frank's set, say a scene is not playing just right. Something in the script. Frank tucks one leg under him in his canvas chair and concentrates on the offending pages. Magically, not a sound on the set! I can't explain it. Respect? Affection? Leadership? If you mentioned this to Frank, I'm sure he would be surprised. Isn't this always true on any director's set? No, it isn't. I have never seen it happen (without endless chiding) on any other director's set.

When time came to shoot the fourth picture in the science series (the one on weather), press of other business made it inconvenient for Frank to direct it, and he honored me by asking me to take it over. (I had been directing *The Loretta Young Show* at that time.) So here I was, directing from his concept and his writing, with his crew. He offered all the help I sought with minor script changes, with casting, with choosing locations, with budget. But on the set, never a suggestion, never a criticism, seldom even a visit. And in the latter case, never without advising me ahead of time! To him I was the *director*, even as he had been. Extraordinary.

When I was new in this business, first under David Selznick, then under the men at Paramount, Metro, and Universal, I was taught that by the time the script was ready for the stages the picture was essentially finished. And that was largely true, despite the overweening books recently by some directors of that period. (It is still true in television.) I suppose Frank was almost the first of the true *auteurs*, the touchstone being, he conceived the project, then *directed the writers*. "Name above the title!" And deservedly.

Once, acting for Frank, I remember fearing that I was trying to make my points too swiftly, trying to go too fast. "Too fast?" said Frank. "Almost never. But let's see. . . ." All of us in the theater, not only actors, but writers and directors as well, have the desire to take the pause, to dawdle, to bask in audience enrapture (we hope). "Too fast? Almost never." It is the admonition that keeps Frank's pictures, always sentimental, from sentimentality. He knows less is more.

—*Letter to the authors from Sherman Oaks, California,*
April 17, 1974.

Through animated cartoons introduced by Richard Carlson and Doctor Frank Baxter, the viewer meets Meteora, supreme goddess of weather. Weather—which not only waters the earth and controls its temperatures, but, as in the case of the Spanish Armada, changes the course of history. Tornadoes and hurricanes (most dreaded storms), are shown in formation, impact, and dissolution. Trade winds, thunder and lightning, weather prediction, the jet stream, and possible control of the earth's weather are all explained and discussed.

Man is working to learn how to live hand in hand with nature, how to control her passions, and how to satisfy his needs. An entirely informative film, *The Unchained Goddess* answers the questions that have been asked by all who look at their environment with curiosity.

RICHARD CARLSON, left, with Dr. Frank Baxter at weather map.

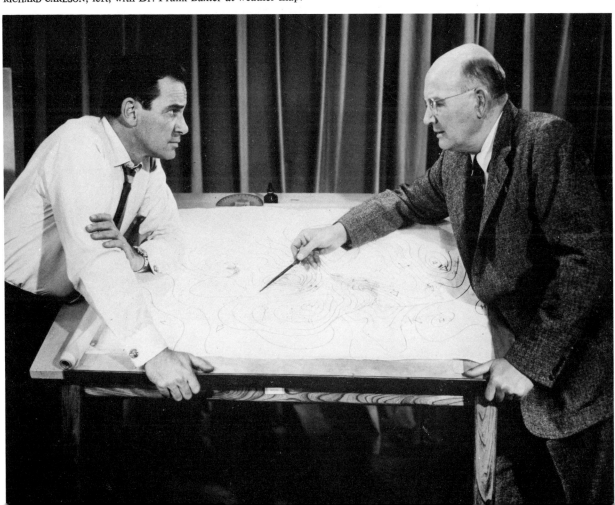

FATHER AND SON—Ally (Eddie Hodges) pleads with his father, Tony Manetta (Frank Sinatra), not to let his uncle and aunt separate them.

A United Artists Picture. A Sincap Production. Produced and directed by Frank Capra. Screenplay by Arnold Schulman, based on his play *A Hole in the Head*. Photographed by William H. Daniels in Cinema-Scope and DeLuxe color. Photographic lenses by Panavision. Art direction by Eddie Imazu. Set decoration by Fred MacLean. Edited by William Hornbeck. Costumes by Edith Head. Music by Nelson Riddle. Orchestrations by Arthur Morton. Songs: "High Hopes" and "All My Tomorrows," by Sammy Cahn and Jimmy Van Heusen. Hair Stylist: Helene Parrish. Makeup by Bernard Ponedel. Sound by Fred Lau. Production Manager: Joe Cooke. Assistant Directors: Arthur S. Black, Jr., and Jack R. Berne. Running time: 120 minutes.

CAST:

Tony Manetta, Frank Sinatra; *Mario Manetta*, Edward G. Robinson; *Mrs. Rogers*, Eleanor Parker; *Shirl*, Carolyn Jones; *Sophie Manetta*, Thelma Ritter; *Jerry Marks*, Keenan Wynn; *Ally Manetta*, Eddie Hodges; *Dorine*, Joi Lansing; *Miss Wexler*, Connie Sawyer; *Julius Manetta*, Jimmy Komack; *Fred*, Dub Taylor; *Mendy*, George DeWitt; *Mr. Diamond*, Benny Rubin; *Sally*, Ruby Dandridge; *Hood*, B. S. Pully; *Alice*, Joyce Nizzari; *Master of Ceremonies*, Pupi Campo; *Cabby*, Robert B. Williams; *Sheriff*, Emory Parnell; *Andy*, Bill Walker.

CAROLYN JONES:

As to my memories of Frank Capra, the Italian leprechaun, I think the thing that impressed me most was his ability to make his actors feel that they were entertaining *him* as well as the audience.

All during the filming of *A Hole in the Head* we all worked a little harder for his quiet chuckle in the comedy scenes or his long, tender sigh in the dramatic ones. Even Eddie Robinson, who was hard of hearing, played to Mr. Capra. We all felt the warmth, affection, and, most important of all, the approval exuding from the gentle man behind the camera.

I miss Frank Capra pictures. I wish he was still making them. I was privileged to know him.

—*Letter to the authors from Palm Springs, California*, May 18, 1974.

EDITH HEAD:

Working with Frank Capra was one of the highlights of my career, not only because he is a super director, but because he is such a charming and wonderful person.

A Hole in the Head

1959

AUNT AND UNCLE—Sophie and Mario Manetta (Thelma Ritter and Edward G. Robinson).

PROSPECTIVE NEW MOTHER, widowed Mrs. Rogers (Eleanor Parker), comforts Ally (Eddie Hodges).

I remember, because the costuming was all extremely important, he had the time to sit down with me and go over the whole meaning of each character, which helped me translate the players into their roles. This was true of every film of his on which I worked.

I do so admire Frank Capra.

—*Letter to the authors from Universal City, California,*
April 16, 1974.

Frank Capra, teamed with Frank Sinatra, formed Sincap Productions to produce *A Hole in the Head,* which was released through United Artists. The color film was a great success, artistically and commercially. The *New York Times* selected it as one of the ten best films of 1959, and the hit song in the film, "High Hopes," won an Academy Award.

The playground world of Miami Beach (some location shooting was done there) is instantly established as a porpoise joyfully leaps high out of the waters of an exhibition tank, and a blimp sails through the clear, sunny sky hauling a net on which appear the title of the film and the names of its stars. A stunning aerial view of ocean, beach, and hotels is the colorful background against which Sinatra sings "All My Tomorrows."

Tony Manetta (Frank Sinatra), ambitious but without business acumen, is about to lose his mismanaged Garden of Eden hotel. A widower, he

LECTURE is given to Tony Manetta (Frank Sinatra) by practical-minded landlord, Mr. Diamond (Benny Rubin), on how not to squander money.

258

CAROLYN JONES, as Shirl, realizes that Tony Manetta (Frank Sinatra) can never be a free spirit like herself. The contrast between her surfboard and his car represents their life styles.

NEPHEW INSPECTED—Doting Aunt Sophie (Thelma Ritter), newly arrived at the Garden of Eden Hotel with her husband, Mario Manetta (Edward G. Robinson), far right, asks Ally (Eddie Hodges) if he is all right. Fred (Dub Taylor) is the hotel's desk clerk.

EXCITING PLANS for flying to Cuba for a few Cha-Cha-Chas ("Fly now, pay later") please Tony Manetta (Frank Sinatra) and Shirl (Carolyn Jones).

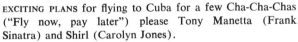

loves and relates well to his serious-minded eleven-year-old son, Ally (Eddie Hodges). His older, successful brother, Mario (Edward G. Robinson), and his wife, Sophie (Thelma Ritter), want to take Ally to their home in New York and bring him up conventionally. The film's story is the story of the struggle of father and son to stay together as the financial crises mount and Tony holds on to the hotel by the merest string.

Tony's old buddy Jerry Marks (Keenan Wynn) has turned selfish and arrogant with success, humiliating and refusing to help Tony.

At one point Mario and Sophie urge Tony to marry and settle down; they've even picked out a suitable widow for him. Tony tells Ally, "If I don't like her and you do, you marry her and take care of me!" Ally tells him, "You've got a hole in the head!" Arm in arm they walk out in the balmy Miami night and sing "High Hopes" in the highest and most infectious of spirits.

The widow turns out to be a beautiful redhead, Mrs. Rogers (Eleanor Parker), but both she and

259

LESSON IN BUSINESS MANAGEMENT is given to Tony Manetta (Frank Sinatra) by Jerry Marks (Keenan Wynn), who is in the process of getting dressed. Later in the film, Jerry will angrily tell Tony, "Never try to promote a promoter."

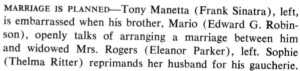

MARRIAGE IS PLANNED—Tony Manetta (Frank Sinatra), left, is embarrassed when his brother, Mario (Edward G. Robinson), openly talks of arranging a marriage between him and widowed Mrs. Rogers (Eleanor Parker), left. Sophie (Thelma Ritter) reprimands her husband for his gaucherie.

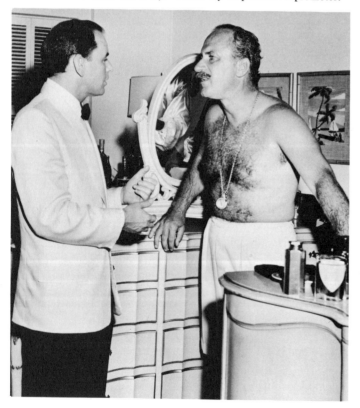

Tony are too sensitive and honest for anything to come of an "arrangement."

Finally, Mario, with Sophie's urging, financially rescues his brother again. Ally is the price Tony must pay, and Ally is about to leave with his uncle and aunt. His father, across the street, opposite the hotel, hides behind a palm tree. Mrs. Rogers, drawn to the boy, says, "Goodbye, Ally. You cry if you want to."

Suddenly, Mario exclaims, "What's going to happen to my brother, standing behind that tree like a crazy man watching his son leave him?"

Next, Tony and Ally, inseparable, are running, fully dressed, in the surf!

Mario and Sophie see that there is something rich and enjoyable in life that they've been missing—so, at least for a brief vacation time, they toss care to the warmly caressing ocean breeze and, like Mrs. Rogers, run down the beach to join the deliriously happy Tony and Ally.

AT THE DOG RACES, Tony Manetta (Frank Sinatra), left, is desperate when he loses all his money. Wealthy Jerry Marks (Keenan Wynn) and Dorine (Joi Lansing) are surprised by his reaction, having been led to believe by him that he could afford to bet.

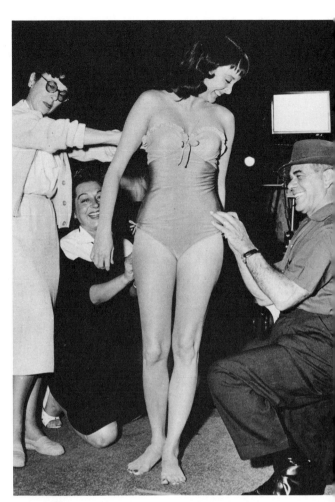

EDITH HEAD, far left, with an assistant, and grinning Frank Capra, right, make adjustments on Carolyn Jones' costume.

DIRECTOR AND STARS—Left to right, Frank Capra, Frank Sinatra and Edward G. Robinson in a gag publicity shot for *A Hole in the Head*.

PLAYFUL DIRECTOR Frank Capra and child star Eddie Hodges frolic on studio street at the time of filming *A Hole in the Head*.

261

DIRECTOR AND CAST—Seated, left to right: Frank Capra, Arthur O'Connell, Hope Lange, Bette Davis, Ann-Margret, and Thomas Mitchell. Standing, left to right: Peter Mann, Mickey Shaughnessy, Glenn Ford, Peter Falk, and Edward Everett Horton. On the set of Mrs. E. Worthington Manville's penthouse terrace.

MEETING IN BULLET-PROOF VAN, nicknamed "Little Switzerland" and made into living quarters where Dave the Dude (Glenn Ford), right, has stashed gangster Steve Darcey (Sheldon Leonard), left, so they can talk business; but Darcey, showing newspaper headline, worries about being caught by the cops. Dave's right hand man is Joy Boy (Peter Falk), center.

FROLICSOME Herbie (Tom Fadden), employee at the Hotel Marberry, jokes with Apple Annie (Bette Davis) after sneaking stationery to her from the hotel.

A United Artists Picture. A Franton Production. Produced and directed by Frank Capra. Associate Producers: Glenn Ford and Joseph Sistrom. Screenplay by Hal Kanter and Harry Tugend, based on a screenplay, *Lady for a Day*, by Robert Riskin, and a short story, "Madame La Gimp," by Damon Runyon. Photographed by Robert Bronner in Panavision and Eastman Color. Process photography by Farciot Edouart. Art direction by Hal Pereira and Roland Anderson. Set decoration by Sam Comer and Ray Moyer. Edited by Frank P. Keller. Women's costumes by Edith Head. Men's costumes by Walter Plunkett. Music scored and conducted by Walter Scharf. Song, "Pocketful of Miracles," by Sammy Cahn and James Van Heusen. Choreography by Nick Castle. Sound recording by Hugo Grenzbach and Charles Grenzbach. Makeup supervision by Wally Westmore. Hair-style supervision by Nellie Manley. Assistant Director: Arthur S. Black, Jr. Running time: 136 minutes.

CAST:

Dave the Dude, Glenn Ford; *Apple Annie*, Bette Davis; *Queenie Martin*, Hope Lange; *Count Romero*, Arthur O'Connell; *Joy Boy*, Peter Falk; *Judge Blake*, Thomas Mitchell; *Butler*, Edward Everett Horton; *Junior*, Mickey Shaughnessy; *Governor*, David Brian; *Steve Darcey*, Sheldon Leonard; *Carlos*, Peter Mann; *Louise*, Ann-Margret; *Police Commissioner*, Barton MacLane; *Inspector*, John Litel; *Mayor*, Jerome Cowan; *Spanish Consul*, Jay Novello; *Newspaper Editors*: Frank Ferguson, Willis Bouchey; *Pierre*, Fritz Feld; *Soho Sal*, Ellen Corby; *Hotel Manager*, Gavin Gordon; *Flyaway*, Benny Rubin; *Cheesecake*, Jack Elam; *Big Mike*, Mike Mazurki; *Captain Moore*, Hayden Rorke; *Pool Player*, Doodles Weaver; *Mallethead*, Paul E. Burns; *Angie*, Angelo Rossitto; *Gloomy*, Edgar Stehli; *Shimkey*, George E. Stone; *Smiley*, William F. Sauls; *Herbie*, Tom Fadden; *Knuckles*, Snub Pollard; *Hotel Employee*, Byron Foulger.

ARTHUR O'CONNELL:

Frank Capra is a darling human being and, without question, one hell of a fine director. His warmth and humor off the set were complemented by his serious and businesslike approach to the work at hand.

Before *Pocketful of Miracles* began shooting, Frank sent for me and arranged to have me work with a Spanish teacher to perfect a believable Spanish accent for my character. After working dili-

GAVIN GORDON, as the Hotel Manager, far right, tells Apple Annie (Bette Davis) that she must leave the premises. His assistant is played by Byron Foulger, and the bell boy is an extra. Annie, with letter from her daughter in hand, exclaims, "Here it is! I told you it was here!"

Pocketful of Miracles

1961

gently four hours a day and then taping the dialogue, we would present ourselves to Frank with our taped efforts. He would listen and make some comments, and we would see him the following afternoon. After three weeks of this, Frank said he would now like to concentrate on my character, rather than my dialect. After bidding the teacher good night, Frank turned to me and said, "Arthur, your character is Spanish—a count, a nobleman—not Mexican!" and he found me another teacher.

The first day I worked, when lunch was called, Frank came over and said if I wasn't having lunch with anyone, he'd like to have lunch with me. Well, it became a practice—when lunch was called he'd signal me, and we'd walk to the executive dining room. A more charming, humorous dinner companion I've never had in my life. He had a million anecdotes about the pictures he'd made and an endless string of jokes, and I wish to Christ I could remember just one of them now. If I remember correctly, however, Frank insisted on picking up the tab nine out of ten times.

We invariably left the dining room laughing, in great humor, as we walked over to the stage; yet as soon as Frank stepped over the threshold, he changed. It would be hard to believe or think this was a man who loved to laugh and tell funny stories. The business at hand was the only important thing, and there was little humor employed to produce what was eventually so humorous and human.

Yet he was certainly not without his understanding of the human condition. When I was contracted to do the picture, the shooting schedule conflicted with the marriage of my daughter, which was to take place in Washington, D.C. Frank, with no questioning, rearranged the whole shooting schedule so that I was able to attend.

Frank Capra is deservedly a man to honor as one of the creators of the Golden Age of Hollywood.

—*Letter to the authors from Los Angeles, California,*
June 10, 1974.

GAVIN GORDON:

When I again worked with Frank Capra, in *Pocketful of Miracles,* he was, of course, very famous, but he was just as warm and friendly as always, although more reserved and with the poise of a man who has achieved his station in life. I felt again the authority, the deep concentration with each small segment as a part of the whole, and found the same patience and thoughtfulness and courtesy.

He knew exactly what he wanted—there could be no doubt about that. Apropos of this, he had an amusing moment with Bette Davis. As the hotel manager, I had a scene with her in one of her more persistent moments in the hotel lobby. She was being a bit on the noisy side. As we began to rehearse, Bette began having ideas, so she began suggesting. No sooner had she begun, than Frank interrupted with a fast, staccato, but not unpleasant, teacher-to-spoiled-child: "Tut, tut, tut, tut." Each *tut* lightly touched. Unmistakable.

A few moments later, another idea sprang forth. Again the reprimanding "Tut, tut, tut, tut." After that, silence. Ideas and new directing thoughts were left to the director.

—*Letter to the authors from Tarzana, California,*
August 18, 1974.

FRITZ FELD:

In 1961 I got a call for an interview with Frank Capra. I was thrilled! To meet the great Capra—that would be a crowning achievement; and to get a part in his production—a real miracle!

I met the casting director at the studio, and we walked over to Stage 5. The red light was flickering—a sign they were shooting.

"What kind of a part am I up for?" I asked the casting director.

"That's up to Mr. Capra. I can't tell you." It sounded mysterious. Then we opened the heavy stage door. It was very quiet on the set, which is typical with a great director at work. We softly approached the set. Capra was rehearsing a scene with Glenn Ford and Peter Falk.

Benny Rubin, a fine comedian and an old friend, came over to see me.

"Fritz, you lucky devil, I see you are up for a part with Capra. Good luck. Hope you get it!" That was all he said, and disappeared.

I saw old friends sitting on the side—the fabulous comedian Edward Everett Horton, Hope Lange, Arthur O'Connell, Thomas Mitchell, Sheldon Leonard, John Litel, Jerome Cowan—what a cast! I saw Arthur Black, the first assistant, trying to get Capra's ear. It looked as if he was telling him that I was waiting.

An hour passed: then Glenn Ford and Joseph Sistrom, the associated producers, and the writer Hal Kanter went into a huddle. The casting director apologized to me, but he didn't realize that I didn't mind waiting for years to meet Frank Capra.

Then suddenly the huddle broke up. Mr. Capra

BENNY RUBIN, right, as Flyaway, an agent who supplies bodyguards, says to Joy Boy (Peter Falk), "Oh, you want four Tom Mixes to protect the Dude." Joy Boy says they should be well dressed and only shoot in self-defense.

"STAY IN THERE AND PITCH, SISTER!" the butler (Edward Everett Horton), who "loves Cinderella stories," advises Apple Annie (Bette Davis), who is at Rodney Kent's borrowed penthouse waiting to be transformed into a lady.

AFTERMATH OF LOVERS' FIGHT—Left to right: Joy Boy (Peter Falk), Dave the Dude (Glenn Ford) and Queenie Martin (Hope Lange). Benny Rubin wrote to the authors of this book from Hollywood, California on March 21, 1974: "In *Pocketful* there was an exciting and funny fight between Glenn Ford and Hope Lange. Every move, punch, gouge, tearing of clothes and things thrown was rehearsed to the letter. NO, not by Glenn or Hope, but by Frank and Joe Sistrom in a bed in Frank's house. Those guys were black and blue."

FRITZ FELD as Pierre ("The Divine") of the Saxon Plaza Hotel ready to transform Apple Annie into "Mrs. E. Worthington Manville."

AMAZED REACTION to real political leaders and society people arriving at the reception. Left to right: Judge Blake (Thomas Mitchell), Junior (Mickey Shaughnessy), Queenie Martin (Hope Lange), Dave the Dude (Glenn Ford) and Joy Boy (Peter Falk). Judge Blake: "This isn't the gang we rehearsed, Dave."

and an entourage of six or eight of his staff members came toward me. My heart started pounding. Capra walked around me in a circle. No one introduced me. I didn't know if I should stand still or turn around. I studied Capra's face, looking for approval. He shook his head to the cameraman. Then I was convinced that I wouldn't get the part—I was out! As quickly as the group arrived, so quickly they disappeared.

I heard the first assistant's voice: "All right. Everybody quiet on the set. Stop talking, nobody move!"

"Action!" said Capra. I was standing sad and forlorn.

After a few moments, the casting director motioned me to follow him. We tiptoed to the door. The red light stopped flickering. We went outside, and I followed him to his office. He gave me a big, fat script. "Congratulations, Fritz. See you tomorrow at eleven in wardrobe."

I was flabbergasted. I rushed across the street to Oblath, the famous coffeehouse. I turned the pages of the script. I couldn't find a part suited for me. No maître d', no waiter, no orchestra leader, no psychiatrist . . . Where am I? What could I be? Ah —Pierre! He transforms Bette Davis from Apple Annie to Mrs. E. Worthington Manville. An elegant beauty consultant. Yes—that was me—that was my part! Small—but I liked cameo work. And with Capra!

The day of the shooting arrived. As Pierre, I entered the scene with an entourage of helpers, beautifully arranged by Capra. I looked Apple Annie over and gave directions to my staff. Then I disappeared into a separate room. Lunch was called. Eddie Horton and Jerome Cowan took me aside. They were trying to help me understand Capra's ways.

"Fritz, be prepared. Capra carefully rehearses each scene many times."

After lunch Mr. Capra said to me: "Fritz, I am not going to rehearse the next scene. You are on your own. Just yell when you are ready."

Behind the door I quickly ruffled my hair, undid my tie, and opened my shirt. "I'm ready!" I yelled.

I heard Capra's voice: "Camera, action!"

I flung the door open. I stopped for a moment in the door frame, obviously disheveled and exhausted from the nearly impossible task of transforming Apple Annie into Mrs. E. Worthington Manville.

"Cut—it's a take," Capra said. "Perfect—thank you, Fritz!"

One take. No rehearsal. I was proud and utterly stunned!

It's customary in Hollywood to go to a party at the finish of shooting a big production. Everyone who worked in the picture is invited. Wives or husbands of the actors and technicians enjoy wonderful food and drinks. My beautiful wife met the great Capra. He was so nice and kind. After the party we went across the street to our parked cars. Cadillacs, Chryslers, Continentals. Would you believe it? Capra drove away in a little Ford! Modest, great, famous, wonderful.

—Letter to the authors from Los Angeles, California,
February 27, 1974.

HAYDEN RORKE:

I have always held Frank Capra in high esteem as a great pioneer in this industry and, in fact, the best in his special kind of comedy.

When I was interviewed by Mr. Capra for a part in *Pocketful of Miracles* some years ago, it was with great trepidation, because I always held him in great awe. Having seen all his pictures and really studied them, I always felt you left his films not only entertained, but inspired with hope. Having worked with many great directors, including Vincente Minnelli, King Vidor, Delmer Daves, Leo McCarey, Tay Garnett, George Cukor, Henry Koster, and others, I couldn't wait to work with Mr. Capra.

My nervousness was immediately put at ease during that interview when he said, 'I've been watching you play suave heavies for years now, and I think it's about time I put you on the other side of the law. How would you like to play a New York cop along with this other converted heavy and fellow Irishman Barton MacLane?"

Working with Mr. Capra on that picture was a most heartwarming and rewarding experience. He has great rapport with an actor. He allows you to bring your own interpretation to the character, only sharpening it with that magical Capra touch that in the end presents an actor at his best.

Filmmaking today is an entirely different ballgame. What a pity that present-day movie audiences do not have the privilege of experiencing the joy and fulfillment of Frank Capra's magical touch.

—Letter to the authors from Studio City, California,
October 2, 1974.

JACK ELAM:

Inasmuch as my role in *Pocketful of Miracles* was so insignificant, it goes without saying that my contact with Mr. Capra was minimal. The picture was made so many years ago that any specifics would have long since escaped me.

My general impression of Mr. Capra, which is still very strong, is that feeling an actor gets when he knows the director is exceedingly talented and secure. There is a polished ease about their demeanor that separates them from the boys.

I feel flattered to have been in a Capra film because he surely, as much as anyone, represents "big time."

—Letter to the authors from North Hollywood,
California, February 19, 1974.

MIKE MAZURKI:

Although I have been privileged to work for many other distinguished directors, unfortunately *Pocketful of Miracles* represents my sole and very brief meeting with Mr. Capra.

Mr. Capra is a man whose directorial expertise, insight, and ability to communicate make him almost unique. It was a great pleasure for me to work with Mr. Capra.

—Letter to the authors from Burbank, California,
April 30, 1974.

FRANK P. KELLER, A.C.E.:

Throughout the years there have been references to parts of pictures called "the Capra touch." It is my belief now that many of these were probably the result of a sudden inspiration and were not planned or thought out in advance. To cite an example from the film *Pocketful of Miracles*, which I had the pleasure of editing, somewhere in the middle of the picture, as written and photographed, was a scene of Apple Annie (played by Bette Davis) in which she reaches into her basket of apples and pulls out a hidden gin bottle. She raises the bottle as a toast to an off-stage character, says, "God bless you, Dude!" and replaces the bottle.

As an apparent afterthought, Annie again lifts up the bottle and says, "God bless everybody!" then takes a swig of gin and puts the bottle back in the basket.

That was the way the scene remained until just before the final editing session. Suddenly one morning, Mr. Capra came in with the bright idea of taking the last half of that scene, just the section with "God bless everybody!" out of its normal context and placing it on the front end of the entire picture,

RETURNING TO SPAIN after a successful visit with "Mrs. E. Worthington Manville" (Bette Davis), the visitors who have caused all the brouhaha, wave to their New York friends. Left to right: Count Romeo (Arthur O'Connell), Louise (Ann-Margret) and Carlos (Peter Mann).

ahead of the main title. This served a delightful dual purpose of setting the spirit of the film and introducing the main character. That type of embellishment is what I consider to be a Capra touch.

—*Letter to the authors from Hollywood, California,*
November 8, 1974.

Twenty-eight years after *Lady for a Day*, Frank Capra Productions bought the remake rights to the film from Columbia Pictures, and Capra remade it in association with Glenn Ford's Newton Productions (the co-venture was called a Franton Production, and it was distributed through United Artists), with a new title, *Pocketful of Miracles*, in color, and with a title song sung during the credits. The song was nominated for an Academy Award; also, Peter Falk, playing the old Ned Sparks role,

was nominated for an Academy Award in the Best Supporting Actor category, and the costume designers were nominated.

Pocketful of Miracles was Frank Capra's last commercial film—a twenty-minute science film, *Rendezvous in Space*, made for New York's 1964-65 World's Fair, is all that followed. When asked why he stopped making movies, Capra replies, "Because I did it all. Now let the younger ones do it."

Pocketful of Miracles has a cast of supporting actors as brilliant as that of the original film, which it resembles in almost all details. The story is identical.

Throughout, the dialogue is fast and trenchant and funny. Mickey Shaughnessy, as Junior, reacts to Apple Annie's transformation: "She's like a cockroach what turned into a butterfly!" As Judge Blake, Thomas Mitchell's superbly high-handed orig-

268

inal rejection of his role as Annie's husband: "Preposterous! A creature of the pavements, a frowsy hag with the breath of a dragon." Jack Elam, as mobster Cheesecake, refusing to play the part of the secretary of the interior because he says a secretary is less important than an ambassador (a part assigned to another mobster), is placated when he is named postmaster general: "That's more like it: I save stamps!" Peter Falk, brilliant throughout as Joy Boy, walks in on a rehearsal of all the mobsters practicing how to bow and asks, "Does the board of health know about this epidemic?"

When Glenn Ford, as Dave the Dude, tells the mob to think of Apple Annie as they would of their mothers, Cheesecake, weeping, says in a poignant aside to Big Mike (Mike Mazurki): "I ought to do something for my mudder. They won't let me see her since they stuck her in solitary." And Judge Blake can speak a favorite Capra thought when he quotes Pascal: "The heart has reasons that reason itself

WAVING GOODBYE, dockside, to the visitors from Spain, are Apple Annie (Bette Davis) as "Mrs. E. Worthington Manville" and Judge Blake (Thomas Mitchell).

BIRTHDAY PARTY for star Glenn Ford on the set of *Pocketful of Miracles* was presided over by Hope Lange, cutting cake, and eager-looking Frank Capra.

knows nothing about." Most moving, Apple Annie (Bette Davis), transformed into a lady she can hardly recognize, gazes at herself in a full-length mirror: "I don't know who that is in there," and then tries to reassure herself of her identity by picking up her basket and saying into the mirror, "Apples?"

The dockside parting between mother and daughter is necessarily tearful, but not unhappy. The Judge, solicitous, whispers to Annie, "Don't cave in now"—moments before he collapses under the emotional strain. Annie recalls her true identity and turns to her disreputable friends with her old voice and intonation: "Hey, hey, hey! Why are you standing there with your mouths open? The crowd on this dock is loaded! Start hustling!"

Frank Capra produced and directed *Rendezvous in Space* (its working title was *Reaching for the Stars*) and also wrote the screenplay. He made this twenty-minute futuristic space film for the Martin-Marietta Corporation, builders of the Titan rocket boosters, who donated it to the Hall of Science building at the 1964-65 New York World's Fair. It was always known that this would be a permanent building, and for eleven and a half years after the Fair closed the film continued to be shown 48 times each week by means of a special wide-angle technique.

Danny Thomas stars in the film, which starts off with color sequence slides of earth taken from outer space and utilizing John Glenn's voice recorded as he described what he saw. We next see a series of both successful and unsuccessful launches, climaxed by the sight of a vehicle going off into space as photographed from a high-flying aircraft. Thomas speaks of the origins of space vehicles, and an excellent cartoon story of the discovery of gunpowder by the Chinese and its original use in rockets is presented.

Danny Thomas does all his talking as a reporter with a microphone in Times Square in New York, and among the many types of people who gather around, two are played by Tom Fadden and Benny Rubin. He finally asks who would like to take a ride in a space "taxi" that shuttles between earth and a manned orbital laboratory (MOL) with supplies and relief crews.

The film stops temporarily while the viewers' attention is directed to a five-eighths-scale space "taxi" (now called the shuttle or reentry vehicle), which is sixty feet above their heads, and moves suspended from a curvature in the ceiling forty feet above it.

Three manikins in the shuttle move and talk, telling the story of the manned orbital laboratory (now called Skylab). As the shuttle progresses across the theater airspace, a large curtain parts, to reveal the American MOL. A docking is effected, lights in the MOL reveal five more manikins similar to those in the shuttle, and one from the shuttle moves into the Skylab area.

Lights on the models go out, and the film resumes with Danny Thomas's predictions of the benefits that will accrue to all men as a result of scientific space exploration.

"I leaped at the opportunity," is Capra's own description in his autobiography of his reaction when invited to make a film relating to his lifelong interest in science.

Rendezvous in Space

1964

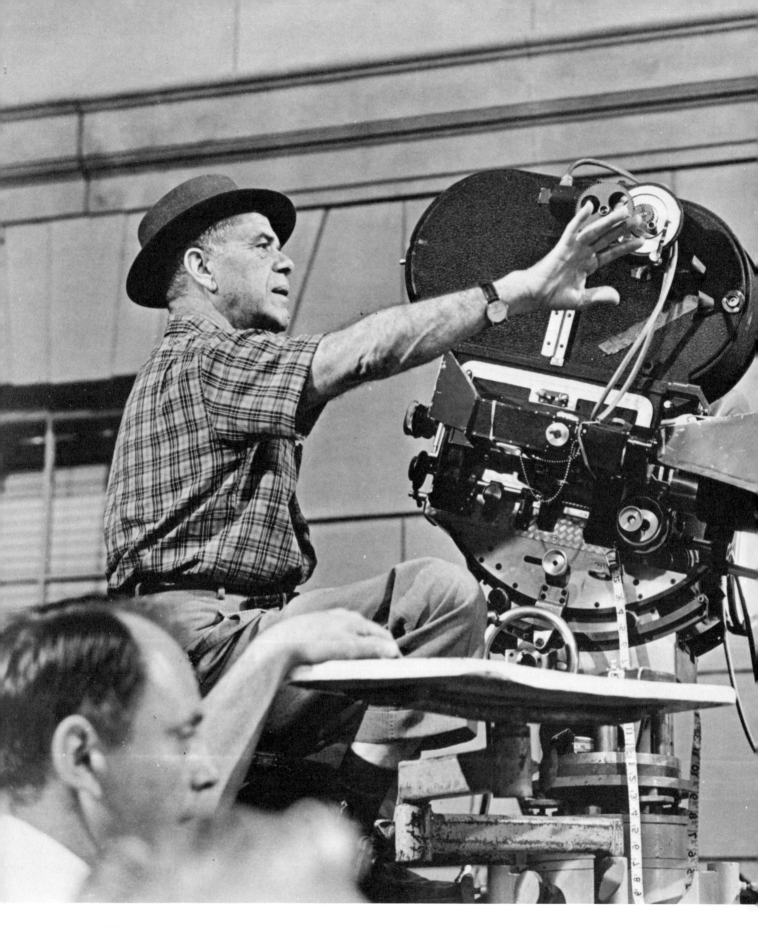

Epilogue

FRANK CAPRA:

I respect films, because I know what goes into them. Nobody starts out to make a bad film. I take my hat off to anyone who can complete a picture. They can't all be successes, because we're dealing with an art form, and there are no formulas. Mathematics and art don't speak the same language.

The best pictures are yet to be made.

—*Statement on* THE MERV GRIFFIN SHOW,
August 14, 1973.

STREET SCENE for *Pocketful of Miracles* is supervised by director Frank Capra at a much more elaborate motion picture camera than he first began using in his silent film days.

273

Index

Index of Names and Titles in Text and Captions

Adair, Jean, 188-192
Agee, James, 197, 198
Agee on Film, 197, 198
Alberghetti, Anna Maria, 247
Albert, Eddie, 252
Alexander, John, 188, 190, 191
Allwyn, Astrid, 166
American Madness, 106-108
Anderson, Bobbie, 222
Anderson, Eddie, 156-162
Andrews, Dana, 219, 220
Andrews, Stanley, 179, 226
Ann-Margret, 262, 268
Anson, A. E., 148
Ardrey, Robert, 23
Arkin, Alan, 154
Armstrong, Louis, 246
Arnold, Edward, 156, 159-162, 167, 171, 173, 176, 177, 179, 183
Arsenic and Old Lace, 187, 190, 192, 193
Arthur, Jean, 12, 28, 135, 138-141, 156, 158-160, 162, 165, 166, 169, 171, 172
Asther, Nils, 111-115
Astor, Gertrude, 39
Attucks, Crispus, 212
Auer, Florence, 236
Auer, Mischa, 156, 158, 159, 162
Ayres, Agnes, 77

Back Street, 104
Bacon, Irving, 140, 176, 183, 236
Baer, Max, 242
Bailey, William Norton, 60, 61
Baird, Bil, 253
Baird, Cora, 253
Baker, Art, 237
Bancroft, George, 140
Barkley, Alben W., 171
Barrymore, Lionel, 19, 156, 158, 159, 161-163, 224, 231, 250
Barton, James, 246, 247, 249
Basquette, Lina, 72-75
Battle of Britain, The, 196, 197, 205
Battle of China, The, 209
Battle of Russia, The, 196, 197, 207
Baxter, Dr. Frank, 252, 253, 255
Baxter, Warner, 130, 132, 133
Beery, Wallace, 23
Bellamy, Ralph, 103-105

Belmore, Lionel, 56-58
Ben-Hur, 31
Bennett, Alma, 43-45
Benny, Jack, 18
Bergman, Ingmar, 2
Bernds, Edward L., 32, 83, 87, 92, 103, 108, 123, 133, 137, 152
Bernstein, Leonard, 171
Bickford, Charles, 242
Birth of a Nation, The, 150, 197
Bismarck, 220
Bitter Tea of General Yen, The, 27, 111, 115, 146
Black, Arthur S., 79, 230, 231, 264
Blaik, Coach Earl "Red", 33
Blandick, Clara, 110
Bogdanovich, Peter, 13
Bond, Ward, 124, 159, 227, 229, 238
Bondi, Beulah, 164, 224, 227, 229
Bonner, Priscilla, 39, 43
Bosworth, Hobart, 90, 91, 93, 118, 120
Bradley, Omar N., 196
Brady, William A., 13
Breese, Edmund, 99
Brennan, Walter, 175-177, 183
Briskin, Samuel, 8, 197, 230
Broadway Bill, 130, 131, 133, 146, 238, 243
Brockwell, Gladys, 43
Browne, Sir Thomas, 32
Buchwald, Art, 16
Buckler, Hugh, 155
Burke, James, 159
Burlesque, 84
Burroughs, John, 23
Bushman, Francis X., 62, 63
Butterworth, Charles, 82
Byington, Spring, 156, 159-162, 183

Cameron, Hugh, 47-49
Capra, Frank, throughout
Capra, Frank, Jr., 30
Capra, Lu, 8, 26, 28, 30
Capra, Lulu, 30
Carey, Harry, 29, 169, 171
Carlson, Richard, 252-255
Carpozi, Jr., George, 138
Carson, Jack, 188
Catlett, Walter, 101, 249

Cavan, Allan, 167
Chadwick, Helene, 62, 63
Chamberlain, Neville, 201
Chandler, Eddy, 159
Chaplin, Charles, 139
Charlesworth, Bob, 133
Chasen, Dave, 32, 88, 89
Chennault, Claire, 211
Cheshire, Harry, 224
Chiang Kai-shek, 209
Chiang Kai-shek, Madame, 209
Churchill, Winston S., 28, 30, 196, 202
Claire, Rene, 139
Clark, Mark W., 196, 215
Clary, Charles, 65
Cobb, Irwin S., 28
Cohan, George M., 168
Cohn, Harry, 13, 26, 27, 58, 69, 71, 73, 79, 80, 88, 92, 137, 180, 243
Cohn, Jack, 75
Colbert, Claudette, 21, 47-49, 123-125, 127-129, 233
Coleman, C. C. (Buddy), 133
Collier, William, Jr. (Collier, Buster), 54, 55, 76, 88, 89
Colman, Ronald, 3, 21, 27, 144-146, 148-150, 152, 154, 155
Compton, Juliette, 82, 84
Conklin, Chester, 246
Connell, Richard, 182
Connolly, Walter, 113, 114, 117, 118, 120, 121, 123, 125, 130, 133, 146
Cook, Joe, 86-89
Cooms, Carol, 230
Cooper, Gary, 17, 18, 135, 136, 138-141, 174-177, 179, 180, 182, 183, 243
Cooper, George, 140
Cooper, Jackie, 18
Corby, Ellen, 224, 229, 249
Cortez, Ricardo, 72, 74
Costello, Maurice, 167
Cowan, Jerome, 264, 266
Cozzens, James Gould, 16
Crawford, Joan, 26
Crisp, Donald, 28
Cromwell, John, 13
Crosby, Bing, 21, 238-244, 246-249
Cukor, George, 267
Cummings, Constance, 106-109

D'Albrook, Sidney, 56-58
Daley, Cass, 246
Dana, Viola, 50-53
Darro, Frankie, 242
Davenport, Harry, 242, 243
Daves, Delmer, 14, 267
Davis, Bette, 262-267, 269
Davis, Edwards, 66
Day, Alice, 60, 61
Day for Night, 2
de Walt Reynolds, Adeline, 249
Dearing, Edgar, 159
Demarest, William, 239, 241, 243
DeMille, Cecil B., 14, 28
Desert Victory, 214
DeVries, Peter, 16, 138
Dickens, Charles, 253
Dietrich, Marlene, 18
Dillaway, Donald, 98, 100
Dingle, Charles, 236
Dirigible, 27, 71, 91-93
Disney, Walt, 199
Divide and Conquer, 202
Donnelly, Ruth, 140, 164, 168
Donovan Affair, The, 77
Doolittle, James H., 24, 196
Doran, Ann, 161, 177, 178
Dostoevski, Feodor, 253
Douglas, Helen Gahagan, 171
Douglas, Melvyn, 171
Douglas, William O., 1
DuBridge, Dr. Lee, 8
Dubuc, Frances Fisher, 176
Dumbrille, Douglass, 135, 137, 141, 238
Dunn, Emma, 135
Dwan, Allan, 14

Eddy, Bob, 24, 26
Edeson, Robert, 64, 66, 67
Edmunds, William, 226
Edwards, Blake, 14
Edwards, Harry, 26
Edwards, Ralph, 8
Edwards, Sarah, 224, 229
Eisenhower, Dwight D., 221
Elam, Jack, 267, 269
Eliot, T. S., 138
Eltz, Theodor von, 60, 61
Ethier, Alphonz (Alphonse), 63, 76

Fadden, Tom, 227, 234, 236, 262, 271
Fairbanks, Douglas, 83
Fairbanks, Douglas, Jr., 64-67
Falk, Peter, 13, 262, 264-266, 268, 269
Farrell, Glenda, 116, 118
Fawcett, George, 85
Faylen, Frank, 224, 229
Fazenda, Louise, 87-89
Feld, Fritz, 264, 266
Finlayson, Jimmy, 246

Flavin, James, 160, 161
Flight, 71, 79, 80
Fonda, Henry, 18
Fontaine, Frank, 246
For the Love of Mike, 26, 47, 48
Forbes, Mary, 156, 159, 160, 162
Forbidden, 3, 103, 104
Ford, Gerald R., 33
Ford, Glenn, 262, 264-266, 268, 269
Ford, John, 15, 31, 168
Foreman, Carl, 197
Foster, Lewis, R., 171
Foulger, Byron, 263
Francisco, Betty, 45
Fresholt, Myrna, 102
Friedkin, William, 14
Fultah Fisher's Boarding House, 1, 24, 35

Gable, Clark, 21, 124, 125, 127-129
Gann, Ernest K., 16
Garnett, Tay, 5, 26, 28, 267
Gary Cooper Story, The, 138
Gencel, Jacques, 244, 246, 248
George S. Kaufman and His Friends, 162
Gifford, Frances, 238, 243
Gilchrist, Connie, 245, 249
Gill, Eric, 23
Gish, Lillian, 19
Gleason, James, 174, 183, 191, 238
Glenn, John, 271
Glory of the Hummingbird, The, 138
Goethe, 253
Goldberg, Rube, 5
Golden, Harry, 16
Goodwin, Harold, 78, 79, 81, 91, 93
Gordon, Gavin, 107, 109-111, 113, 263, 264
Graham Greene on Film, 139, 171
Grahame, Gloria, 224, 225, 229
Grand Hotel, 150
Grant, Cary, 17, 186, 189, 191-193
Graves, Ralph, 50-53, 68-71, 78-85, 90, 91, 93
Gray, Coleen, 21, 238, 240, 241, 243
Greene, Graham, 139, 171
Griffin, Merv, 32
Griffith, D. W., 19, 28, 33, 83, 150
Grimes, Karolyn, 230
Gunther, John, 197
Gypsy, 234

Hager, George, 133
Hagney, Frank, 224
Hale, Alan, 129
Hale, Louise Closser, 98, 100, 101
Halton, Charles, 225
Hardy, Oliver, 241, 243
Hardy, Sam, 94-96
Hardy, Thomas, 36
Harlow, Jean, 98-101
Harriman, W. Averell, 196

Harris, Mildred, 65, 66
Harris, Phil, 246, 247
Harvey, Paul, 238
Hawkins, Jimmy, 230
Hazlitt, William, 32
Head, Edith, 257, 261
Heller, Robert, 196
Hemo the Magnificent, 252
Henderson, Del, 64, 66, 67
Henry, Bill, 196
Hepburn, Katharine, 5, 233-237
Here Comes the Groom, 244-249
Here Is Germany, 218
Herlihy, James Leo, 16
Herriman, George, 23
Herring, Aggie, 51, 53
Hersholt, Jean, 28, 72-75
Hilliard, Ernest, 57, 59
Hilton, James, 150, 196
Hinds, Samuel S., 118, 156, 162
Hirohito, 219, 221
Hitchcock, Alfred, 2, 18, 108, 196
Hitler, Adolf, 182, 198, 200, 202, 203, 205, 207, 209, 212, 218, 220, 221
Hobbes, Halliwell, 98, 101, 156, 158, 159, 162
Hodges, Eddie, 256, 258, 259, 261
Hole in the Head, A, 12, 257, 258, 261
Holloway, Sterling, 107, 252
Hollywood, 14
Holman, Harry, 104, 129, 231
Holt, Jack, 27, 68-71, 76-81, 90, 92, 93
Homer, 23
Homma, Lieutenant General, 221
Hornbeck, William, 196
Horton, Edward Everett, 23, 145, 146, 148, 150, 154, 191, 192, 262, 264-266
Howard, John, 144, 145, 150-152, 154, 155
Howard, Tom, 87-89
Howell, Helen, 26
Hughes, Langston, 212
Hull, Josephine, 188-192
Hunter, Evan, 17
Hurst, Fannie, 104
Husing, Ted, 26
Huston, Walter, 106, 108, 109, 199, 202, 203, 207, 209, 212, 218, 219
Hymer, Warren, 176

If Winter Comes, 234
It Happened One Night, 2, 13, 19, 28, 123, 125, 139, 140, 146
It's a Wonderful Life, 2, 13, 19, 23, 28, 223, 225-227, 229, 230

Jaffe, Sam, 17, 146, 148, 150, 152, 155
Jazz Singer, The, 26
Jefferson, Thomas, 1

Jewell, Isabel, 27, 146, 148, 150, 151
Jimmu, God-Emperor, 219
Johnson, Kay, 109
Johnson, Van, 235-237
Joko, v
Jones, Carolyn, 8, 257, 259, 261
Jones, James, 17
Joy, Nicholas, 249

Kabibble, Ish, 241, 242
Kaltenborn, H. V., 173
Kanin, Garson, 14
Kantor, Hal, 264
Kantor, Mackinlay, 17
Karloff, Boris, 190, 191
Karns, Roscoe, 93, 125
Karns, Todd, 229
Kaufman, George S., 162
Keith, Robert, 245
Keller, Frank P., 251, 253, 267
Kelley, George, 133
Kelly, Gene, 19
Kelton, Pert, 160
Kesselring, Joseph, 190
Kibbee, Guy, 29, 116-118, 164, 167, 171
Kilbride, Percy, 239, 243
King, Henry, 14
Kipling, Rudyard, 1, 35, 36
Knight, Eric, 196, 197
Know your Ally: Britain, 203
Know Your Enemy—Japan, 219
Koster, Henry, 267
Kubrick, Stanley, 14
Kuhn, Fritz, 201

La Cava, Gregory, 23
La Rocque, Rod, 179
Ladies of Leisure, 82-84
Lady for a Day, 116-118, 120, 121, 268
Lady Vanishes, The, 18
Lamour, Dorothy, 246
Lane, Charles, 158, 187, 188, 238
Lane, Priscilla, 186, 187, 191, 192
Lang, Fritz, 15, 139
Langdon, Harry, 2, 13, 19, 24, 26, 38-45
Lange, Hope, 262, 264-266, 269
Lange, Michele, 244
Lansbury, Angela, 234-237
Lansing, Joi, 261
Lantz, Walter, 9
Later, Al, 133
Laughton, Charles, 146
Lease, Rex, 74, 75
Lee, Lila, 78-81
Lehman, Ernest, 17
Lenya, Lotte, 19
Leonard, Sheldon, 226, 227, 262, 264
Lewis, Mitchell, 60, 61, 179
Libbot, Irving (Buster), 133
Lincoln, Abraham, 1

Lindbergh, Charles, 218
Lippman, Irving, 133
Litel, John, 264
Littlefield, Lucien, 110
Litvak, Anatole, 196, 197
Livingston, Margaret, 60-63
Lloyd, Frank, 28, 33
Lloyd, Harold, 249
Lloyd, Jimmy, 133
Long Pants, 26, 43
Loo, Richard, 113, 114
Lorenzo Goes to Hollywood, 176
Loretta Young Show, The, 255
Lorre, Peter, 190, 191
Lost Horizon, 3, 17-19, 21, 27, 143, 144, 146, 148-150, 153-155
Love, Bessie, 56-59
Loy, Myrna, 130-133
Lubitsch, Ernst, 2, 139, 150, 152, 196
Luce, Clare Boothe, 173
Lyon, Ben, 47-49

MacDonald, J. Farrell, 177
MacLane, Barton, 267
Madame La Gimp, 117
Magnificent Dope, The, 18
Maltin, Leonard, 133, 138
Mann, Hank, 188
Mann, Peter, 262, 268
Manners, David, 94-97
Margo, 21, 152, 155
Marina, 138
Marshall, George C., 28, 30, 195, 196, 199, 221
Mason, Shirley, 54, 55
Massey, Raymond, 190, 191
Matinee Idol, The, 57-59
Mature, Victor, 19
Mayo, Bobby, 159
Mazurki, Mike, 267, 269
McAdam, Michael R., 197
McCabe, John, 133, 138
McCarey, Leo, 2, 17, 267
McCullough, Philo, 65
McGovern, George, 168
McIntosh, Burr, 51, 53
McNamara, Edward, 188
McWade, Margaret, 141
Meek, Donald, 156, 159, 162
Meet John Doe, 2, 17, 26, 175, 178, 180, 182, 183
Menjou, Adolphe, 3, 102-105, 235-237
Mercer, Beryl, 95, 96
Meredith, Scott, 162
Merv Griffin Show, The, 26, 32, 273
Middleton, Charles, 132
Miller, Ann, 156, 159, 160, 162
Miller, Marvin, 250
Minnelli, Vincent, 267
Mir, David, 56-58
Miracle of Morgan's Creek, The, 23
Miracle Woman, The, 95, 99

Mitchell, Grant, 188
Mitchell, Thomas, 27, 145, 146, 148, 150, 151, 154, 165, 166, 169, 171, 224, 229, 230, 262, 264, 266, 268, 269
Mong, William V., 40
Montague, Walter, 24
Moore, Colleen, 19, 153
Mori, Toshia, 111, 113
Mr. Deeds Goes to Town, 2, 13, 17-19, 21, 135, 137-141, 146, 168
Mr. Smith Goes to Washington, x, 2, 12, 13, 16-19, 21, 29, 165, 168, 171, 173, 180
Munson, Lyman, 8
Murphy, George, 21
Murrow, Edward R., 218
Muse, Clarence, 21, 87, 90, 91, 131-133, 238, 240, 242, 243
Mussolini, Benito, 221
Myrtil, Odette, 244, 248

Name Above the Title, The, 14, 23, 153
Nazis Strike, The, 196, 201
Negro Soldier, The, 212
Nelson, Lord, 26
Nelson, Sam, 92
New Yorker, The, 32
Norton, Barry, 117, 118, 120, 121
Nugent, Frank S., 172

Oakman, Wheeler, 66, 67
O'Brien, Liam, 249
O'Brien, Pat, 107, 109
O'Connell, Arthur, 262-264, 268
One Foot in Heaven, 23
Our Mr. Sun, 252
Owen, Reginald, 98, 100, 101

Pallette, Eugene, 167, 171
Parker, Eleanor, 258-260
Parker, Jean, 116-118
Parma, Leon, 33
Parsons, Louella, 148
Pascal, Blaise, 269
Pasternak, Joe, 123
Peckinpah, Sam, 15
Pedi, Tom, 236
Peers, Joan, 86, 88, 89
Penn, Arthur, 15
Perlberg, William, 27
Peterson, Edgar, 196
Pickford, Mary, 83
Pieces of Time, 13
Pitts, ZaSu, 159
Platinum Blonde, 99, 100
Pocketful of Miracles, 13, 229, 262-265, 267-269, 273
Poe, Edgar Allan, 253
Power of the Press, The, 65
Prelude to War, 196, 198, 199

Preminger, Otto, 15
Presnell, Robert, 182
Prevost, Marie, 85
Private Reader, The, 141

Quisling, 203

Rain or Shine, 86-88
Rains, Claude, 29, 166, 167, 171, 173
Ralston, Jobyna, 64-67
Randolph, Lillian, 224
Rankin, Arthur, 62, 63
Reaching for the Stars, 271
Real Stars, The, 133, 138
Real Tinsel, The, 152
Reed, Alan, 247
Reed, Donna, 222-225, 229-231
Rembrandt, 36
Renault, Mary, 17
Rendezvous in Space, 268, 271
Revier, Dorothy, 69-71, 76, 77
Reyburn, Lucille, 26
Rhein, George, 133
Riding High, 21, 238, 239, 241-243
Riefenstahl, Leni, 195
Riegles, Roy, 80
Ripley, Arthur, 24
Riskin, Robert, 27, 100, 118, 121, 139, 175, 176, 178, 180, 182, 183, 249
Ritt, Martin, 15
Ritter, Thelma, 257, 259, 260
Rivkin, Alan, 196
Roach, Hal, 73
Robinson, Edward G., 8, 257, 259-261
Robson, May, 116-121
Roche, John, 77
Rogers, Will, 23, 128
Roosevelt, Franklin Delano, 28, 109, 190, 195, 203, 215, 217
Roosevelt, Theodore, 191
Rorke, Hayden, 267
Rosanova, Rosa, 74
Roscoe, Alan, 43, 80
Rosenberg, Bernard, 152
Ross, Harold, 32
Rubin, Benny, 13, 26, 47, 58, 59, 258, 264, 265, 271
Runyon, Damon, 26, 117, 118
Russell, Rosalind, 21, 27

Salem, Peter, 212
Sandburg, Carl, 1
Say It With Sables, 62, 63
Seddon, Margaret, 141
Selznick, David, 255
Sennett, Mack, 5, 6, 7, 9, 24, 26, 69, 246
Seuss, Dr. (Ted Geisel), 5, 197

Shaughnessy, Mickey, 262, 266, 268
Shaw, Irwin, 17
Shelton, Turner, 8,
Sherman, Lowell, 82, 83
Shirer, William L., 196, 217
Sidney, George, 47-49
Silverstein, Harry, 152,
Sinatra, Frank, 12, 256, 258-261
Sistrom, Joseph, 264, 265
Smith, Alexis, 248, 249
Smith, C. Aubrey, 148
Smith, Ella, 84, 85
Smith, H. Allen, 17
Smith, Howard, 236
Smith, Margaret Chase, 168
So This Is Love, 55
Soderling, Walter, 179
Sparks, Ned, 118, 137, 268
Spiegelgass, Leonard, 196, 197
Stalin, Joseph, 28, 196
Stander, Lionel, 135, 137, 141
Stanwyck, Barbara, x, 1, 3, 27, 82-85, 94-97, 102-105, 110-115, 174-177, 179, 180, 182-184
Stapleton, Jean, 21
Starring Miss Barbara Stanwyck, 84, 85
State of the Union, 5, 233, 234, 237
Sterling, Ford, 47, 48
Stevens, George, 15, 197, 230
Stewart, James, x, 12, 17-19, 29, 156, 158-162, 164-167, 170-172, 222-227, 229-231
Stewart, Mary, 17
Stone, Grace Zaring, 27
Stone, Irving, 18
Stone, Lewis, 234
Strange Case of the Cosmic Rays, The, 253
Strong Man, The, 26, 39
Sturges, Preston, 2
Submarine, 8, 69, 71
Syzk, Arthur, 221

Taylor, Dub, 156, 159-162, 259
Thalasso, Arthur, 39, 40
That Certain Thing, 51, 69
This Is Your Life, 8
Thomas, Danny, 271
Thomas, Jameson, 125
Tiomkin, Dimitri, 154, 199
Tone, Franchot, 249
Toomey, Regis, 26, 176, 177
Tracey, Spencer, 5, 17, 233-237
Tramp, Tramp, Tramp, 26
Travers, Henry, 227, 230
Treen, Mary, 225, 229
Triumph of the Will, 195
Truffaut, Francois, 2
Truman, Harry S, 237

Tschaikovsky, 208
Tunisian Victory, 214
Turner, Maidel, 129, 249
Two Down and One to Go, 221

Unchained Goddess, The, 254, 255
Uris, Leon, 18

Van Doren, Mark, 139, 141
Veiller, Anthony, 196, 202, 203, 209
Venutti, Joe, 242
Vidor, King, 15, 267
Vinson, Helen, 130, 131, 133
Virtue Is a Dirty Word, 73
Von Sternberg, Joseph, 18

Walburn, Raymond, 130, 133, 138, 239, 241
Walker, Johnnie, 54-59
Walker, Joseph, 10, 27, 32, 123, 133
Wallace, Irving, 197
Walsh, Raoul, 15
Walthall, Henry B., 28, 148, 150
War Comes to America, 214
Warner, H. B., 145, 148, 154, 155, 161, 222, 224, 229, 249
Warner, Jack, 180, 190
Washburn, Beverly, 244, 246, 248
Washington, George, 1
Watkin, Pierre, 161, 179, 236
Way of the Strong, The, 61
Wellman, William A., 16
West, John, 8
Westmoreland, William C., 197
Whitlock, Lloyd, 167
Why We Fight, 1, 195-199, 201, 202, 205, 207, 209, 214
Willat, Irvin, 69
William, Warren. 116-121
Williams, Charles, 225, 229
Williams, Robert, 98-101
Willkie, Wendell, 218
Winston, Harold, 237
Wolfe, Ian, 161, 248, 249
Woody Woodpecker, 9
Wray, Fay, 27, 90, 92, 93
Wyatt, Jane, 27, 144, 146, 149, 155
Wyler, William, 15, 31, 197, 230
Wyman, Jane, 245, 247-249
Wynn, Keenan, 259-261

Yarbo, Lillian, 156, 160, 162
You Can't Take It With You, 2, 5, 17, 18, 27, 28, 157, 159-163
Young, Loretta, 99-101
Younger Generation, The, 73-75
Your Job in Germany, 219

Zanuck, Darryl F., 197
Zinnemann, Fred, 15